T0305250

Community Co-Production

Community Co-Production

Social Enterprise in Remote and Rural Communities

Edited by

Jane Farmer

La Trobe University, Australia

Carol Hill

University of Glasgow, UK

Sarah-Anne Muñoz

University of the Highlands and Islands, UK

Edward Elgar

Cheltenham, UK • Northampton, MA, USA

Published by
Edward Elgar Publishing Limited
The Lypiatts
15 Lansdown Road
Cheltenham
Glos GL50 2JA
UK

Edward Elgar Publishing, Inc.
William Pratt House
9 Dewey Court
Northampton
Massachusetts 01060
USA

A catalogue record for this book
is available from the British Library

Library of Congress Control Number: 2012935283

ISBN 978 1 84980 840 8

Typeset by Servis Filmsetting Ltd, Stockport, Cheshire
Printed and bound by MPG Books Group, UK

Contents

Figures

Tables

Maps

Contributors

Sara Bradley has a BA (Hons) from Oxford University and PhD in Social Gerontology from the University of Aberdeen. Her main area of interest is ageing and older people. Sara has worked mainly in the voluntary sector in employment, disability and health, as well as older people's issues. She is also a Research Fellow at the Centre for Rural Health (University of the Highlands and Islands).

Jane Farmer is Professor of Rural Health Management & Policy and Head of the La Trobe University Rural Health School (Australia) and was previously Co-Director of the Centre for Rural Health (University of the Highlands and Islands, UK). Jane has researched health and social services delivery in rural areas for 15 years, moving from studies that considered the role of diverse health and social care professionals in rural teams to the role of communities in designing and providing services, shaping and forcing change.

Carol Hill is a Senior Lecturer in Health and Social Policy at the University of Glasgow School of Interdisciplinary Studies, and Director of the Crichton Centre for Research in Health and Social Issues. Her overarching interest is in the complex relationship between ideology, the economy, health and social policy, and the policy process, and their impact on the delivery of agendas for health with links to current discourse on the (contested) rights and responsibilities of citizenship.

Sarah-Anne Muñoz is a Geographer based at the Centre for Rural Health (University of the Highlands and Islands, UK) where she is a Research Fellow. Her research interests are in health and place, as well as third sector service delivery and the role of community activities in health and wellbeing outcomes. She is currently funded by the Arts and Humanities Research Council and Scottish Funding Council to look at the health benefits of hospital grounds green space.

Katy Radford is a Social Anthropologist working with communities in areas of social justice and inclusion. She is a Research Associate with the Institute for Conflict Research in Northern Ireland (UK) and an advisor to the Commission for Victims and Survivors. She is currently working on issues of commemoration and memorialisation for the Community Relations Council and the Heritage Lottery Fund.

Sally Shortall is a Reader in Sociology at Queen's University Belfast (UK). She has published on rural development theory and practice, community and stakeholder engagement in policy processes, and the position of women in the farming industry. Following a year in the Department of Agriculture and Rural Development as a Research Fellow of the Economic and Social Research Council, she is currently writing on the social construction of rural policy priorities.

Sarah Skerratt is a Senior Researcher and Team Leader at the Scottish Agricultural College (SAC) (UK). She has 24 years' experience in analysing the differences between policy vision and experience-on-the-ground in rural areas and communities, with a particular focus on rural community development policies and strategies, and initiatives led by communities. She is Editor of SAC's *Rural Scotland in Focus* Reports, and convenor of the Round Table Debate Series bringing together stakeholders from across the private, public and third sectors.

Artur Steinerowski is a Researcher in the Rural Society Team at the Scottish Agricultural College (UK). His research focuses on improving quality of life and sustainability of rural communities. Artur is currently investigating aspects of rural social entrepreneurship and social enterprises and has an interest in operational aspects of innovative forms of businesses/entrepreneurship that bring social outcomes and societal development.

Kate Stephen was the Project Manager for the O4O Project in Highland, Scotland (UK). Her background is in community development and community care; she has a BSc in Rural Development and is currently engaged in doctoral research in the area of rural health.

Sandy Whitelaw is a Lecturer in Health and Social Studies within the School of Interdisciplinary Studies (University of Glasgow, Dumfries Campus, UK). He has worked within the field of public health in both the UK National Health Service and various Higher Education institutions. Sandy has experience in project work, lecturing and research in various public health areas.

Foreword

Too often older people are perceived as being a 'drain' on public services, and depicted as passive recipients of services designed and provided by others. The work of the O4O: Older People for Older People project seeks to counteract these popular misconceptions and postulates a model where older people are actively involved in the design and delivery of the services their generations receive. It recognises that older people have amassed a wide range of skills and experiences which should be used positively, and proposes that a community social enterprise model, working in partnership with the public sector, is particularly suited to this type of service delivery. The delivery of public services in rural areas faces particular challenges that are compounded by demographic change as younger people leave for study and work and older people move in to enjoy a scenic and tranquil retirement. Many of these older people remain fit and active for decades and could potentially be the natural leaders of social enterprises offering services to others in their community. The O4O project examined service provision in rural areas in Scotland, Northern Ireland, Greenland, Sweden and Finland, and the factors which influence the success of this model of service delivery.

It gives me particular pleasure to write the foreword to this book as one of the partners in the O4O project was the Crichton Centre for Research in Health and Social Issues based on the University of Glasgow's campus in Dumfries. I look forward to its conclusions bringing positive benefits to older residents in rural Scotland and across Europe's Northern Periphery Regions.

Elaine Murray
Member of the Scottish Parliament for Dumfriesshire Constituency

Introduction

Jane Farmer, Carol Hill and Sarah-Anne Muñoz

Across Europe, citizens are being encouraged by the state to get involved in their neighbourhood activities, community groups and civic life; in public sector consultations and decision-making processes, and even in the delivery of services that once lay firmly within the domain of the public sector. Within and between the European Union's (EU) nation states this emerging 'civil society' policy environment (Alcock, 2011) for service delivery is being played out in contextually specific ways. It is also occurring within the shared conditions of a global economic crisis, strained public sector budgets, varying degrees of civic unrest in relation to government cuts and a demographic shift resulting in increased proportions of older people in contemporary society.

Against this backdrop, the Conservative–Liberal Coalition government in the United Kingdom (UK) has drawn upon the Conservative Party's 'Big Society' agenda to promote local, needs-led service delivery via non-state providers and encourage citizens to work towards the creation of 'a society where people come together to solve problems and improve life for themselves and their communities; a society where the leading force for progress is social responsibility, not state control' (Conservative Party, 2010:1). Elsewhere in the EU, citizens are similarly being asked to engage in activities that sit within the social economy with its long roots to voluntarism, philanthropy, co-operatives and organisations that use business practice to achieve social aims. For example, across Scandinavia social businesses are promoted as a means of combating social exclusion through work integration. Sweden has notably instituted a centrally driven agenda to encourage service user choice and create new opportunities for non-state provision. In other EU countries the rhetoric surrounding the movement to engage civil society is focused on the development of partnership working between the social economy and the state (Addari et al, 2008). This nuanced business-like approach to meeting social need requires sections of the public sector to become proactive in engaging service users in decisions affecting the nature and delivery of their services. This scenario sees sub-contracting to, and procuring from, social economy organisations as a means of achieving greater public and service user engagement and contributing to users and professionals working in partnership to design and deliver public services (Boyle & Harris, 2009); that is, co-production. This model of service delivery is assumed to bring added value by helping to maintain the vibrancy of communities, harnessing the latent entrepreneurial power of citizens and encouraging innovation and efficiency. Service provision by community or social economy providers is also understood to enhance wellbeing and feelings of empowerment and encourage the 'reinvention' of communities (Aigner et al, 2001) through integration, participation and social inclusion (Lee, 2003).

In contrast to these affirmative approaches, a strand within current critical social science discourse, social policy literature, think-tanks and the mass media questions whether a shift in responsibility for service design and delivery from the state to citizens/civil society is necessary, realisable and likely to result in positive outcomes for service recipients and society in general. Kisby (2010), for example, questions whether capacity exists in the form of additional volunteering, whilst Evans (2011) argues that the promotion of empowerment through citizen engagement in service delivery is simply a device to conceal public sector cutbacks and make them more palatable, and McCabe (2010) suggests that, rather than becoming empowered, citizens will become over-burdened to the detriment of service delivery. Others, such as Bednarek (2011), question the ability of communities and the social economy to respond adequately to the 'opportunities' offered by the policy trajectory and regard Big Society-type initiatives as having the potential to reinforce geographies of disadvantage since not all communities will have latent social entrepreneurs who will spring into civic action.

The extent to which communities are willing to embrace the co-production agenda, or have the skills and capabilities to bring citizen energy into play are relatively under-explored, as are the support mechanisms required to pump-prime civil participation (Boyle & Harris, 2009). Indeed, agendas to increase the number of community-run social economy organisations often portray stereotypical situations in which disadvantaged urban communities might benefit from their development, but give little consideration to their occurrence within diverse contexts, including rural areas, or around provision for, and by, specific demographic groups.

In this book, we consider the implications of applying policy that promotes service delivery by social economy organisations in the context of rural communities and older people's services. We examine the policy contexts, aspects of the process, the complexities of attempting to establish social enterprises, question the meaning and utility of sustainability, demonstrate the problems of evaluating and measuring outcomes and, using the findings from a large case study of developing social enterprises in rural Europe, point the way to achieving community service co-production through social enterprise.

SOCIAL ENTERPRISE AS A SERVICE PROVIDER

The current civil turn in policy has identified social economy organisations as a means of channelling citizen enthusiasm and action into bodies that work to produce societal benefit. In this respect, the last 20 years have seen *social entrepreneurship* and *social enterprise* emerge as terms to describe the process of, and organisational model for, achieving social benefit through trading activity although there is no consensus on their meaning, or where social enterprise sits within the social economy or in relation to the public sector and private enterprises. Despite this ambiguity, social enterprise has been conceptualised as a new type of organisation; one that sits at the crossroads of the public, private and voluntary sectors (Nyssens, 2006) and trades primarily for social benefit.

Social Enterprise

Although a social enterprise is generally conceptualised as an organisation that trades for social purposes, contemporary research, literature and policy all highlight difficulty of definition (Haugh & Kitson, 2007; Nicholls & Cho, 2008; Ridley-Duff, 2008; Townsend & Hart, 2008; Neck et al, 2009). In its widest sense, social enterprise embraces the gamut of social economy organisations engaged in trading activities including community enterprises, social firms, social businesses, mutuals, fair trade companies and voluntary organisations that trade (Pearce, 2003). But partly because ideas about the social economy as a service provider are still evolving, academics and policymakers tend to use social enterprise as a 'catch all' term. At policy level, social enterprise is promoted as a cost-effective, flexible and innovative means of addressing the challenges of localised service provision (Scottish Social Enterprise Coalition (SSEC), 2009) and perceived as a useful solution in disadvantaged or difficult-to-supply areas. This is because it can draw on local people to ensure that services are relevant and attuned whilst simultaneously developing skills, confidence and social capital. This focus on generating social benefit through enterprise activity is reflected in a much cited definition from the UK Department of Trade and Industry (DTI) *viz*, 'A social enterprise is a business with primarily social objectives whose surpluses are principally reinvested for that purpose in the business or in the community, rather than being driven by the need to maximise profit for shareholders and owners' (DTI, 2002:7).

Social enterprises range from those producing products to those delivering services. They promote economic development and tackle social issues (DTI, 2002, 2005) by providing the means for individuals and communities to: improve their local neighbourhood; develop the skills and talents of local people; bring excluded groups into the labour market; create wealth and jobs; deliver value-for-money services in a wide range of sectors; promote active citizenship; and catalyse innovative solutions to local needs (Social Enterprise London, 2006). For Ridley-Duff and Bull (2011:60), social enterprise within the European context has the flavour of collective action and goals around the 'incremental building of social capital' whilst in the United States of America (USA) it is seen as individual-led businesses that are a 'market response to social issues'. Unsurprisingly, within this broad church of social enterprise conceptualisation, organisations employ different ways of combining social and economic objectives and models of social enterprise differ within and between countries.

Social Entrepreneurship

Though first defined more than 250 years ago (Austin et al, 2006), entrepreneurship remains a complex, variously understood and variously presented notion (Berglund & Johansson, 2007; Gartner, 1990). This complexity is reflected in Harding's definition of entrepreneurship as 'any attempt at new business or new venture creation, such as self employment, a new business organisation, or the expansion of an existing business by an individual, team of individuals or established business' (Harding, 2006:7). Reflecting this, social entrepreneurship has become a label for enterprising activity with community goals that is designed to generate profit for re-investment in a social business or a community (Harding, 2006); that is, an activity with 'an entrepreneurial embedded social purpose' (Austin et al, 2006:1). Thus, the process of social entrepreneurship is one in which social inequalities and imperfections are addressed in an entrepreneurial way (Steinerowski et al, 2008).

Although definitions and descriptions of social entrepreneurship appear fairly broad, common themes are identifiable. These include: an enterprise or business dimension to the process; an interest in innovation and change in relation to social issues; the need for independence from the state; and the (re-)investment of monies to meet social objectives. By extension, social entrepreneurs are viewed as key actors in the entrepreneurship process and are, according to Bornstein (2004:1), 'people with new ideas to address major problems, who are relentless in the pursuit of their visions'. Social entrepreneurs look for opportunities to add social impact throughout their value chain and are often presented as romantic heroes; creative risk-taking actors who tackle social problems using new approaches, untapped resources and 'his or her bare hands' (Nicholls and Cho, 2008:111).

Community Social Enterprise

Social enterprise is generally linked with the individualising concept of social entrepreneurship. However, the recent emergence of concepts such as 'The Big Society' in UK policy discourse evokes the notion of mass emergence of community groups eager to use their energy to invigorate neighbourhoods and help their neighbours. This is at odds with commentary about social enterprise and social entrepreneurship. Empowering communities to transform public services is key to the Big Society agenda and reflects the government's desire to empower citizens and communities to take responsibility for local challenges by becoming actively involved in the planning and delivery of services (Cabinet Office, 2010a, 2010b; Conservative Party, 2010). Yet whilst the place of social enterprise seems assured, there is obscurity around how the ideology of co-production will be translated into action on the ground and the underlying assumption that ubiquitous co-productive solutions will emerge from communities in the form of action from pre-established neighbourhood groups. It is thus useful to develop understanding of how communities can translate their current and latent activity into service provision and the benefits and burdens produced. Boyle and Harris (2009) suggest that insights are required into the realities of implementing 'collective co-production' for different communities and social groups. These issues are addressed within this volume, in chapters that examine the extent to which it is possible to actively make community social enterprises happen; the processes and challenges of developing such organisations in local contexts; the challenges for communities and citizens of getting involved; and the sustainability of the enterprises and activities created.

Community Social Enterprise for Older People's Services

Within the EU and USA the proportions of older people in the population are increasing as a result of demographic trends, including the low natural growth seen in the majority of European regions (<2.5%).[1] Most countries in the developed world are experiencing a decrease in the average number of births per woman and a concomitant increase in the dependency ratio, such that between 2000 and 2009 the proportion of the EU population aged 80+ increased from 3.4% to 4.6% and those aged between 65 and 79 increased from 12.3% to 12.7%.[2] These trends underpin concerns at both national and local levels about the ability of services and budgets to meet the needs of higher proportions of older people, particularly frailer older people who are known to consume high levels of health and social services.

Apocalyptic descriptions of ageing populations are often accompanied by calls for innovative, potentially non-state provided, service solutions. This suggests that the sector is ripe for community-based social enterprise service provision; as does the assumption that the growing proportion of older people harbours an under-utilised army of volunteers with the capacity and desire to participate in service delivery. The challenges of delivering appropriate services to ageing populations offer a contemporary context for discussion around the civil society turn in policy and service provision.

As an approach, community social enterprise appears to offer a variety of benefits including acting as a counter to the challenge of providing local, needs-led state-funded services and as a means of engaging an untapped source of free labour from amongst younger, fitter 'baby-boomers' and early retirees. Indeed, Scott (2011) suggests that an outcome of the use of 'moral persuasion' to 'encourage' fitter retirees to volunteer and participate in social enterprise creation is likely to be the harnessing of latent entrepreneurial skills within communities. And, through contributing to the maintenance of physical and mental activity and social interaction, there will be health and wellbeing benefits for those who engage in enterprise development. Furthermore, harnessing their life experience and networks to create and run organisations that provide services for other older people (such as social support, domestic help, shopping, transport, exercise schemes, health care, community alarm schemes, snow-clearing and fuel provision) should encourage a shift in the paradigm that views older people as a societal burden. Whilst services such as those listed might be criticised for not being professional or medicalised, they are specifically tailored to older people's needs and designed to enhance their quality of life. They also address areas of provision that may be difficult for statutory providers.

An attraction of community social enterprise lies in its articulation with the concept of enhanced services; that is, supporting and working in partnership with the public sector to maintain health and wellbeing. This aligns with the twin thrusts in contemporary social policy to keep people out of long-term institutional care and avoid crisis admissions. Ultimately, such costly institutional or technical service interventions are not beneficial to the wellbeing of older people whereas facilitating older people to help themselves, and each other, through collective activities aligns with wider health policy around illness prevention and health maintenance. Community social enterprise thus has credence as an approach to care because of its potential to maintain older people in their communities and because it implies multi-dimensional beneficial health and healthcare system impacts.

Service Provision in Europe's Rural Areas

Population ageing is most pronounced within Europe's rural regions due, in part, to the out-migration of younger people and the in-migration of older people from urban areas seeking a perceived higher quality of life. These regions are also home to the highest cost of service provision *per capita* and where, contrary to perception, older people often experience loneliness and isolation linked to the out-migration of younger family members, changing community structures and dispersed settlement patterns. Unsurprisingly, therefore, the ageing populations in rural areas are placing increasing demands on public sector service provision – and will continue to do so as the proportion of those aged over 55 years increases. Concomitantly, local services such as shops, banks, schools, post offices and health services, and the availability of professional jobs have been in decline across rural and remote areas (Sederberg, 1987; Kearns & Joseph, 1997; Civil Renewal Unit, 2006; Argent, 2008; Sawer, 2008). As many aspects of service provision affect quality of life, it is likely that their reduction will impact adversely on the health and wellbeing of older people in rural areas. This likelihood is compounded by a cycle of decline resulting in fewer jobs for young people and higher-paid professionals which raises the likelihood of sparse, disparately located concentrations of retired, part-time or low-paid workers developing in remote and rural areas. In terms of planning and service provision, this scenario will lead to sporadic case loads and mitigate against the possibility of justifying locally based full-time continuing jobs for health and social service professionals (Bryant & Joseph, 2001).

Within the health and social care professions, a move to specialisation and the technicalisation of work has seen a concentration of career opportunities which, together with a perception that the exciting jobs are those with high volumes of specialist cases (and therefore urban-based), has made it difficult to attract ambitious professionals to generalist rural work. In a similar vein, a push for economies of scale through team-working and service hubs has encouraged health and social care to provide services through outreach or 'drive-in, drive-out' models of care to the detriment of community-located services. Thus, across rural Europe there is a growing sense of panic about how to provide services to rural areas in a context where demand is likely to rise and access to health service staff likely to decline. In this context, policymakers and service providers are keen to consider novel ways of providing services that involve communities and citizens.

Rural social enterprises are likely to experience many of the same structural challenges faced by public sector service providers, including limited access to finance and information (Osborne et al, 2002; Farmer et al, 2008), but more profoundly, given their already diminished experience of service provision, rural citizens may resent the imposition of responsibility for developing and delivering services and associate social enterprise provision with second-rate services (Farmer et al, 2008). However, other contextual factors suggest that a rural environment is conducive to social enterprise as social networks are denser (Hofferth & Iceland, 1998); and their impacts of high levels of trust and active civic participation (Dale & Onyx, 2005) are key components of the social capital associated with social enterprise development, as is the existence of co-dependence, reciprocity and collective activity. These characteristics imply that rural areas should represent a nurturing context for social enterprises (Shucksmith et al, 1996; Granovetter, 2005).

THE OLDER PEOPLE FOR OLDER PEOPLE (O4O) PROJECT

Given rural population ageing, the challenges of rural service delivery and a policy turn favouring the engagement of civil society, the O4O project set out to test the extent to which state-driven policies promoting community social enterprise can be enacted and the extent to which community social enterprise can be facilitated and produce the outcomes and benefits suggested by policymakers. The benefits of social enterprise are often discussed in relation to deprived urban neighbourhoods but rural regions across Europe also share challenges that indicate they too may provide a needy environment for community social enterprise delivery. The O4O project (funded by the EU Northern Periphery Programme from 2007–2011) aimed to work with communities across five European regions (see Map I.1) to facilitate community social enterprise for the delivery of older people's services in rural settings. Project staff worked with communities in Scotland, Greenland, Sweden, Finland and Northern Ireland to identify older people's needs and establish community social enterprises that local citizens thought would enhance the quality of life of local older people.

The O4O project was specifically designed in response to the costs and

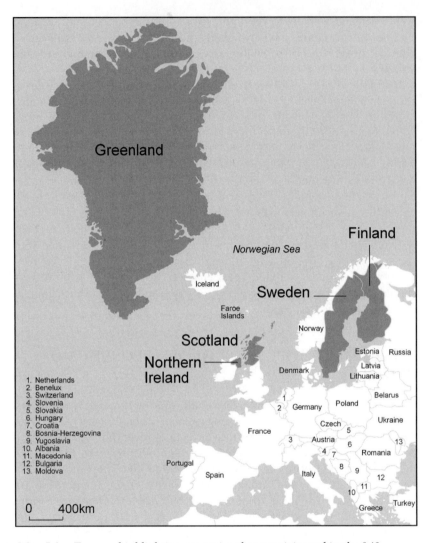

*Map I.1   Europe, highlighting countries that participated in the O4O
            project*

difficulties of providing services for rising proportions of older people
within remote and rural communities and tested policy ideas around the
promotion of service co-production through social enterprise. It engaged
with the notion that many older people remain fit and active long after
retirement and saw them as a resource for social entrepreneurship;

potential social entrepreneurs with the life experiences, skills and wisdom to establish, lead and manage community-based social enterprises. O4O also sought to determine whether there is the potential to build on older people's willingness to volunteer so that the 'younger, fitter old' might support the 'frailer, older old'. Current policy and research suggest a theoretical process of value creation from O4O-type social enterprises in which the engagement of older people in the development of community-led service provision has additional benefits. These include helping to keep older people active for longer with resultant positive impacts on their physical and mental health and the development of trust and social networks within the community. This is seen in Figure I.1, which outlines the process of social enterprise development and outcomes.

The aim of implementing O4O in rural communities was to engage older people in service co-production. To achieve this, O4O Project Managers were employed in each of the countries and regions involved, with a remit to mentor community members and groups through the process of community social enterprise development. The Project Managers, some of whom contribute to chapters within this book, used an action research approach to capture information on the processes in which they were involved. From the outset it was envisaged that whilst each of the participating communities would aspire to develop an ideal type of social enterprise – that is, a social business model – their different contextual factors, state of readiness and choice of service(s) to deliver made it highly likely that a range of forms of community social enterprise would transpire. Indeed, the production of different types of organisations and services was of particular interest and a range of comparative contextual information was collected for each region so that the emergent models might be compared with knowledge about the environment within which they grew. O4O Project Managers supported communities to develop organisations that met their objectives and, as Tables I.1–I.5 demonstrate, this resulted in the production of different organisation and service types.

Whilst the particularities of each of the communities involved in O4O contributed to differences in the community social enterprise models they developed, these differences were also partially attributable to, and shaped by, the wider socio-economic and political contexts of the participating countries.

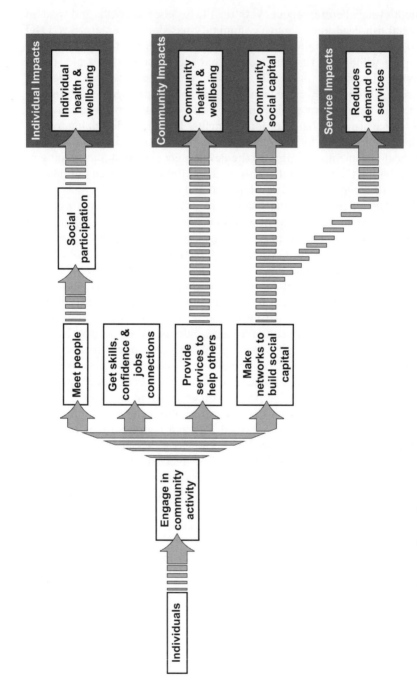

Figure I.1 A theory of social enterprise processes and outcomes production

Table I.1 O4O project emergent community social enterprise types – Scotland

Country	Social enterprise context	Community/ies	Description of O4O development	Emergent organisational type at O4O project end	Community social enterprise model
Scotland	A social enterprise (social business) sector is relatively well established and supported by public policy.	Ardersier	An informal voluntary group was established to produce an oral history DVD.	An informal group of oral history volunteers and a community development company.	Company limited by guarantee.
		Tongue	A multi-faceted transport scheme was developed including volunteer drivers.	The transport scheme was set up as a sub-group of an existing community development company (company limited by guarantee).	Company limited by guarantee.
		Lochinver	Following closure of a public sector centre for older people, a community group formed an organisation to run the centre.	The community group organisation (Community Care Assynt) was established as a not-for-personal-profit legal form and won a contract from the public sector to run the local centre.	Community Interest Company (CIC).

Table I.2 O4O project emergent community social enterprise types – Northern Ireland

Country	Social enterprise context	Community/ies	Description of O4O development	Emergent organisational type at O4O project end	Community social enterprise model
Northern Ireland	A social enterprise (social business) sector is relatively well established and supported by public policy.	Ards Peninsula	Developed a pilot community radio station.	A pilot radio station staffed by volunteers.	Voluntary group that may not continue beyond project-end.
		Markethill	Development of social enterprise activities relating to a drop-in centre and outreach centre.	An existing charity worked to develop a plan for engaging in trade through a socially entrepreneurial approach.	Charity that trades.
		Cookstown	Development of social enterprise activities linked to a lunch club, restaurant and drop-in centre.	An existing charity expanded trading activity.	Charity that trades.

Table I.3   O4O project emergent community social enterprise types – Greenland

Country	Social enterprise context	Community/ies	Description of O4O development	Emergent organisational type at O4O project end	Community social enterprise model
Greenland	Social enterprise sector almost non-existent.	Aruk, Paamiut, Kuummiut, Kulusuk & Ittoqqortoormiit	Activity groups of older people formed in each community, e.g. needlework, befriending.	Informal community groups with volunteers and a trained volunteer 'leader'.	Informal voluntary group.

Table I.4 O4O project emergent community social enterprise types – Finland

Country	Social enterprise context	Community/ies	Description of O4O development	Emergent organisational type at O4O project end	Community social enterprise model
Finland	Strong public sector service provision with social enterprise generally performing a work integration function.	Nurmes	O4O Project Manager worked with an existing 'association' to increase community capacity for volunteering, e.g. through development of guidance for volunteers.	Social economy organisation established as an 'association' with focus on volunteering.	Village association.
		Vuonislahti & Koli	Replication of the 'association' model developed in Nurmes.	Social economy organisation established as an 'association' with focus on volunteering.	Village association.

Table I.5 O4O project emergent community social enterprise types – Sweden

Country	Social enterprise context	Community/ies	Description of O4O development	Emergent organisational type at O4O project end	Community social enterprise model
Sweden	Strong public sector service provision with social enterprise generally performing a work integration function.	Sundom	Community secured funding from the public sector to deliver IT training.	Specific projects within the remit of an existing 'association'.	Co-operative.
		Jamton	A café and meeting place in a grocery store. An employee was hired for grocery deliveries and recycling collections.	Public sector subsidy for employment of 'hard-to-reach' groups used to support hiring a delivery/ collection person. Scheme may be extended using volunteers.	Work integration function added to existing private business.
		Niemsel	Within a private school, the community created a hub for older people's services.	A private school association that facilitates volunteering and aspires to facilitate social enterprise.	An association working towards social business creation.

Scotland

Scotland has a total resident population aged 16+ of just over 5 million. Approximately 18% of the population is of pensionable age, with 7% aged over 75 years.

The O4O Project Manager worked with communities in the Highland region, which is Scotland's largest region in terms of geographical size and is classified as rural by the Scottish government. The region is internally varied and encompasses remote, dispersed settlements, small coastal and market towns, and the regional capital, Inverness, which has approximately 45,000 residents. Within Highland, 19.5% of the population is of

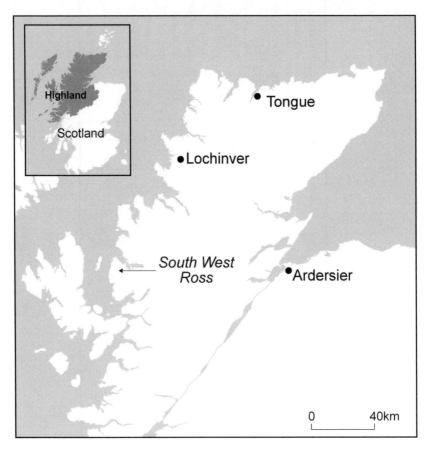

Map I.2   Highland region within Scotland and location of communities that participated in the O4O project within the Highland region

pensionable age and 39.6% fall under the Scottish government's defini-tion of an older person (i.e. 55 and over) compared with 35.4% within the Scottish population as a whole. O4O worked with four communities in the Highland region (see Map I.2): *Tongue* and *Lochinver* have small popu-lations of between 500 and 700 people and are situated over one hour's drive from Inverness; *South West Ross* consists of a cluster of three small settlements with a combined population of around 1,500 and *Ardersier* is a former industrial/military town of around 1,000 residents less than 20 miles from Inverness. A Project Manager was employed to work with citizens across these four locations over a period of three years and in three of the four Highland communities this process resulted in a community social enterprise being established. The needs that communities chose to address reflect previously identified concerns about poor rural transport, older people's day and residential care, and social isolation.

Scotland sits within the UK context where social enterprise models are promoted in policy, fairly well recognised within the general popu-lation and have existing support bodies such as the Scottish Social Enterprise Coalition and various legal structures available to them. Three of Scotland's Highland communities worked towards establishing for-mally constituted social enterprises using not-for-personal-profit business formats available in the UK including a company limited by guarantee (Ardersier and Tongue) and a community interest company (Lochinver).

Northern Ireland

Northern Ireland's population of approximately 1.6 million comprises roughly 3% of the UK population. Just over 16% of the Northern Irish population is of pensionable age. Within Northern Ireland, the popula-tion is concentrated in the capital city of Belfast and the surrounding rural areas, giving a population density of 122 per square kilometre. The O4O Project Manager was based in Belfast but worked with communities in the rural areas of: *Cookstown*, which has a population of around 11,000 and is one of the largest towns within County Tyrone; *Markethill*, which is a small market village in County Armagh with around 1,200 residents; and *Kircubbin*, a settlement of around 2,000 residents that sits on the Ards Penninsula in County Down (see Map I.3). As with Highland in Scotland, social enterprise models have been adopted by some existing social economy organisations within Northern Ireland and the concept of social business is, to a degree, established. However, the Northern Irish context is particular in relation to its history of social, political and economic unrest which has been seen as damaging to social capital and civil society activity. As a consequence, the O4O Project Manager worked

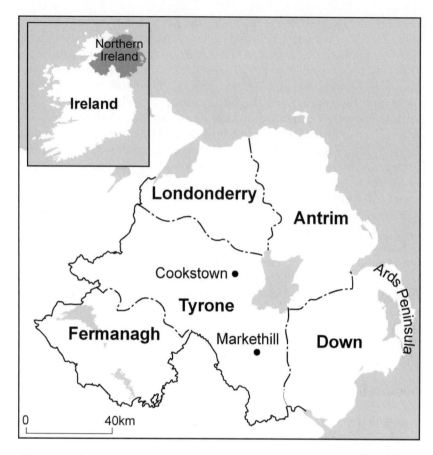

Map I.3   Communities in Northern Ireland that participated in the 040 project

with existing voluntary groups and charities with a view to building their capacity for social entrepreneurship. This involved business management and governance training for a voluntary group that went on to develop trading activities for social benefit (Cookstown), a 'drop-in' centre with an existing voluntary group (Markethill) and a pilot community radio station (Kircubbin).

Greenland

With a population of only 56,500 people Greenland is characterised by an extremely low population density of 0.07 people per square kilometre. This

*Map I.4   Greenland, showing the location of the communities that
            participated in the O4O project*

reflects the distribution of the population around coastal towns and villages at considerable distances from each other. Around 26% of the population live in the capital city of Nuuk, in the Kommuneqarfik Sermersooq
region in the south of Greenland which spans from the east to west coast
and comprises the five municipalities that participated in O4O. The two
O4O Project Managers were based in Nuuk but worked with five settlements dispersed around the east and west coasts of the country (see Map
I.4): *Arsuk*, a small village of around 150 residents situated to the south
of Nuuk; *Paamiut*, a fishing town of around 1,600 residents in southwest
Sermersooq that is a six hour boat ride from Arsuk; *Kulusuk*, a village

of around 280 people on an island to the east of the region, served by an airport; *Kuummiut*, a village of around 360 citizens located on the region's east coast and 30 kilometres north of Kulusuk; and *Ittoqqortoormiit*, a village of around 450 people, one of Greenland's most remote communities and the most northerly of the communities with which O4O Project Managers worked.

At the start of the O4O project, the Greenlandic team felt that very little was known about the characteristics of older people, their needs and capacity to be involved in volunteering. Social enterprise was an unfamiliar format, with little activity within the country that could be defined under this banner and none related to older people's services. The O4O Project Managers travelled extensively. They held several community meetings in each participating town or village and collected information on older people's lives and their service using interview, survey and community discussion methods. Working groups were established to bring older people together, to engage in activities that they had identified as beneficial, and were supported to submit applications for grant-funding for their groups. This is seen as the first stage in building community capacity for more formalised social enterprise service provision and co-production.

Sweden

Sweden has almost 10 million inhabitants but its population density of around 20 people per square kilometre is illustrative of its large rural areas outside the urban centres – particularly in the north of the country where the population densities are lower and distances between communities greater. Norrbotten county, which participated in O4O, is located in the north of Sweden (see Map I.5). It has borders running from the coast to Swedish Lapland and a population of almost 200,000, of which 21% are retired. The Project Manager was based in Norrbotten's capital city, Lulea, and worked with three rural communities to develop community social enterprises: *Sundom*, a coastal village of about 180 residents situated some 20 miles northeast of Lulea; *Niemisel*, a village with a population just over 100, lying further inland than Sundom and some 30 miles north of Lulea; and *Jamton*, a coastal village of around 240 residents and the most northerly of the Swedish O4O communities.

Sweden has a long history of welfare state provision but the social enterprise concept is gaining momentum as the state looks for innovative ways to meet certain service delivery challenges, including older people's care. There is also a tradition of work integration social enterprises which are part-funded by the state and provide employment opportunities for

Map I.5   Sweden and neighbouring countries, highlighting the Swedish communities that participated in the O4O project

hard-to-reach groups, and of community associations that tend to operate under what are seen as the voluntary model in definitions of the social economy. Within this context, the O4O Project Manager worked with communities to develop a phased process for facilitating social entrepreneurship opportunities around: a private school initiative (Niemisel); a meeting place within a grocery store, with associated grocery delivery and recyclable collection services provided through a work integration organisation (Jamton); and an inter-generational IT training programme run through an existing older people's voluntary organisation (Sundom).

Finland

Situated in the north-east of Europe, Finland has a population of almost
5.5 million, a population density of roughly 16 people per square kilometre
and, away from the capital city, Helsinki, is largely rural. Finland's North
Karelia region, which is located in the central east of the country border-
ing Russia, participated in O4O (see Map I.6). The Project Manager was
based in the town of Nurmes, which has a population of around 8,500
people. He worked with citizens within *Nurmes* and the small villages
of *Vuonislahti*, which has a population of 250 residents (rising to 750 in

*Map I.6   Finland and neighbouring countries, highlighting the Finnish
communities that participated in the O4O project*

the summer due to second-home ownership) and *Koli*, which has 300 residents. Both villages are in Lieksa, situated on the opposite shore of Lake Pielinen from Nurmes and are accessible by car ferry in the summer or ice road in the winter. Like Sweden, the Finnish context is one in which citizens have high expectations of public sector service delivery and this saw the Finnish Project Manager work to extend existing voluntary sector support for older people as a mechanism for building community capacity. This was done by developing volunteer guidance documents (Nurmes) and replicating existing voluntary organisational models (Vuonislahti and Koli).

THE O4O EXPERIENCE OF DEVELOPING SOCIAL ENTERPRISE: A SUMMARY

The community social enterprises that emerged through O4O had different aims and organisational structures that were conditioned by both the priorities of the communities involved in their creation and wider contextual features. The Project Managers found that facilitating community social enterprise was a gradual process, with some communities unwilling or 'unable' to create a social business. As a consequence, the variety of emergent O4O social enterprises reflects the community capacity-building work begun by O4O Project Managers as part of a wider aim of working towards an ideal-type model of community social enterprise for service provision. In Greenland, where social enterprise as an organisational form is virtually unknown, the organisations developed amounted to little more than informal local groups, bringing people together to talk, to consider their needs and how these might be addressed. In contrast, in Scotland, which in terms of the countries participating in O4O has one of the most established social enterprise sectors, the process of developing community social enterprise occurred at a far quicker pace and resulted in social enterprises legally constituted as companies within the life-time of the project.

The different organisations emergent from O4O can be seen to be at different stages on a trajectory towards community social enterprise as social business, with the goal either to obtain contracts from the public sector or to sell directly to service users. Accordingly, when the authors in this volume discuss community social enterprise they are referring to a variety of social economy organisational types that emerged by working with citizens to create solutions to their identified priorities.

WHAT FOLLOWS IN THIS BOOK

The work of the O4O project provides evidence-informed commentary on community social enterprise development issues, including the impacts of contextual features, the roles of different players, the extent to which communities can and should be requested to be resilient and look after themselves, the kinds of enterprises communities build, the nature of community enterprise (as compared with individual social enterprise), and issues around sustainability and measurement of impacts and success. By drawing on evidence from O4O, this book addresses the need for greater evidence on the potential role of communities in co-producing their services. Due to its large focal case study of O4O, the book concentrates on community social enterprise within rural areas, but the themes and findings discussed have implications for other locations as there are no typical communities and policy needs to move away from its focus on social enterprise as a way of addressing stereotypical decayed urban communityscapes. This book also considers a specific type of social enterprise; one that governments, communities and opinion leaders widely assume it is possible to build, but is as yet under-researched. The community social enterprises at the heart of this book are, in a sense, a range of small projects to develop self-sustaining social economy organisations of various types that sit on the cusp between community associations, volunteering organisations and social businesses – yet they are very much attuned to the *zeitgeist* of embracing social responsibility for one's community combined with operating on business principles.

In Chapter 1, Hill explores demographic, economic and ideological trends; the socio-political factors that both drive and constrain the development of community social enterprises as service providers in rural areas and the reality of/potential for policy implementation. Skerratt, in Chapter 2, continues the contextualisation of social enterprise by providing a comparative analysis of existing national structures and processes affecting their development as service providers. Together, these chapters set the context for the rest of the volume. Chapters that follow highlight the strengths and weaknesses of small, local community social enterprises as a genre and open up discussion of new areas including the apparently conflicting portrayal of social entrepreneurs as heroic individuals and policy which assumes communities can be socially entrepreneurial. In Chapter 3, Muñoz and Steinerowski explore this apparent conflict by identifying the entrepreneurial skills needed for community social enterprises within remote and rural areas and testing the feasibility of policies that promote the notion that communities ought to be involved in service delivery – and that it will be beneficial. Farmer and Stephen discuss this further in Chapter 4 by reflecting on a Project Manager's lived experience of implementing O4O, how local context affects social enterprise development, and the pros and cons of a bottom-up approach.

The O4O case study has facilitated exploration of how many of the issues play out in relation to two problematical areas for local and national governments; that is, how to provide services at the nexus of two highly expensive service imperatives: services for older people (with high service demands) and services for rural areas (which lack economies of scale, have difficulties recruiting workers and may be constrained by community norms). In Chapter 5, Radford and Shortall use evidence from O4O to reflect on whether communities are ready to engage with the process of setting up and running social organisations by drawing on the particular context of community engagement in Northern Ireland.

The authors acknowledge that governments are promoting community social enterprise as having multiple benefits and do not seek to undermine that argument *per se*. Rather, our interest is in exploring and critiquing the extent to which it might be possible to engineer the building of ubiquitous community social enterprises and in probing issues around their establishment and lifecourse. Whitelaw, in Chapter 6, reflects on the meaning of, and potential for, organisational sustainability of community social initiatives and suggests that a more nuanced understanding of sustainability is called for. Authors explored elements in the process of community social enterprise development; specifically, what affected process and what elements in the process helped or hindered social enterprise development. This relates to a need to understand the theoretical importance of measuring the value of social organisations for different stakeholders and the difficulties of capturing value and impact. This is discussed by Farmer and Bradley in Chapter 7.

The O4O case study has allowed the authors to observe the process of expanding community social enterprise in different countries, regions and communities which helped to illuminate the role of contextual factors and agency in social enterprise development. This book draws on theory, evidence and empirical findings and its authors are a similarly mixed bag of theorists, pragmatists and practitioners whose approaches represent the multiple perspectives necessary to examine the concept of community social enterprise. Consequently, the book is intended to be pragmatic but also thoughtful and analytical. It is meant to be helpful to the range of stakeholders, including community members, planners, service providers and policymakers, and to bridge the worlds of practice and academic research.

Much is made by politicians of the promise that communities should, can and will co-produce with the state, and of the attendant range of benefits, so it should be no surprise that the authors were concerned to test policymakers' claims that this was achievable. Sometimes the results were surprising. O4O was a highly complex project; it involved real people, real communities and real service delivery issues, and as a consequence was often painful in aspects of its delivery. In their Conclusion, Hill, Farmer and Muñoz analyse the body of evidence within the book to comment on the feasibility of the ubiquitous emergence of community social enterprises as rural service providers. They highlight particularly challenging issues and offer concrete recommendations for the future, if governments and societies continue along the road towards a changed paradigm of service delivery; one for the people, by the people. It may be difficult but just possible . . .

NOTES

1. Eurostat. Available at http://epp.eurostat.ec.europa.eu (accessed 17 February 2012).
2. Eurostat. Available at http://epp.eurostat.ec.europa.eu (accessed 17 February 2012).

REFERENCES

Addari F., Deakin C. & Elsworth S. (2008), *Learning from Abroad: The third sector's role in public service transformation*, London: ACEVO.

Aigner S.M., Flora C.B. & Hernandez J.M. (2001), 'The Premise and Promise of Citizenship and Civil Society for Renewing Democracies and Empowering Sustainable Communities', *Sociological Inquiry*, 71(4), pp. 493–507.

Alcock P. (2011), *Big Society or Civil Society? A new policy environment for the third sector,* Third Sector Research Centre. Retrieved from: http://tinyurl.com/3hka4ha (accessed 1 July 2011).

Argent N. (2008), 'Perceived Density, Social Interaction and Morale in New South Wales Rural Communities', *Journal of Rural Studies*, 24, pp. 245–261.

Austin J.E., Stevenson H. & Wei-Skillern J. (2006), 'Social and Commercial Entrepreneurship: Same, different, or both?', *Entrepreneurship Theory and Practice*, 30(1), pp. 1–22.

Bednarek A. (2011) 'Responsibility and the Big Society', *Sociological Research Online*, 16(2). Available at http://www.socresonline.org.uk/16/2/17.html (accessed 17 February 2012).

Berglund K. & Johansson A.W. (2007), 'Constructions of Entrepreneurship: A discourse analysis of academic publications', *Journal of Enterprising Communities*, 1(1), pp. 77–102.

Bornstein D. (2004), *How to Change the World: Social entrepreneurs and the power of new ideas,* New York: Oxford University Press.

Bryant C. & Joseph A.E. (2001), 'Canada's Rural Population: Trends in space and implications in place', *Canadian Geographer*, 45(1), pp. 132–137.

Boyle D. & Harris P. (2009), *The Challenge of Co-Production.* Retrieved from: http://www.nesta.org.uk/library/documents/Co-production-report.pdf (accessed 1 July 2011).

Cabinet Office (2010a) *The Coalition: Our programme for government*, London: HM Government.

Cabinet Office (2010b), *Building the Big Society*. Retrieved from: http://www.cabinetoffice.gov.uk/media/407789/building-big-society.pdf (accessed 1 July 2011).

Civil Renewal Unit (2006), *Community Assets: The benefits and costs of community management and ownership*, London: Department for Communities and Local Government.

Conservative Party (2010) *Big Society, Not Big Government: Building a Big Society*, London: Conservative Party.

Dale A. & Onyx J. (2005), *A Dynamic Balance: Social capital and sustainable community development*, Vancouver: UBS Press.

DTI (2002), *Social Enterprise: A strategy for success*, London: DTI.

DTI (2005), *A Survey of Social Enterprises Across the UK*, London: DTI.

Evans K. (2011), 'Big Society in the UK: A policy review', *Children and Society*, 25(2), pp. 164–171.

Farmer J., Steinerowski A. & Jack S. (2008), 'Starting Social Enterprises in Remote and Rural Scotland: Best or worst of circumstances?', *International Journal of Entrepreneurship and Small Business*, 6(3), pp. 450–464.

Gartner W.B. (1990), 'What Are We Talking About When We Are Talking About Entrepreneurship?', *Journal of Business Venturing*, 5(1), pp. 15–28.

Granovetter M. (2005), 'The Impact of Social Structure on Economic Outcomes', *Journal of Economic Perspectives*, 19(1), pp. 33–50.

Harding R. (2006), *Social Entrepreneurship Monitor: United Kingdom 2006*, London: London Business School.

Haugh H. & Kitson M. (2007), 'The Third Way and the Third Sector: New Labour's economic policy and the social economy', *Cambridge Journal of Economics*, 31(6), pp. 973–994.

Hofferth S. & Iceland J. (1998), 'Social Capital in Urban and Rural Communities', *Rural Sociology*, 63(4), pp. 574–598.

Kearns R.A. & Joseph A.E. (1997), 'Restructuring Health and Rural Communities in New Zealand', *Progress in Human Geography*, 21(1), pp. 18–32.

Kisby B. (2010), 'The Big Society: Power to the people?', *Political Quarterly*, 81(4), pp. 484–491.

Lee A. (2003), 'Community Development in Ireland', *Community Development Journal*, 38, pp. 48–58.

McCabe A, (2010), *Reflections on Community Engagement, Empowerment and Social Action in a Changing Policy Context,* University of Birmingham: Third Sector Research Centre. Available from: http://www.tsrc.ac.uk/Research/BelowtheRadarBtR/tabid/450/Default.aspx (accessed 1 July 2011).

Neck H., Brush C. & Allen E. (2009), 'The Landscape of Social Entrepreneurship', *Business Horizons*, 52, pp. 13–19.

Nicholls A. & Cho H. (2008), 'Social Entrepreneurship: The structuration of a field' in Nicholls A. (Ed.), *New Models of Sustainable Social Change*, Oxford: Oxford University Press, pp. 99–119.

Nyssens M. (Ed.) (2006), *Social Enterprise: At the crossroads of market, public policies and civil society*, London: Routledge.

Osborne S.P., Beattie R.S. & Williamson A.P. (2002), *Community Involvement in*

Rural Regeneration Partnerships in the UK: Evidence from England, Northern Ireland and Scotland, London: Policy Press.

Pearce J. (2003), *Social Enterprise in Anytown*, London: Calouste Gulbenkian Foundation.

Ridley-Duff R. (2008), 'Social Enterprise as a Socially Rational Business', *International Journal of Entrepreneurial Behaviour & Research*, 14(5), pp. 291–312.

Ridley-Duff R. & Bull M. (2011), *Understanding Social Enterprise: Theory and practice*, London: Sage.

Sawer P. (2008), *Villagers Cut Off After Closure of Rural Banks*. Retrieved from: http://www.telegraph.co.uk/earth/earthnews/3321560/Villagers-cut-off-after-clo sure-of-rural-banks.html (accessed 1 July 2011).

Scott M. (2011), 'Reflections on "The Big Society"', *Community Development Journal*, 46(1), pp. 132–137.

Sederberg C.H. (1987), 'Economic Role of School Districts in Rural Communities', *Research in Rural Education*, 4(3), pp. 125–130.

Shaw E. & Carter S. (2007), 'Social Entrepreneurship: Theoretical antecedents and empirical analysis of entrepreneurial processes and outcomes', *Journal of Small Business and Enterprise Development*, 14(3), pp. 418–434.

Shucksmith M., Chapman P., Clark G.M., Black J.S. & Conway E. (1996), *Rural Scotland Today: The best of both worlds?*, Aldershot: Ashgate Publishing Limited.

Social Enterprise London (2006), *Characteristics of Social Enterprises* [online]. Available from: http://www.sel.org.uk/ (accessed 1 July 2011).

SSEC (2009), *Policy and Resources*. Retrieved from http://www.scottishsocial enterprise.org.uk/policy/ (accessed 1 July 2011).

Steinerowski A., Jack S. & Farmer J. (2008), 'Who are the Social Entrepreneurs and What do they Actually do?', *Frontiers of Entrepreneurship Research*, Babson College, Boston, pp. 693–708.

Townsend D.M. & Hart T.A. (2008), 'Perceived Institutional Ambiguity and the Choice of Organizational Form in Social Entrepreneurial Ventures', *Entrepreneurship Theory and Practice*, 32(4), pp. 685–700.

Acknowledgements

We would like to acknowledge the work of the O4O project partners in the Karelia and Kainuu regions of Finland; in Sermersooq, Greenland; Lulea, Sweden; Northern Ireland; and the Dumfries & Galloway and Highland regions of Scotland. We specifically acknowledge input of the O4O regional leaders, Jane Farmer, Carol Hill, Asko Saatsi, Sally Shortall, Marianne Pedersen, Rosemarie Elsner and Pia Johnsen, and Project Managers, Arja Jamsen, Rosemarie Elsner, Pia Johnsen, Katy Radford, Kate Stephen and Matz Engman. The project is also indebted to a number of research assistants and to the support and co-ordination staff in each of the participating countries and regions.

The main funder of the O4O project was the EU Northern Periphery Programme. Funding was matched by contributions to the project in each region, details of which are available on www.o4os.eu. The pilot projects and services initiated during the lifetime of the project would not have happened had it not been for the unpaid effort and commitment of volunteers, most of whom were older citizens. We wholeheartedly express our appreciation, and that of the project staff, to these volunteers.

Jane Farmer, Carol Hill and Sarah-Anne Muñoz

1. The signs all point to community social enterprise – don't they?

Carol Hill

INTRODUCTION

Over recent decades policies on ageing and older people have risen dramatically up political agendas across the UK, Europe and beyond. They are driven by growing awareness of the demographic shifts impacting on the age profile of many advanced industrial nations and the inherent challenges of meeting the needs of increasing proportions of older people. More recently, the specific remote and rural dimension to these challenges has been acknowledged as policy makers seek to determine how best to ensure appropriate levels of health and social welfare within a framework of finite, and even declining resources.

Notwithstanding other differences within the national health and welfare systems of the northern periphery countries (Scotland, Northern Ireland, Sweden, Finland and Greenland) participating in the O4O: Older People for Older People project (O4O) that informs much of this book, each takes pride in its tradition of delivering universal tax-based national health and welfare systems which include provision, in varying degrees, for the health and personal care needs of older people. They are also committed to policy frameworks that value older people as both individuals and a resource for society, and seek to develop services on the basis of local need and resources that promote social inclusion and impact at community level.[1]

In the Nordic countries the role of the state in financing, organising and delivering welfare benefits has long been conditioned by the 'political goal of encouraging strong social cohesion' and underpinned by a set of ethical principles around the promotion of equity and equal entitlement, and access to social and health services, education and culture (Nordic Council, n.d.; Johansson & Hvinden, 2007). Reliant on relatively high levels of taxation, the Nordic system was challenged by the fall-out from the economic downturn of the late 1980s and early 1990s (and the subsequent 2007 global financial crisis) which pushed Sweden and Finland to seek new ways of making their welfare systems more effective. This opened the way for a gradual softening of the once clear distinction between private and public Nordic health care (Magnussen et al, 2009) and facilitated entry of what Skerratt describes in Chapter 2 as the 'Nordic model of social enterprise' into the broad field of health and social care service delivery. This has a degree of resonance with the position in Greenland, an autonomous country within Denmark since 2009 but also the recipient of high levels of benefits and pensions for its indigenous people from Denmark, on which it is still reliant for a sizeable proportion of its government revenue.[2] In addition, as a society in which gendered familial responsibility for older people remains the expected norm and where the political agenda prioritises policies relating to children and young people over those for the elderly, the impact of the out-migration of young adults and young retirees to Denmark is a cause for concern.

As countries within the UK, Scotland and Northern Ireland are subject to the crude political consensus existent during the early decades of the post-1948 welfare state which delivered a newly interventionist state with a collectivist approach to the delivery of welfare services and benefits underpinned by the ideals of universalism and comprehensiveness. There has since been a significant and increasing shift away from the prioritisation of social rights to a new politics of social obligation and personal responsibility which began in the 1970s. In Northern Ireland this, as Radford and Shortall discuss in Chapter 5, is reflected in the elevation of social enterprise in policy, and an accompanying pledge to engage more older people in its development and delivery. A similar view prevails in Scotland although the trajectory towards 'social obligation and personal responsibility' is perhaps less prevalent. As Jeffery (2010) argues, the devolved Scottish parliament has remained committed to inclusion and participation and the various Scottish governments, whether led by the Labour, Liberal or Scottish National Party, have been ideologically positioned to the left of centre. As such they have sought to retain a more traditional, social democratic model of public sector service provision, particularly in the field of social policy – which includes policies on ageing and older people (Keating, 2005).

In recent times a combination of structural features has brought each of these models under increasing strain and produced an urgency within policy communities to seek out and promote new and sustainable models of care to both supplement and, where feasible, replace state-delivered health and social welfare services. In remote and rural areas this trend has gained added impetus due to the above average cost of providing quality services at local level to small, dispersed populations containing higher than average numbers of older people, which can also mitigate against provision of private sector care services (Philip et al, 2003; Civil Renewal

Unit, 2006; Sawer, 2008). Accordingly, within related policy discourse the potential of communities, third sector providers and social enterprise as vehicles for service delivery within the health and social welfare sectors has become the subject of increased attention. This has resulted in a commitment to social enterprise, variously defined,[3] across most of the northern periphery countries, including the UK, and consideration of how to engage older people in their design and delivery as a means of harnessing their latent entrepreneurial potential (see, for example, Department of Trade and Industry (DTI), 2002; Wickham, 2006; Bridge et al, 2008; Bull 2008). This, according to Aigner et al (2001), is partially because service provision through social organisations is understood to bring benefits that are additional to cost savings, including wellbeing and empowerment, but also because they are thought, by governments, to 'regenerate' communities and encourage integration, participation and social inclusion (Lee, 2003). Conversely, others argue that such policies simply reflect a pragmatic approach to maintaining public services and an ideological interest in promoting individual responsibility (Poland et al, 2000).

Public policy does not occur in a vacuum and in this chapter I adopt a multiple lens approach to explore various rationales for the current thrust in policy towards social enterprise as a vehicle for developing and (co) delivering services to meet the health and wellbeing needs of older people; specifically within the UK but also with reference to other European Union (EU) northern periphery countries. Particular consideration is given to: the demographic shift that is particularly pronounced in remote and rural areas; the impact of the 2007 global economic crisis; and, using the UK as exemplar, an ideological trajectory that over the past three or four decades has, to varying degrees, underpinned a momentum in policy towards neo-mutualism. It is suggested that cumulatively, these particular landscapes are both framing policy development and the elevation of social enterprise within it.

THE DEMOGRAPHIC IMPETUS

Driven by falling fertility rates[4] and increased life expectancy[5] the world's population is ageing faster than at any time in history, meeting the United Nation's definition of an ageing society, one in which at least 7% of the population has reached the age of 65 years or more, for most of the last decade (Economist Intelligence Unit (EIU), 2009). This world-wide trend, which has seen the number of older people triple over the last 50 years and will see it more than triple over the next, is at its most immediate in developed countries. For example, across Europe nearly 1.6 million people are currently aged 65 or more and current projections are that the figure will exceed 20% of the European population by 2025 (EIU, 2009).

Within the EU, where the proportion of those aged between 65 and 79 increased from 12.3% to 12.7%, and those aged 80 and over from 3.4% to 4.6% between 2000 and 2009, identifiable demographic trends underpin the trajectory towards an ageing population. The majority of regions, including Highland (Scotland, UK), Norrbotten (Sweden), North Karelia (Finland) and Northern Ireland (UK) which were involved in O4O, are experiencing negative or low natural growth.[6] At the same time, the average number of births per woman in the EU has fallen from 2.5 in the early 1960s to the current 1.6, taking it below the 2.1 'replacement level' of the population, whilst the working age population is decreasing and life expectancy, which has increased by about 10 years over the last 50 years, is predicted to further increase into the future (Eurostat Population Statistics, March 2010).

Rurality, remoteness, dispersed populations characterised by the out-migration of young people and in-migration of retirees, and the concentration of higher than average proportions of older people in particular geographic locations are significant common spatial demographics of the EU northern periphery regions that participated in O4O. Each of these regions is projected to witness a continuing and significant increase in the proportion of their populations aged over 65, and in particular aged over 75, in the coming decades. In Scotland, for example, the pensionable population is predicted to increase from the 1998 figure of 17.9% to one of 24% by 2036; but when disaggregated by local authority the more predominately rural local authorities are shown to have significantly higher proportions than their urban counterparts (General Register Office Scotland (GROS), 2008). This is clearly seen in Dumfries and Galloway, one of Scotland's two oldest local authorities,[7] where, in 2006, 24% of its population was already of pensionable age. That figure is projected to rise to 30% by 2031 (EIU, 2009) with the fastest growing demographic cohort being those aged over 65, whose numbers are projected to rise by 56%, of which 83% will be aged over 75, by 2033. Over the same period the working age population is set to fall by 10.8% (GROS, 2008-based population projections) and the indications are that the dependency ratio will increase from 60:100 to 68:100 by 2033. This is not untypical of the remote and rural regions of the European Union's northern periphery, where it is recognised that any adverse shift in the dependency ratio will impact disproportionately on the care of the elderly, due to their heavy reliance on informal carers. Reflecting this, most countries addressing the issue are, understandably, inclined to focus on ways of improving and expanding services that enable older people to remain in their own homes rather than investing in additional institutional care, because it is economically more attractive and usually more in line with the wishes of older people.

In terms of service utilisation old age is patently not, of itself, an illness but as a cohort older people are known to consume the highest proportion of health and social care budgets (Asthana & Gibson, 2008; Asthana et al, 2009).This reflects the relationship between ageing and increased susceptibility to various chronic conditions and mild disabilities, which impact on health and social care spending *per capita*, which further increases with the onset of the most severe disabilities in the later years of life. In the UK, for example, those aged 65 and over are known to visit their General Practitioner seven times per annum, compared to only four by those aged between 16 and 44, and to account for two-thirds of hospital beds (EIU, 2009). Currently, 820,000 people are thought to suffer dementia and with that figure predicted to rise to 1 million by 2026 and 1.7 million by 2051, the burden on the UK National Health Service (NHS), residential care homes and informal carers is all too obvious. A similar pattern is evident across Europe, where it is predicted that the number of dementia sufferers will also soar over the next 30 years, and given that only 2% of sufferers are under 65 years and that risk doubles every 5 years thereafter, the indications are that by the age of 90, 22% of men and 30% of women will be affected by some form of dementia (Humphries et al, 2010).

In more general terms, the health and social care needs of older people are universal but in remote and rural areas their increasing proportions present a growing challenge to ensuring geographic equity of access to services. Current efficiency-oriented trends for the delivery of health and social care have induced a shift from locally located services to outreach, or 'drive in, drive out', services and the concentration of specialist services, multi-agency hubs and career opportunities in areas of high volume (NHS Scotland Remote and Rural Steering Group, 2008; Organisation for Economic Cooperation and Development (OECD), 2008, 2010). However, as Mungall (2005:1) argues, notwithstanding the benefits of centralisation, which include opportunities for up-skilling and increased levels of specialisation leading to better outcomes for patients/clients, the 'utilisation of services is inversely related to the distance of the patient from the hospital; so-called "distance decay"'. Thus, sparse, disparately located older populations in remote and rural areas can be argued as mitigating against the utility and efficacy of attempts to exploit medical and economic efficiencies of scale. In addition, whilst for many rural older people the tranquillity and security of their physical environment, its sense of community and culture of mutual support is advantageous (Black et al, 1994; Wenger, 1995), others experience loss of independence and loneliness through the fragmentation of their kin networks, restricted mobility through poor health and inadequate public transport provision (e.g. Findlay et al, 1999; Sloman, 2003), and difficulties in accessing health and social services. When compounded by low income these negative aspects of rural life can also result in poverty and social exclusion which have implications for mental and physical wellbeing (e.g. Black et al, 1994; Shucksmith, 1996; Philip & Shucksmith, 2000).

Any increase in the proportions of older people in society and change in the dependency ratio that impacts on the level of public finance available simply to maintain the *status quo* for service provision is likely to have a more profound impact on service delivery in remote and rural areas. This points to the urgency of finding novel, more imaginative ways of ensuring that the needs of older people in such areas are met. Thus, social enterprise is often promoted in policy as a viable option where cost, recruitment difficulties, and thin or failed markets hamper private or public sector provision and where it is thought that the ethos of social enterprise could harness the higher levels of social capital in rural areas.

THE ECONOMIC IMPETUS

Adding to demographic pressures on health and welfare spending are the consequences of, and policy responses to, the global financial and economic turmoil which began in 2007 and brought about a dramatic slowdown or depression in most economies in the developed world including, to varying degrees, those nations participating in O4O. In Sweden and Finland, efficient market regulation (Midttun and Witoszek, 2011) and state action to protect their banking systems following a series of crises in the late 1980s and early 1990s cushioned the impact of the 2007 global turmoil but neither their economies nor that of Denmark,[8] Greenland's primary source of government finance, were unscathed by the lack of global liquidity. Thus, despite their relative strengths, Sweden, Finland and Greenland all experienced increased unemployment and adverse fluctuations in gross domestic product (GDP), and remain vulnerable in a relatively unstable operating environment (e.g. Jonugn, 2009; Naudé, 2009; The Economist, 2009a, b; Midttun & Witoszek, 2011).

In the UK, where the impact of the economic crisis was profound, the state's response has been conditioned by its belief that high levels of government borrowing and spending are both damaging and unsustainable. To achieve its stated aim of reducing the structural deficit over four years, from 2011/12 to 2014/15, the Conservative-led coalition government has made a commitment to reduce borrowing and spending over the same period. On its own figures, the cuts in public spending that are key to this strategy, and set out in the government's October 2010 Comprehensive Spending Review (CSR), will see the loss of many thousands of public sector jobs. Within the UK, the biggest share of English Local Authorities' spending is on social care, for which they received £14.4 billion of state funding in 2010/11 and for which, under the CSR, they face cuts of 27% over the next four years. It is true that as part of their settlement these Local Authorities will receive an additional £2 billion for social care but this sum is not ring-fenced and is vulnerable in an environment in which the same Local Authorities are being asked to make efficiency savings of 7.1% per year. Indeed, even were this increase directed entirely to social care it would fall short of the minimum 4% increase required just to keep pace with the demands of increased numbers of older people (Ramesh, 2010).

Also within the UK, Scotland acquired devolved status in 1998 (Scotland Act 1998) giving it a parliament with the power to enact legislation in areas of devolved policy, including health and social services. This autonomy has seen the emergence of a distinct Scottish policy on ageing and older people and as part of that, the introduction of free personal and nursing care (FPNC) in 2001. However, whilst Audit Scotland's 2008 review of FPNC recognised it as an important policy for the nation's older people, because it acknowledged their concerns to retain the independence of living in their own homes, it also noted that the cost in the first four years of delivery had been around £0.66 billion more than would have been spent under the previous means-tested system. This increase in expenditure is a result of unanticipated levels of demand for residential, and more significantly FPNC at home, which has led Jeffery (2010) to argue that the policy was made without full consideration of either demand or cost. Given that demand, and therefore the cost of FPNC, is set to increase alongside growth in Scotland's older population, the potential strain on the Scottish budget is likely to see the nation facing budgetary constraints on a par with its English neighbours for whilst the Scotland Act gave the Scottish parliament devolved power within the UK, the main fiscal powers currently remain firmly embedded in London and ensure the Scottish parliament's dependence on Westminster for the bulk of its finance. Under the CSR, this is set to decrease by £5 billion (£6.8%); a real term cut of 10.6% over the four year period from 2011/12 to 2014/15.

The ethos of the Scottish, or what Skerratt identifies in Chapter 2 as a 'Celtic', approach to policy for the care of older people resonates with that of the O4O's Nordic partners whose commitment to 'a decent life for all' (Midttun and Witoszek, 2011:7) and view of the state as 'an ally especially of the weaker, more vulnerable citizens' (Trägårdh, in Midttun and Witoszek, 2011:18) is reflected in their approach to older people's care. Both the Celtic and the Nordic states seek a balance between individualism and collectivism and recognise the virtues of a pluralistic system characterised by a range of statutory and non-statutory service providers; yet neither is immune from the adverse financial forces prevalent in a globalised capitalist economy and are consequently 'open to' and 'actively seeking' novel forms of service delivery including social enterprise.

Just as demographic shifts bring social and economic challenges for health care systems so the growing external and internal strains on public sector budgets add impetus to the urgency of finding alternative means of delivering services (Kvist, 1999). These stresses are being felt across Europe's northern periphery where nation states are engaging in welfare restructuring with increasing determination and where the indicators are that governments are increasingly keen to share the responsibility for meeting these needs by bringing ideas about co-production and the role and responsibilities of citizens to the forefront of policy discourse. This shift is pragmatically driven – a reflection of the need to reduce state spending – but also has strong ideological undertones. In the UK for example, the thrust for co-production and community and citizen engagement can be argued to represent an apogee in an ideologically driven trend that has been reshaping the nature and purpose of state funded welfare since the 1960s.

IDEOLOGICAL IMPETUS: THE UK AS EXEMPLAR

Social Welfarism

As is well established, the election of Britain's first Labour government in 1945 was due in no small part to its commitment to introduce the recommendations of the 1942 Beveridge Report; the effective blueprint for the British welfare state. Labour's election heralded a wholesale ideological shift from centuries of *laissez-faire* to a social welfarist approach that saw the state take on the primary role of managing the economy in order to protect and promote the economic and social wellbeing of its citizens 'from the cradle to the grave'. The particular characteristics of Britain's post-war welfare state were subsequently developed by a number of influential theorists including T.H. Marshall, whose conceptualisation of citizenship added universal state-guaranteed social rights to existing civil and political rights (Marshall, 1950); Richard Titmuss, who developed the notion of social policy as a means of social integration (Titmuss, 1968); and Anthony Crosland (1956), who adopted a more benign view of the private sector, emphasised equality of opportunity and encouraged a shift in Labour's focus from central planning and public ownership to the better distribution of the benefits of economic growth. The Conservative government that followed Labour in 1951 subscribed to a form of 'one nation' conservatism that emphasised the duty of government to improve the condition of the people and enabled it, whether for ideological or pragmatic reasons, or for both, to maintain Labour's policy direction. This produced the broad cross-party consensus, or shared policy framework, which included commitment to the mixed economy, Keynesian economics and the collectivist welfare state, that lasted into the 1960s when, as Alcock (2007) infers, the consensus began to unravel. James Callaghan's 1970s Labour government rejected Keynesian demand management, cut public spending and took a pragmatic approach to high levels of unemployment. Concomitantly, the New Right, as advocates of neo-liberalism, came to the fore as an intellectual and political force and profoundly altered the direction of debate about the social responsibilities of the state to its citizens – and *vice versa*. Thus, as I continue to discuss below, the ideological legitimisation of the place of community social enterprise in the mixed economy of health and welfare is occurring as a consequence of incremental, yet relatively profound, developments in thinking about the roles and responsibility of 'the government' and 'the governed' over the past four decades.

Neo-liberalism

Under the leadership of Margaret Thatcher, the neo-liberal Conservative government that came to power in the UK in 1979 subscribed to the view that the period of consensus on the economy and on welfare had 'increased the power of the state to such an extent that individuals were being swamped and subjugated in the interests of the common good' (Taylor, 2007:69). It thus rejected collectivism in favour of individualism and self-help. For Thatcher's Conservatives, influenced by key neo-liberal thinkers such as Milton Friedman, Friedrich von Hayek, Robert Nozick and Keith Joseph, it was essential that the role of the state in the economic and social domains be minimised in order to empower individuals to accept responsibility for their own and familial wellbeing. This, it was believed, would eradicate the de-incentivising culture of welfare-dependency and enable its replacement by policies that valued individual freedom and choice; elevated personal responsibility; and recognised pluralism of provision as the approach to service delivery most likely to promote enterprise, secure innovation and facilitate freedom of choice. Indeed, both Friedman and Hayek expressly criticised the way in which the welfare state had quashed the potential of private markets and individual initiative to compete and provide services, and thereby minimised consumer choice (Alcock, 2007), whilst Friedman (1962) also highlighted the potential of the voluntary sector. This ideologically driven departure from collectivism in favour of competition via private markets and individual initiatives is clearly at odds with the post-war consensus and is argued to be an important milestone on the road to social enterprise.

Although very much moderated by the prevailing economic conditions and the centrality of the welfare state in the mindset of the electorate, neo-liberal thinking is to be seen in a range of Conservative reforms to Britain's health and welfare services from 1979. These include Griffiths' 1983 review of the management of the NHS which advocated devolved management and sought to introduce an entrepreneurial and accountable culture more closely akin to the decision-making structures found in the business sector. This paved the way for the advent of the internal market – an attempt to imitate the commercial environment with contracts and prices; buyers and sellers. However, as Le Grand and Bartlett (1993) have argued, it was not until their third term in office, from 1987, that the Conservative government felt able to launch their strongest assault on social welfarism. But their innate concerns with efficiency, value for money and market-type solutions are clearly evident in their early reforms which provide context for the possible emergence of a general, mixed economy of welfare and, further down the line, social enterprise *per se*.

The essence of 1980s neo-liberal thinking is similarly apparent in the encouragement given to individuals to take out private health insurance, for which coverage increased from 4% to c.12% of the adult population between 1978 and 1990 (Baggott, 2004:104), and in the National Health Service and Care in the Community Act 1990. That Act resurrected the policy/management division proposed by Griffiths in 1983 and, in allowing services for NHS patients to be purchased on their behalf by GP fund-holders and District Health Authorities, established the division between purchasers and providers in health care and introduced elements of competition and choice. The Act was also a rejection of institutionalisation; a policy that was in part cost-related since social security spending on residential care had risen from £10 million in 1981 to £2 billion by 1991 (Page, 2007:86), but also ideologically driven since, in a reflection of arguments put forward by Townsend (1962) and others (e.g. Goffman, 1961), institutional care was increasingly recognised as negating individual choice, freedom and responsibility. Thus, in relation to the care of the elderly, the 1990 Act imposed a duty on local authorities to assess individual needs, and plan and provide for their care 'within the community', thereby enabling individuals to remain 'at home' and 'socially included'. It also elevated the role of kin and communities over that of the state.

The Thatcher footprint on UK social welfare is evident across a range of measures designed to increase consumer choice and the plurality of service providers; limit the responsibility of the state; and create a more self-interested, independent and entrepreneurial citizenry that would assume greater responsibility for their, and their families', health and well-being. Ultimately, the extent of the Conservative reforms was tempered by political considerations (Alcock, 2007:202) but nearly two decades of neo-liberal government (from 1979 to 1997) engendered a significant mind-shift amongst the public and political elites equating to a rejection of Marshall's view of social rights as the companion of citizenship status and the elevation of the market and personal responsibility. That said, the influence, and therefore impact, of the neo-liberal ethos varies across the UK and has been more powerful in England than in the devolved countries, including Scotland and Northern Ireland (e.g. Mooney and Wright, 2009; McCafferty and Mooney, 2010).

The Third Way

Paradoxically, as Thatcherism waned as a political force during the 1990s so some of the ideas most closely associated with it were taken up by Parties previously opposed. The 1997 New Labour government led by Tony Blair accepted much of the so-called 'Thatcher settlement' which, in economic terms, had rejected Keynesian economic planning in favour of economic liberalism and in social terms had looked to create a society populated by self-interested individuals responsible for both their own wellbeing and that of their kin (Atkins, 2010). In opposition, New Labour increasingly appeared to share the Conservative government's concerns about both 'nanny statism', with its perceived culture of dependency, and the size and growth of welfare expenditure, leading, ultimately, to its conceptualisation of welfare as an enabling tool which, if properly deployed, could make retrenchment of the welfare state possible through a process of enabling individuals until they were able to act independently of it. This stance can be seen in, for example, New Labour's *Welfare to Work* programme, which incorporated an element of compulsion, and its *Sure Start* programme, which focused on intervening in people's lives to shape aspirations and abilities. Policies such as these reflected New Labour's commitment to equality of opportunity and facilitated the presentation of health and welfare reform as the basis of a new contract between 'the government' and 'the governed' that owed much to the work of Anthony Giddens, a major influence on Third Way politics. Giddens argued that individuals or groups who benefit from social goods should 'use them responsibly and give something back to the wider community in return' (Giddens, 1998:52).

This ethic lay at the heart of Third Way politics which, in seeking to rede-
fine, and strike a balance between, an individual's rights and their responsibilities, and to make the former contingent upon the latter, represented
a significant shift from the UK Labour Party's historic commitment to
equality through redistribution, unconditionality and universalism.

Under New Labour, the ethos of programmes like *Welfare to Work*
and *Sure Start*, along with the principle that an individual's rights should
be contingent upon their acceptance of a level of personal responsibility and recognition of obligations to wider society, were established in
other state-funded domains, including health. The case for this was made
clear by Prime Minister Tony Blair when he stated that 'Government
can't be the only one with the responsibility [it] must be shared and the
individual helped but with an obligation also to help themselves' (Blair,
2006:3). Atkins argues that such notions of personal responsibility and
self-reliance were taken from the New Right (Atkins in Griffiths &
Hickson 2010:42).

According to Rawlins, inculcating 'a sense of shared responsibility
amongst the citizenry is part of New Labour's conception of an "enabling
state"' (Rawlins, 2008:136). This attitude towards behaviour can be seen
in a range of health-related policy initiatives in relation to, for example,
smoking, physical activity and healthy eating that were designed to ensure
the maintenance of health (Public Health White Paper, 2004), and can be
argued to be a continuum of the emphasis on 'individual responsibility'
for health and wellbeing previously seen in the neo-liberal approach of the
Conservative administrations from 1979 to 1997.

The extent to which New Labour's policies were translated into practice was undoubtedly mitigated by its relative increase in spending on
health and social care, which also helped to alleviate potentially difficult
rationing decisions and allowed treatment to those whose behaviour was
'irresponsible'. Policy was also blown off course by the government's
interest in inequalities and the structural forces on health which allowed
room both for competing perspectives on health and appreciation of its
determined nature. However, the broad principle of 'the individual being
responsible for their health' was undoubtedly established and further
extrapolated into a *community* context through trailblazing initiatives
such as the 1998 *Health Action Zones* (HAZ) and programmes such as
Building Healthy Communities (BHC): the former to promote a new way
of local working and delivering better services by breaking through organisational boundaries; and the latter predicated on the belief that individual
behaviour change could be fostered through community participation and
action and that this, in turn, would support and empower not only individuals in the maintenance of their health, but also that of their families

and their communities (Hill et al, 2004). Community empowerment is also strongly evident in the 1999 *Healthy Living Centre* (HLC) initiative which, backed by £300 milllion of lottery funding, targeted the most deprived sectors of the population and aimed to mobilise community activity to improve health and inequalities. Significantly, it was expected that the HLC initiative would see local communities and users become involved in all aspects of the design and delivery of funded projects, and that the NHS would actively seek and support innovative projects, and stimulate and support communities to develop proposals focused on health promotion (in its widest sense) that would bring together a mix of old established and newly identified stakeholders to work in new partnerships. This approach, in terms of empowering communities and engaging them in the delivery of health and wellbeing agendas, is, as I discuss below, also evident in the current Conservative–Liberal Democrat coalition government's 'Big Society' agenda; a current policy priority with objectives of 'empowering communities, encouraging social action and philanthropy, and opening up the delivery of public services to diverse suppliers' (Schmuecker, 2011:2).

In its approach, and in the mechanisms used for the *delivery* of services, New Labour embraced much of the neo-liberal, market-oriented entrepreneurial line developed by its Conservative predecessors. This is evident in, for example, its support for public–private partnerships within the NHS (despite its earlier criticism of the Conservative Party when introducing the policy for non-NHS projects in 1992); foundation hospitals; and the development of private treatment centres within the NHS. It also encouraged public and social entrepreneurialism; casting the public sector as commissioners and opening up provision across a range of areas, including health and welfare, to the private and third sectors, and sought to value the expertise of alternative service providers in that process (Blair, 2006:2–3). However, as seen in both the HAZ and BHC initiatives, and as argued by Atkins (2010), whilst elements of neo-liberalism are clearly traceable in New Labour policies, the notion of 'community', based on the assumption that human nature is as much 'co-operative as well as competitive, selfless as well as self-interested' (Atkins, 2010:41), was also core to the Third Way. For New Labour 'community' offered the conditions in which individuals could flourish and was thus essential to its overall strategy to reinvigorate civil society through the promotion of localism, elevation of the third sector and co-operative – that is, non-state, non-commercial – endeavour (Ellis, 2010), and the attempt to integrate local projects into wider, national strategy (Lister, 2002). These are all elements of the neo-mutualist approach seen in the 'Big Society' policy agenda of the Conservative–Liberal Democrat coalition government that succeeded New Labour in 2010.

The Big Society

Despite a degree of uncertainty amongst political elites of all persuasions, policy makers, service providers, including the third sector, and the public at large, the UK's Conservative-led coalition government, elected in 2010, committed to its notion of the 'Big Society' as a basis to its reform of the public sector. Resonating with the neo-liberal views of Conservative administrations from 1979 to 1997, and much of New Labour's Third Way ideology and policy uptake, advocates for the Big Society start from the premise that people have erroneously come to *expect* the state to provide for them and there is a need to bring about change in the societal mindset. Their rhetoric implies the intention to distinguish between that which is perceived as good, that is 'the socially interventionist community', and that which is not good, that is 'the socially interventionist state' (Tonge, 2010:35), and seeks to promote the former whilst reducing the latter.

Traces of the ideas inherent in 'Big Society thinking' had previously been given expression under New Labour in what Lister (2002:245) refers to as its 'big tent' philosophy. This inclusive approach to welfare stretched across the ideological, political and practice domains to bring together tradition- ally disparate, even contradictory, ingredients to achieve a pragmatically defined end-point at which the 'practice domain' involved a mixed economy and strong communitarian ethic. This approach is seen in Professor Lord Darzi's 2008 review of the NHS in England, which recommended greater personalisation of services and extension of patient choice, and acknowl- edged that implementation would require mechanisms to encourage and support a wide range of organisations to acquire the capacity to develop and deliver a diversity of services. The review also highlighted the role that third sector organisations could play in supplying primary care.

The philosophy of the 'Big Society', with its emphasis on the values of personal responsibility, localism and collective initiative, were articulated by Prime Minister David Cameron in a 19 July 2010 speech (reported in *The Independent*, 2010) and combined strands of contemporary liberal- conservatism with the inner logic of 'path dependency' which restricts policy initiatives to step adjustments to existing foundations as a conse- quence of embedded and inherited institutional arrangements. However, for contemporary liberal-conservatives New Labour's approach was characterised by 'top down government which had the effect of sapping responsibility, local innovation, and civic action [and had] turned able, capable individuals into passive recipients of state help' (*The Independent*, 2010). Thus, with a 'nod' to both Thatcherism and the Third Way, the 'Big Society' first of all seeks retrenchment, to minimise state activity in public policy to: reduce dependency; counter the inefficiencies of 'top down' government schemes and facilitate decentralisation of power to communities, neighbourhoods and individuals; and open up public services to new providers including social enterprise and the third and private sectors. Secondly, it seeks to foster a culture of philanthropy, social action and voluntarism in order to: build capacity; stimulate diversity; innovation and responsiveness, and empower individuals and communities to take charge of their own destinies.

As I have suggested, many of the ideals inherent in 'Big Society' philosophy, particularly its emphasis on 'individual responsibility', 'localism', 'community' and 'voluntarism', can be argued to be elements of an organic, ideological continuum with emphases that, to varying degrees, are as much core to New Labour's Third Way as to Thatcherism. It also appears to continue New Labour's engagement with mutualism, albeit this is contested territory, with former contender for the party leadership David Milliband, in a May 2011 speech, arguing that 'Big Society' rhetoric on a more responsive society signified the Coalition government's re-occupation of political ground previously held by Labour (*The Telegraph*, 2011) whilst 'Big Society' advocates claim the rediscovery of mutualism as an act of restitution, arguing that it represents the 'rediscovery of *Conservative* rights regarding institutions which [had] been ignored by free market neoliberals' (Ellis, 2010:144) and a means by which to reverse the failings of post-war social democracy and renew civil society (Ellis, 2010).

For advocates of the 'Big Society', revitalisation of the third sector and the restoration of its place within a mixed economy of welfare are essential for the wider renewal of civil society and it should be possible, indeed desirable, to throw open the supply side of health and welfare services to allow provision by a broad variety of groups, with payment by the state determined by results. This policy is perceived to be ideologically and economically advantageous since it offers individuals greater choice over the services they use and, by ensuring that funding follows client choice and paying public service providers by results, it should encourage enterprise and provide value for money.

IS THE COMMUNITY SOCIAL ENTERPRISE POLICY 'INEVITABLE' OR 'DOABLE'?

As I suggested in the introduction to this chapter, the thrust of contemporary ideological, economic and demographic trends, which form the international context for health and welfare policies, appears to be creating an inexorable momentum towards localised service delivery through the medium of social enterprise. However, this route is not without its critics (e.g. Mohan, 2011; Schmuecker, 2011) and, as various of O4O's projects uncovered, there are a range of institutional and community barriers to spontaneous and successful 'Big Society-type' social enterprise that bring 'inevitability' and 'doability' into question. As Farmer and Stephen discuss in Chapter 4, the potential for spontaneous emergence of social entrepreneurs in small communities is limited and those seeking to generate community social enterprise are likely to find themselves both spanning the paradigms of 'community development' and 'social business' and acting as a bridge for bringing resources to the local community. Embedded community tensions and social norms have the ability, as Radford and Shortall discuss in Chapter 5, to destabilise and even destroy potentially sustainable social enterprises, and in each of the O4O partner countries skilled community activists were essential sources of support for communities seeking to identify and secure funding for their community enterprise and acquire the skill-sets to develop it. Funding was invariably in the form of grants which, as Whitelaw discusses in Chapter 6, brings forth a range of questions about the sustainability of this mode of service delivery that are unlikely to be addressed in the current economic climate. Even in the UK, where the *Big Society Bank* (BSB) has been established to 'connect social entrepreneurs to the capital markets so that they can access growth capital' (The Cabinet Office, 2011:2), the likelihood of it providing capital to help small, nascent social enterprises in remote and rural areas become investable is minimal – even where community need is established. Indeed, the BSB expressly restricts its 'investment capital to social ventures capable of expanding to deliver significant social impacts as well as a financial return' (The Cabinet Office, 2011:3). This raises concerns about how this source of funding might be made available to the type of small community social enterprises that the Big Society philosophy appears to advocate – given their *raison d'être* is social rather than financial return and the inherent difficulties of evaluating the social impacts discussed by Farmer and Bradley in Chapter 7.

The Big Society's social enterprise agenda elevates the role of volunteers in the design and delivery of services and assumes the ability of communities to attract and retain sufficient and appropriately skilled volunteers to devise their own solutions to social problems. Yet it appears to give little consideration to the willingness and/or capacity of communities to meet these specifications. Within the UK, rates of volunteering have been stable for many years but whilst there are currently 900,000 voluntary sector organisations with the capacity to mobilise millions of volunteers (Association of Chief Executives of Voluntary Organisations (ACEVO), 2011:19) their distribution is uneven and ranges from a low of 0.9 per 1,000 population in some local authority areas to a high of 7.7 in others[9] (ACEVO, 2011:39). Currently, just 31% of the population (typically middle-class, middle-aged, well-educated, long-term home owners resident in more affluent areas) provide almost 90% of voluntary hours and 80% of charitable giving (Wardell et al, 2000; Barlow & Hainsworth, 2001; ACEVO, 2011:39). In the absence of a substantial shift in the social and geographical distribution of volunteers this uneven spread of philanthropy and volunteering capacity inevitably raises concerns about over-reliance on volunteers and the potential (non)emergence of the localised infrastructures required for community-led social enterprise in areas where it is most needed.

CONCLUSION

In visualising a society in which individuals are socially minded, (re) engaged in local politics and of a mind to take responsibility for themselves and their local communities; conjoining the language of 'social responsibility' and 'the public good'; seeking to supplement the realms of state and market activity with an active society; and in its elevation of the third sector as part of a wider renewal of civil society, 'Big Society' philosophy essentially advocates a revised, mutualistic approach to service delivery. In a number of respects this approach harks back to the nineteenth century when welfare was delivered by a range of friendly societies, municipally owned organisations and philanthropists, and when volunteering was recognised as a means of meeting need and building character. Of course, this view tends to overlook the failings of nineteenth-century social welfare provision and is clearly an idealised view of the pre-1948 relationship between 'mutualism', 'welfare' and 'needs' in the UK. Nonetheless, it resonates with the UK government's desire to see a shift in the public mindset to one in which individuals cease to see the state as the first port of call and take greater responsibility for meeting needs through volunteering and mutual activity. This is not new. For New Labour, the 2010 coalition's predecessor in UK government, an inclusive society was also one that imposed responsibilities on individuals and communities which, together with its rejection of the 'false choice' between social and personal responsibility, formed the basis of New Labour's conception of citizenship. And prior to New Labour, various neo-liberal Conservative administrations had sought to minimise the role of the state, elevate the role of the market, and prioritise individual and familial rights and responsibilities.

Thus, as I have suggested throughout this chapter, the thrust of contemporary demographic, economic and ideological shifts appears to be underpinning an approaching apogee on a policy line straddled in the UK by governments of various persuasions since the 1970s; one that has been edging towards the identification of neo-mutualist activity, such as community social enterprise, as an appropriate, novel and cost-effective means of replacing state activity by engaging citizens in the identification and delivery of local, needs-oriented services. Reflecting this, O4O was able to test whether the concept of community-based social enterprises led by a particular cohort of citizens – active older people – could indeed identify needs and deliver appropriate and sustainable services to other older people in rural communities. As various authors discuss in the chapters that follow, the project uncovered a range of issues around the 'readiness' and 'capacity' of volunteers in such communities to undertake complex community initiatives. It also established significant latent potential and drew out a range of 'lessons for policy makers' if they are to ensure a level playing field for communities with varying capacity and social capital and enable the strength of the policy rhetoric to be matched in implementation.

NOTES

1. See, for example, Prime Minister's Office, Finland (2010), Ministry of Health and Social Services, Sweden (2001), The Scottish Government (2007) and The Office of the First Minister and Deputy First Minister Northern Ireland (2005).
2. Though awarded self-rule in 2009 Greenland currently receives 57% of its government revenue from Denmark.
3. Chapters 2 and 3 offer detailed discussions of *social enterprise* as a contested term and its different structures and ethos both within the UK and across EU northern periphery countries.
4. The 55 years between 1950 and 2005 saw global fertility per woman almost halve, to 2.6 children. This trend, though slowing, is expected to continue (EIU, 2009).
5. Humanity's median age has risen by 5 years, to 29.1 years, since 1990. A similar increase is projected over the next 20 years (EIU, 2009).
6. *Natural growth* is the difference between the number of live births and the number of deaths.
7. The other is Eilean Siar, the Western Isles region of Scotland.
8. Whilst the 2008 World Economic Forum's Competitiveness Index ranked Denmark amongst the top three countries its position has slipped as a result of the global financial crisis, which had a more profound impact on Denmark than on other Nordic countries due to its housing bubble (Midttun & Witoszek, 2011).
9. These statistics exclude central London boroughs where many national organisations are based.

BIBLIOGRAPHY

ACEVO (2011), *Powerful People, Responsible Society: The report of the Commission on Big Society*, London: ACEVO.
Aigner S.M., Flora C.B. & Hernandez J.M. (2001), 'The Premise and Promise

of Citizenship and Civil Society for Renewing Democracies and Empowering Sustainable Communities', *Sociological Inquiry*, 71(4), pp. 493–507.

Alcock C. (2007), *Introducing Social Policy*, London: Longman.

Asthana S. & Gibson A. (2008), 'Deprivation, Demography, and the Distribution of General Practice: Challenging the conventional wisdom of inverse care', *British Journal of General Practice*, 58, pp. 720–728.

Asthana S., Gibson A., Bailey T., Hewson, P. & Dibben C. (2009), *Developing a Person Based Resource Allocation Formula for Setting Practice-Level Mental Health Budgets: 2009/10 and 2010/11*. Report to the Department of Health (Policy Research Programme), University of Plymouth.

Atkins J. (2010), 'Assessing the Impact of the Third Way' in Griffiths S. & Hickson K. (Eds.), *British Party Politics and Ideology after New Labour*, Basingstoke: Palgrave Macmillan, pp. 39–52.

Audit Scotland (2008), *A Review of Free Personal and Nursing Care*. Retrieved from: http://www.auditscotland.gov.uk/docs/health/2007/nr_080201_free_personal_care.pdf (accessed 31 October 2011).

Baggott R. (2004), *Health and Health Care in Britain*, Basingstoke: Palgrave Macmillan.

Barlow J. & Hainsworth J. (2001), 'Volunteerism Among Older People With Arthritis', *Ageing and Society*, 21, pp. 201–217.

Black S., Chapman P., Clark G. & Shucksmith M. (1994), *The Good Life? Rural disadvantage and older people in Scotland*, Edinburgh: Age Concern Scotland.

Blair T. (2006), Speech on Healthy Living, 26 July. Retrieved from: http://webarchive.nationalarchives.gov.uk/+/http://www.number10.gov.uk/Page9921 (accessed 28 April 2011).

Bridge S., Murtagh B. & O'Neill K. (2008), *Understanding the Social Economy and the Third Sector*, London: Palgrave Macmillan.

Buchanan I. (2010), 'Policy Context: The place of social enterprise in UK contemporary policy' in Gunn R. & Durkin C. (Eds.), *Social Entrepreneurship: A skills approach*, Bristol: Policy Press, pp. 7–19.

Bull M. (2008), 'Challenging Tensions: Critical, theoretical and empirical perspectives on social enterprise', *International Journal of Entrepreneurial Behaviour and Research*, 14(5), pp. 268–275.

Civil Renewal Unit (2006), *Community Assets: The benefits and costs of community management and ownership*, London: Department for Communities and Local Government.

Crosland A. (1956), *The Future of Socialism*, 2006 edition edited by Leonard D., London: Constable & Robinson Ltd.

Department of Trade and Industry (2002), *Social Enterprise: A strategy for success*, London: DTI.

Economist Intelligence Unit Ltd. (2009), *Healthcare Strategies for an Ageing Society*, London: Economist Intelligence Unit Ltd.

Ellis C. (2010), 'Mutualism and the Reinvention of Civil Society: A conservative agenda?' in Griffiths S. & Hickson K. (Eds.), *British Party Politics and Ideology after New Labour*, Basingstoke: Palgrave Macmillan, pp. 138–149.

Eurostat Population Statistics (March, 2010). Retrieved from: http://epp.eurostat.ec.europa.eu/statistics_explained/index.php/European_cities_-_demographic_challenges (accessed 21 April 2011).

Findlay A., Short D., Stockdale A., Findlay A., Lin N. Li & Philip L. (1999), *Study of the Impact of Migration in Rural Scotland*, Age Concern Scotland, Scottish

Consumer Council & the Senior Studies Institute, University of Strathclyde, Edinburgh: The Scottish Office Central Research Unit.

Finlayson A. (2010), 'Did Blair Advance Social Democracy?' in Griffiths S. & Hickson K. (Eds.), *British Party Politics and Ideology After New Labour*, Basingstoke: Palgrave Macmillan, pp. 11–17.

Friedman M. (1962), *Capitalism and Freedom*, Chicago: University of Chicago Press.

General Register Office Scotland (2008), *Population Projections Scotland (2008 based)*. Retrieved from: http://www.groscotland.gov.uk/statistics/theme/population/projections/scotland/2008-based/index.html (accessed 7 March 2011).

Giddens A. (1998), *The Third Way: Renewal of social democracy*, Cambridge: The Polity Press.

Goffman E. (1961), *Asylums: Essays on the social situation of mental patients and other inmates*, London: Penguin.

Griffiths R. (1983), *NHS Management Inquiry Report*, London: DHSS.

Griffiths S. & Hickson K. (Eds.) (2010), *British Party Politics and Ideology after New Labour*, Basingstoke: Palgrave Macmillan.

Hill C., Blamey A. & Mackenzie M. (2004), *The Commissioned Evaluation of Building Healthy Communities*, Dumfries: Crichton Centre for Research in Health and Social Issues.

HM Government (2010), *The Coalition: Our programme for government*, London: HM Government.

HM Treasury (2010), *Spending Review*, Cm 7942, London: Crown Office.

Humphries R., Forder J. & Fernández J.L. (2010), *Securing Good Care for More People*, London: The King's Fund.

Jeffery C. (2010), *Older People, Public Policy and the Impact of Devolution in Scotland*, Edinburgh: Age Scotland.

Johansson H. & Hvinden B. (2007), 'Re-activating the Nordic Welfare States: Do we find a distinct universalistic model?', *International Journal of Sociology and Social Policy*, 27(7/8), pp. 334–346.

Jonugn L. (2009), *The Swedish Model for Resolving the Banking Crisis of 1991–93. Seven reasons why it was successful*, Brussels: DGECFIN, European Commission. Retrieved from: http://ec.europa.eu/economy_finance/publications/publication14098_en.pdf (accessed 8 March 2011).

Keating M. (2005), 'Policy Convergence and Divergence in Scotland under Devolution', *Journal of Regional Studies*, 39(4), pp. 453–463.

Kvist J. (1999), 'Welfare Reforms in the Nordic Countries in the 1990s: Using fuzzy-set theory to assess conformity to ideal types', *Journal of European Social Policy*, 9(3), pp. 231–252.

Le Grand J. & Bartlett W. (Eds.) (1993), *Quasi-markets and Social Policy*, Basingstoke: Macmillan Press.

Lee A. (2003), 'Community Development in Ireland', *Community Development Journal*, 38, pp. 48–58.

Lister R. (2002), 'New Labour: A study in ambiguity from a position of ambivalence', *Critical Social Policy*, 21(4), pp. 425–447.

Magnussen J., Vrangbaeck K. & Saltman R.B. (2009), *Nordic Health Care Systems: Recent reforms and current policy challenges*, Buckingham: Open University Press.

Marshall T.H. (1950), *Citizenship and Social Class and Other Essays*, Cambridge: Cambridge University Press.

McCafferty P. & Mooney G. (2010), 'Resisting the Neoliberal "Modernisation" of Public Services in Contemporary Scotland: The case of public service workers' in Davidson N., McCafferty P. & Miller D. (Eds), *Neoliberal Scotland: Class and society in a stateless nation*, Newcastle: Cambridge Scholars, pp. 161–179.

Midttun A. & Witoszek N. (Eds) (2011), *The Nordic Model: Is it sustainable and exportable?*, Oslo: UIO, Norwegian School of Management.

Milliband D. (2011) Speech at Hay-on-Wye, 29 May, reported by James Kirkup in *The Telegraph*, 30 May.

Ministry of Health and Social Services, Sweden (2001), *Social Services Act*. Retrieved from: http://www.scribd.com/doc/32167396/Social-Services-Act-in-Sweden (accessed 23 February 2011).

Mohan, J. (2011), 'The Big Society in Practice: The challenges of increasing volunteering, charitable giving and civic partnership' in *Britain in 2011*, Swindon: ESRC.

Mooney G. & Wright S. (2009), 'Introduction: Social policy in the devolved Scotland: Towards a Scottish welfare state?', *Social Policy and Society*, 8, pp. 361–365.

Mungall, I.J. (2005), 'Trend towards Centralisation of Hospital Services, and its Effect on Access to Care for Rural and Remote Communities in the UK', *The International Electronic Journal of Rural and Remote Health Research, Education, Practice and Policy*, 5(390), pp. 1–8. Retreived from http://www.rrh.org.au/articles/subviewnew.asp?ArticleID=390 (accessed 21 April 2011).

National Health Service and Community Care Act 1990. Retrieved from: http://www.legislation.gov.uk/ukga/1990/19/contents/enacted (accessed 21 April 2011).

Naudé W. (2009), *The Financial Crisis of 2008 and the Developing Countries*, Discussion paper No. 2009/01, Helsinki: UNU-WIDER.

NHS Scotland Remote and Rural Steering Group (2008), *Delivering for Remote and Rural Healthcare*, Edinburgh: NHS Scotland.

Nordic Council (n.d.), 'Norden'. Retrieved from: http://www.norden.org/en (accessed 3 May 2011).

OECD (2008), *OECD Policy Reviews: Scotland, UK: Assessment and recommendations*. Retrieved from: http://www.scotland.gov.uk/Resource/Doc/212 557/0056531.pdf 11/1/11 (accessed 11 January 2011).

OECD (2010), *Health at a Glance: Europe 2010*, OECD Publishing. Retrieved from: http://dx.doi.org/10.1787/health_glance-2010-en (accessed 6 March 2011).

Page R.M. (2007), *Revisioning the Welfare State*, Buckingham: Open University Press.

Philip D., Gilbert A., Mauthner N. & Phimister E. (2003), *Scoping Study of Older People in Rural Scotland*, Edinburgh: Scottish Executive Social Research Unit.

Philip L. & Shucksmith M. (2000), 'The Character of Poverty in Rural Scotland', *Social Justice Annual Report Scotland 2000*, Edinburgh: Scottish Executive.

Poland B.D., Green l. & Rootman I. (2000), *Settings for Health Promotion: Linking theory and practice*, London: Sage.

Prime Minister's Office, Finland (2010), *Ageing Report: Overall assessment of the effects of ageing and the adequacy of preparation for demographic changes*. Retrieved from: http://www.vnk.fi/julkaisut/julkaisusarja/julkaisu/en.jsp?oid=258437 (accessed 23 February 2011).

Professor Lord Darzi (2008), *High Quality Care For All: NHS next stage review final report*, Cm 7432, London: Crown Office.

Public Health White Paper (2004), *'Choosing Health: Making healthy choices easier'*, Cm 6374, London: HMSO.

Ramesh, R. (2010), 'Spending Review, 2010 (Social Care)', *The Guardian*, 21 October, p. 13.

Rawlins E. (2008), 'Citizenship, Health Education and the Obesity Crisis', *ACME: An International E-Journal of Critical Geography*, 7(2), pp. 135–151. Retrieved from: http://www.acme-journal.org/vol7/ERa.pdf (accessed 25 April 2011).

Rochester C., Paine A.E., Howlett S. with Zimmeck M. (2010), *Volunteering and Society in the 21st Century*, Basingstoke: Palgrave Macmillan.

Sawer P. (2008), *Villagers Cut Off After Closure of Rural Banks*. Retrieved from: http://www.telegraph.co.uk/earth/earthnews/3321560/Villagers-cut-off-after-clo sure-of-rural-banks.html (accessed 25 April 2011).

Schmuecker K. (2011), *Can the Big Society be a Fair Society? A North East perspective*, Newcastle: Institute for Public Policy Research.

Shucksmith M. (1996), *Disadvantages in Rural Areas*, Salisbury: Rural Development Commission.

Sloman, L. (2003), *Rural Transport Futures: Transport solutions for a thriving countryside,* London: Transport 2000.

Taylor G. (2007), *Ideology and Welfare*, Basingstoke: Palgrave Macmillan.

The Cabinet Office (2010), *Building the Big Society*. Retrieved from: http://www.cabinetoffice.gov.uk/media/407789/building-big-society.pdf (accessed 28 February 2011).

The Cabinet Office (2011) , *The Big Society Bank ('BSB') Outline Proposal*, May. Retrieved from: http://www.cabinetoffice.gov.uk/sites/default/files/resources/big-society-bank-outline-proposal.pdf (accessed 13 June 2011).

The Economist (2009a), 21 April.

The Economist (2009b), 17 August.

The Independent (2010), 'The Big Society: A genuine vision for Britain's future – or just empty rhetoric?', 20 July.

The Office of the First Minister and Deputy First Minister Northern Ireland (2005), *Ageing in an Inclusive Society – Promoting the social inclusion of old people*. Retrieved from: http://www.ofmdfmni.gov.uk/ageing-strategy.pdf (accessed 23 February 2011).

The Office for National Statistics (2010), *Social Trends No. 40, 2010 Edition*, The Office for National Statistics. Retrieved from: http://www.ons.gov.uk/ons/rel/social-trends-rd/social-trends/social-trends-40/index.html (accessed 23 February 2011).

The Scottish Government (2007), *All Our Futures; Planning for a Scotland with an ageing population*. Retrieved from: http://www.scotland.gov.uk/Publications/2007/03/08143924/0 (accessed 23 February 2011).

The Telegraph (2011), 'David Milliband: Labour should back the Big Society', 30 May.

Titmuss R.M. (1968), 'Universalism and Selection', reprinted in Pierson C. & Castles F.G. (Eds.) (2000), *The Welfare State: A reader*, Cambridge: Polity Press, pp. 42–52.

Tonge J. (2010), 'Response' in Griffiths S. & Hickson K. (Eds.), *British Party Politics and Ideology After New Labour*, Basingstoke: Palgrave Macmillan, pp. 34–35.

Townsend P. (1962), *The Last Refuge*, London: Routledge & Kegan Paul.

Townsend P. (1979), *Poverty in the United Kingdom: A survey of household resources and standards of living*, Harmondsworth: Penguin.

Wardell F., Lishman J. & Whalley L. (2000), 'Who Volunteers?', *British Journal of Social Work*, 30(2), pp. 227–248.

Wenger G.C. (1995), 'A Comparison of Urban with Rural Support Networks: Liverpool and North Wales', *Ageing and Society*, 15, pp. 59–81.

Wickham P. (2006), *Strategic Entrepreneurship*, Harlow: Prentice Hall.

World Economic Forum (2011), *Shared Norms for the New Reality. The Nordic Way*, Davos: World Economic Forum. Retrieved from: http://www.norden.org/en/about-nordic-co-operation/areas-of-co-operation/the-nordic-welfare-model/about-the-nordic-welfare-model (accessed 16 May 2011).

2. Developing rural social enterprise: the relevance of context

Sarah Skerratt

CONTEXT MATTERS

Contemporary literature around rural community development highlights the contingent role of *context* in the nature and success of development (Henderson & Vercseg, 2010; Mackleworth & Caric, 2010). Context is experienced at a local level, in terms of social relations (Oldenburg, 1999, 2002; Putnam, 2000; Hailey, 2001; Cleaver, 2004; Davies, 2007, 2009), and also operates 'vertically', in that it comprises the policy, legislative and sectoral landscape within which communities operate (Sorensen & Epps, 1996; Gray & Sinclair, 2005). Thus, as Cleaver (2001) contends, to focus solely on communities and their activities would incorrectly abstract them from day-to-day realities, including relations with a range of agencies and stakeholders. Communities, local enterprises and agents thus do not operate in a vacuum; rather, initiatives are often dependent on external directions and options. Research into the capitals of development (Flora et al, n.d.) highlights that political and bridging social capital are required – that is, individuals and communities need to know how to relate to those outside of their immediate sphere in order to shift their development trajectory (O'Brien et al, 1991, 1998). Rural leadership research (Sorensen & Epps, 1996; Gray & Sinclair, 2005; Skerratt, 2011) also points to the need for successful communities and leaders to acknowledge and work with wider relationships beyond the immediate locale. Given this context it is important that analyses of community-level activity development, including the building of (formal and informal) organisations for service delivery such as in the O4O: Older People For Older People project (that aimed to work with older people in rural communities to establish community social enterprises for service delivery), examine various levels of action that are relevant to localities. Research should accurately reflect reality more by including the wider context within which enterprises, individuals and communities operate.

A strand in the literature suggests that communities should not be 'expected' to deliver all services (Bridger & Luloff, 1999; Cleaver, 2001; Skerratt, 2010a). Aspects of delivery, infrastructure, strategy and investment remain in the domain of the public, and to a lesser extent (certainly in rural areas) private, sectors. As Edwards (2009:19) states:

> there is a danger in expecting too much from associational life, as if it were a 'magic bullet' for resolving the intractable social, economic and political problems ... Increasingly, it seems, voluntary associations are expected to organise social services, govern local communities, solve the unemployment problem, save the environment, and still have time left over for rebuilding the moral life of nations.

Edwards' view runs counter to the romanticising of community with its capitals being able to deliver to *all* outcomes – what Edwards calls the civil society revivalist movement (2009:107). There is a need to recognise the importance of multi-level activity, and ideally the integration of such activity, where community actions are enhanced and supported by other agents in the public and private sphere (Henderson & Vercseg, 2010).

Cultural norms support certain developmental trajectories as appropriate or inappropriate (Sorensen & Epps, 1996; Khotari, 2001; Brennan & Luloff, 2007; Mackleworth & Caric, 2010). Norms operate at community level, as well as at regional and national levels of government and within other public sector agencies. These may relate to 'entitlements' of individuals and communities, of service standards and their distribution and of 'eligibility' according to established criteria. These variables are all relevant, perhaps particularly to those in remote and rural areas (Skerratt, 2010b), where the range of alternatives and options is typically far more limited than in urban settings. Knowing what is considered acceptable by people living in such areas is pertinent to understanding what happens.

In this chapter, the ways that context as defined above influences a component of community civil society – that is, the formation and sustainability of community social enterprises – are considered. A case study of the European Union-funded O4O initiative provided examples of attempts to develop community social enterprises in rural regions of Scotland, Northern Ireland, Sweden, Finland and Greenland. As well as an action element that drove and supported the establishment of community social enterprises, the project captured data around the context of community social enterprise development in participating countries. This process, *Context Mapping*, was achieved through three sets of questionnaires, four sets of interviews with O4O Project Managers in different countries and iterative group discussions of summarised multi-country questionnaire responses from project partners. These latter discussions allowed cross-national differences, similarities and assumptions to be uncovered, debated and understood.

The Context Mapping process helped to identify what influences in the macro environment may help or hinder the development of community social enterprises for service delivery, allowing identification of priorities for change to be addressed if social enterprise is to grow from a multi-sector, multi-level perspective across different regions. This chapter takes an international-comparative perspective and considers the context affecting development of social enterprise, the context affecting the specific dimension in which O4O sought to develop (older people's services) and examines how contextual factors combine to affect outcomes. The chapter also reflects on how knowledge of context helps to explain what happens or even to predict what will, or is unlikely to, happen. It considers the place of Context Mapping methodology in the context of multi-country comparative studies about social and organisational developments.

CONTEXT MAPPING METHODOLOGY

A multi-method approach was employed to collect contextual data, comprising three elements: three iterations of in-depth written questionnaires, four iterations of telephone interviews with O4O Project Managers, and three discussion forums at international partners' workshops. Findings were analysed thematically (Patton, 1990); that is, the themes which emerged for each of the questions (both questionnaire and telephone) were identified, and similarities and differences were presented at partner workshops, clarified and discussed. Thereafter, an overall, thematic description of similarities and differences in context was formulated. First, O4O country teams consisting of Project Managers and country team leaders were required to complete three written questionnaires. These asked for in-depth information on: the policy context for social enterprises; the legal and financial structures for establishing social enterprises; structures and the extent of volunteering; models of older persons' care; and expectations regarding which agencies would provide care. The second strand of data collection was through telephone interviews with in-country O4O Project Managers at intervals during the project's lifetime (four iterations in total). An identical core set of questions was used on each occasion, so that data could be assessed longitudinally to compare and verify perspectives. Thirdly, group discussion of the findings was facilitated at international workshops. This allowed for two outcomes: participant validation of the findings, and discussion of similarities and differences between countries.

FINDINGS

In this section the respective contexts for social enterprise across the five participant countries are considered, by examining how social enterprise is defined and structural issues including finance and state support and the state of the concept of volunteering, a key source of human resources for social enterprises, across participant countries. The particular sectoral context for development in O4O is then discussed (i.e. older people's services) and commentary provided on the potential effects of 'differences in context' on the outcomes for different countries seeking to develop community social enterprises for older people's services. The quotes are from O4O Project Managers in each of the O4O partner countries.

The Concept of Social Enterprise

There is an extensive English-language literature, reflected on by Muñoz and Steinerowski in Chapter 3, that highlights how the concept of social enterprise is ill-defined and contested. Findings from the Context Mapping on social enterprise highlight that social enterprise was differently understood, defined and enacted in the different countries involved in the O4O project. The key axis of difference was between models described by partners from Finland, Sweden and Greenland, and those described by Scottish and Northern Irish participants. In the former, named for shorthand the 'Nordic' model, social enterprise can be summarised as private or voluntary sector organisations that have, as a component of their workforce, employees who would otherwise find it difficult to find employment due to physical or emotional ill-health, long-term unemployment or homelessness (www.finlex.fi; Huotari et al, 2008). Typically, approximately one third of the workforce must comprise such employees for a business to be classed as a social enterprise. The following quotes by Project Managers in Finland, Greenland and Sweden describe what social enterprise means in the three countries:

> Social enterprises make as good a profit as they can as they are private companies. Social enterprises are not different from other companies. They produce goods and services for the market and try to make a profit. A social enterprise can operate in any sector or line of business. It pays all its employees a salary under a collective bargaining agreement. However, social enterprises have fewer possibilities to succeed and make profit. The employees have reduced ability to work and that is why social enterprises can have some compensatory support from government. (Project Manager, North Karelia, Finland, May 2009)

> Social enterprises can exist within the voluntary, public and business sectors. 'Social activities' within this specific context are defined as jobs where the

Municipality gives grants to pay the wages of an individual, or lump sum benefits. Various social enterprise companies take staff on, through subsidised wages, and help them with rehabilitation through flexible working. They also help individuals to remain in employment. (Project Manager, Greenland, May 2009)

Social enterprises have a purpose of integrating people who are far removed from the labor market, society and working life . . . They are independent from public activity. Over the past decade, social enterprises have been launched all around Sweden . . . to combat social exclusion. (Project Manager, Luleå, Sweden, May 2009)

In Scotland and Northern Ireland, a 'Celtic' model is in place. Although there is no universally agreed definition the most widely used is from the UK Department of Trade and Industry (2002): 'A Social Enterprise is a business with primarily social objectives whose surpluses are principally reinvested for that purpose in the business or in the community, rather than being driven by the need to maximise profit for shareholders and owners.' Unlike the Nordic model there are no specific requirements regarding the composition of the labour force; rather the focus is on meeting social objectives and returning profits to the community or social business. The following are definitions provided by the O4O Project Managers in Scotland and Northern Ireland:

Social enterprises are autonomous organisations that trade in goods and services primarily for a social purpose often to benefit a local community . . . they have clear social aims . . . The impact is not purely to be found in wealth generation, but can be measured in job creation and a wider social impact at a community level that in turn addresses the social determinants of a community's well-being. (Project Manager, Northern Ireland, May 2009)

In the majority of cases, social enterprises in Scotland generate income. This does not mean that they are self-sustainable. In many cases, they rely to some extent on external financial support. If profit is gained, it has to benefit a community . . . Rather than being driven by the need to maximise profit for shareholders and owners, business solutions used by a social enterprise are used to achieve public good. (Project Manager, Highland, Scotland, May 2009)

These terminological differences between the Nordic and Celtic models are important and only emerged because of the iterative information-finding, discussion and verification process of Context Mapping. Until mid-project, all project partners were carrying only their own definitions of social enterprise in their heads, assuming these were the shared norm. Although all project partners were pursuing their models of social enterprise on the ground, the lack of definitional clarity was causing confusion.

Two consequences resulted from this confusion. First, the 'social enter-prise model' described in O4O publicity material, the O4O website and other shared O4O literature was that of the Scottish project leaders, and partners from Greenland, Sweden and Finland found it hard to reconcile their understanding of a social enterprise with the organisational model being proposed by Scotland, the team that was leading the project, for implementation. This meant that the Scandinavian partners found it much harder to convey O4O objectives to *their* stakeholders in a way that was meaningful. Secondly, this led to delays in building shared understanding of what needed to be achieved on the ground in the Scandinavian context, due to an assumed shared understanding between project coordinator and partners. This situation reflects what has been termed 'the taken-for-granted assumptions that are part of one's culture' (Cohen, 1982:83). Different understandings of the concept of social enterprise are one example of the taken-for-granted assumptions that the Context Mapping sought to identify and examine.

Support for Social Enterprises

In considering how communities might obtain funding to start and sustain social enterprises, national and regional perspectives were examined through the Context Mapping process which provided insights about the structural context within which community social enterprises seek to become established and survive. In all of the Nordic countries involved in O4O funding was available for social enterprises. In Finland a social enterprise, which may be in the private, public or third sector, had the same status as any other company in terms of its eligibility for private and public financing for business start-up. Specifically they were eligible for start-up grants for up to 18 months, employment cost subsidies and Employment Policy Assistance for a social enterprise seeking to employ 'difficult to employ' people. Loans were also available for small enter-prises. Similarly, in Greenland the government provided grants to social enterprise start-ups and, again, employment cost subsidies for those hard to employ. There were also small foundations and charities which gave grants for social activities. In Sweden, where a culture of funding from charities, trusts and lottery-type funds was not apparent, the European Social Fund (ESF) was viewed as the main source of funding for social enterprises.

The situation in Northern Ireland and Scotland, in terms of the avail-ability of, and eligibility for, funding and financial support for social enterprise was found to be significantly different from that pertaining in the Nordic countries. In Northern Ireland, potential funding sources were diverse but without a defined source for social enterprises. Banks were regarded as unsympathetic and whilst there was some small grant funding from government departments this was aimed at short-term projects. Many social economy businesses in Northern Ireland were within the church-based sector and their constitutions precluded them from taking money from the Big Lottery funds distributor.

Scotland had two, limited, sources of funding specifically designed for social enterprises, the Social Entrepreneurs Fund and the Millennium Awards Trust, but the majority of funding was sought from within the main funding landscape, where funders included the Scottish Investment Fund, Third Sector Enterprise Fund, Big Lottery, and Lloyds TSB Foundation for Scotland. Funds and loans were available, but most were over a shorter term and some required partial pay-back.

When examining regional development agencies' interactions with social enterprises, equivalent contrasts could be seen. Scotland and Northern Ireland's regional development agencies (Highlands & Islands Enterprise, Scottish Enterprise and Enterprise NI) each had a specific objective and funding schemes to encourage social enterprise start-ups. Luleå in Sweden could access four regional development agencies, each of which was experienced in providing matched funding for European Union-funded schemes, many of which were favourable to organisations with social objectives. In North Karelia, Finland's regional development agency was geared to supporting commercial business. In Greenland, consultants operated out of the development agencies to provide guidance; in the 'O4O region' of Greenland, there was an association advisor in Kommuneqarfik Sermersooq who provided practical and financial advice.

The evidence from the Context Mapping showed, therefore, that Scotland and Northern Ireland had funding contexts that were most conducive specifically to social enterprise development, with schemes badged for social enterprise. However, and conversely, a plethora of other funding agencies that did not single out social enterprises also made it challenging for such enterprises to identify potential funding streams. Swedish and Finnish enterprises could potentially access finance through regional agencies. In most O4O countries, therefore, social enterprises would be required to rummage through a diverse bag of different sources of funding as there was little evidence of banks with structure to support the sector.

A similar picture could be seen with the availability of advice to establish a social enterprise. Thus, for the two models identified (Nordic and Celtic), Scotland was the most well served, with a well-developed advice network, with advice in the Nordic countries tailored largely to commercial enterprises rather than to the needs of social enterprises. The Context Mapping showed that in Scotland navigating the extensive advice landscape was a challenge, and in the other O4O countries identifying potential advice was the main difficulty. Specifically, Scotland's support structure was well established; in fact, there were extensive sources of advice, including Highlands and Islands Enterprise (Inverness); Highlands and Islands Social Enterprise Zone (Inverness); Business Gateway (Inverness); Scottish Social Enterprise Coalition (Edinburgh); First Port (Edinburgh); and the Social Enterprise Academy (Edinburgh). Invest Northern Ireland provided advice and assistance for its clients but to access this a business must have met criteria including a £100,000 turnover in business and exporting potential. Whilst some social enterprises may meet these criteria, the majority are ineligible. Invest Northern Ireland may have provided advice, and other enterprise organisations might have been of assistance, but there was a lack of access to tailored social enterprise advice. In Sweden and Finland, while free advice, support and training was available from government and regional agencies (e.g. the North Karelia Enterprise Agency (Pohjois-Karjalan Uusyrityskeskus ry), Objectives for Enterprise and Finnvera plc in Finland and Coompanion in Sweden), this was for commercial businesses and enterprise, with no specific recognition of the needs of social businesses. Similarly in Greenland, there were consultants employed in the development agencies to provide guidance to companies, associations and individuals.

Volunteers: The Human Resources of Social Enterprise

From O4O's inception, it was clear that the participant countries had different traditions and understandings of the concept of 'volunteers'. In O4O, volunteers were defined by the Project Managers as unpaid community members who provided their time and skills to support development of community social enterprises and provided services for them. Based on this definition, Scotland and Northern Ireland have a long tradition of formal volunteering and voluntary organisations. Many of these organisations play a role in service provision and some have become large not-for-profit social enterprises, voluntary organisations and hybrid (public/private and voluntary/paid) organisations. In Inverness, the largest centre in the Scottish Highlands, there was evidence that 30% of those aged 50–59; 26% of those aged 60–74 and 15% of those over 75 provided voluntary services in non-profit organisations at the time of the O4O project (source: Context Mapping questionnaire response, Highland region). In Northern Ireland, there were over 1200 voluntary sector groups providing a range of services. These were often free or charged a small amount towards costs and provided the following range of services: transport; lunch clubs; social activities; physical activities; health promotion; counselling; education and training; befriending; domiciliary care; community pharmacists; benefit and welfare advice; advocacy; campaigning and lobbying; financial services; home maintenance and security services; residential and nursing care; and housing.

The Northern Ireland Volunteer Development Agency's (2007) *It's All About Time* report highlighted that the overall economic value of formal volunteers' contribution, based on the Northern Ireland average hourly wage, is £504 million/year. Older volunteers in the 50+ age group are most likely to volunteer once a week and give more time than any other age group. There were two agencies which acted as the leading structures for volunteering development and recruitment in Northern Ireland: the Volunteer Development Agency, which has a remit to increase awareness of, and recognition for, the importance of volunteering as an expression of active citizenship; and the Volunteer Services Bureau, whose role is as a local development agency providing the infrastructure to support, encourage and promote citizenship and participation through voluntary activity. Despite a well-developed voluntary sector, in Scotland and Northern Ireland the public is used to most service delivery from public services, free at the point of delivery and financed through taxation.

Project partners from Sweden (Luleå), Finland (North Karelia) and Greenland expressed interest in establishing formal volunteering as there was no tradition of voluntary organisations in these countries and a high expectation of paid public sector employees providing a wide range of services. Whilst volunteering does occur in these countries – for example, North Karelia in Finland had 214 voluntary organisations that provide some form of services to older people – it was often linked with seniors, pensioners, religious, sports and activity organisations where members help each other or provide benevolent services to the community. In Sweden, volunteering was provided by the Church of Sweden, the Pensioners National Organisation (PRO) and the Pensioners Association of Sweden (SPF).

Scandinavian Municipality providers desired a shift in culture towards the public accepting that volunteers can provide enhanced services that support public sector provision or help to improve older people's quality of life. As voluntary organisations targeted at providing services were few, municipalities were wrestling with the challenge of how to get these started or accepted by the public as providers. Some volunteering was supported and run by Luleå Municipality, for example.

In Greenland, O4O project workers described a paternalistic situation where, in the past, the Danish government had provided high levels of benefits and pensions for indigenous Greenlanders. In Greenland, help and support for older people (outside the public sector) were provided by the

Senior's Association; the Association of the Disabled; Qeersaat (sports); Oqilaatsukkut (choir); Sanningasoq Tungujortoq (Blue Cross); Angutit Erinarsoqatigiit (men's choir); NIPE (choir); Peqatigiinniat (Christian association); and individual volunteers (reading, lectures, showing of films, music and organised walks).

In all of the participant countries the provision of support to older people was in a state of change, and state and local public services were interested in how to generate more volunteer workers to provide services that would enhance older people's quality of life and help to keep them living in their homes and communities, out of hospitals and residential care. Greenlandic, Swedish (Luleå) and Finnish (North Karelia) participants were intrigued as to how Scotland and Northern Ireland could attract such a high level of 'free' labour in the form of volunteering and voluntary organisations in order to address this need. The place of each country regarding volunteering is illustrated through the following quotes:

> There is not a wide culture or a tradition of volunteering, of doing things for no pay. (Project Manager, North Karelia, Finland, May 2009)

> We have not focused on 'volunteering' or 'voluntary services', as that would not be very productive. Instead, we have made sure that we have focused on 'safe, helping, secure visiting etc. in our village'. Voluntary services are not seen as something positive in Sweden because we have a history that the State or Municipality takes care of you after a lifetime of work. Therefore, to sell O4O to elderly people, you have to talk about it helping others to feel safe in their village. (Project Manager, Luleå, Sweden, November 2009)

> Getting volunteers and communities to do things for themselves. It's been very tough to motivate people to do this. They say 'why should we do this?' and 'it was done for us in the past'. We are seen as taking away from what the public sector should be doing. We need people with enthusiasm who see that this is positive for the community. (Project Manager, Highland, Scotland, May 2009)

> We say that 'YOU are the answer'. O4O gives an opportunity for you to be seen as good practice – we write up the process that they've gone through, and identify aspects with them which they can then sell as leverage for meeting targets in local government. (Project Manager, Northern Ireland, November 2009)

All participants said there was a perception in their region that volunteering is connected with loss of state entitlements. This is illustrated in the following quotes:

> Communes [municipalities] are increasingly being encouraged to take care of their problems. It is a very big challenge for us to get older people to understand

to do things for themselves. This generation is used to things being provided for them. (Project Manager, Greenland, May 2009)

Others have been recipients of services for ever, both individuals and communities. They can complain about the services, but they don't have to run them and they have no responsibility for them. For getting funding, or for managing a budget. It takes so much more energy to manage these things than it does to complain about them. (Project Manager, Highland, Scotland, May 2009)

SOCIAL ENTERPRISE AND OLDER PEOPLE

Having considered contrasts and similarities between Greenland, Sweden (Luleå), Finland (North Karelia), Scotland (Highland) and Northern Ireland in terms of the context for establishing social enterprise, discussion now turns to a consideration of the context for the specific older people's sector that was the focus of the O4O project. We examine elements of the economy of service provision for older people, including what services are expected, who is expected to pay and who is expected to provide. Whilst the O4O project sought to look at how community social enterprises could provide services for older people, such as transport, domestic help, lunch clubs and meeting places, the information captured by the Context Mapping largely pertains to aspects of older people's more formal social and health care provision. It provides insights as to how community social enterprise for and by older people might proceed in the different regions and what factors might influence its development.

Services and Payments

As part of considering the existing market context of service provision, including the range of services provided and the extent to which people perceive receipt of services as a state or a personal responsibility, partners in O4O were asked to state the range of services that older people would receive from the public sector in their region and indicate individuals' responsibility for payment. The range of services suggested and the extent to which services were chargeable, means-tested or free at the point of delivery were examined for each country (Table 2.1).

Table 2.1 highlights the variety in types of services provided by municipalities, councils and health services. It shows that in most countries services are targeted at frailer older people and are generally more targeted at technical support for those with illness rather than social types of support that address social and psychological wellbeing maintenance. This perhaps reflects a traditional model of providing 'intensive' technical

Table 2.1   Examples of public sector services for older people in O4O partner countries/regions

Country	Chargeable services	Means-tested – provided in relation to pay	Free services
Northern Ireland	Personal care: help with eating, dressing, washing and bathing, getting in and out of bed (subsidised).	None.	Attendance allowance: tax-free benefit paid to people aged 65+ who need help with personal care. Many voluntary sector services such as befriending schemes.
Scotland	Chiropodists, opticians, dental care, lunch clubs (subsidised), telecare (subsidised).	Shopping, personal hygiene/ washing, support work, local essential travel, laundry.	Health care, free personal care for over 65s, district nurse, travel to hospital, equipment to help people stay in own homes, services accessed via hospital (at the intermediate care stage).
Sweden (Luleå)	Most services are chargeable.	Not applicable.	Activities at specific meeting places for older citizens.
Finland (North Karelia)	Private nursing and health care, support services at home, rehabilitation services (day/night care).	Institutional care services, support in caring for close relatives, home renovation, domestic support, housing allowance.	Phone counselling, social and patient attorney, mental health outpatient department, senior gymnasium and fitness welfare clinic, social worker and disabled soldier services, family doctor, physiotherapy, outpatient department, day surgery, short-term institutional care, special worker services at health care centre, day care centres.
Greenland	Transportation services are numerous but include those for the disabled and food services.	Domestic help for those with supplementary income, government financial support, support for those with special dietary requirements.	Municipal authorities offer personal and practical assistance, e.g. domestic help, day centres and senior citizens' homes, professional domestic nursing assistance for the elderly and disabled.

services for a small proportion of vulnerable/frail older people. With changing demography and ideas about health moving towards an understanding of the importance of wellbeing and social support to help keep people out of institutional care, public services need to move towards providing structure for health maintenance. Finland's provision hints at attention to health maintenance services, including free gym, web services, counselling and day centre activities, whilst Scotland's free services are still oriented at the ill and frail and keeping them out of institutional care.

Of the countries considered, the North Karelia region of Finland identified the most extensive range of free public services for older people. Notably, Sweden's Municipality-provided services all have standard charges. This information provided an indication of the types of services people might regard as being provided for 'older people' and also of potential attitudes to personal or state responsibility for aspects of looking after older people. This therefore relates back to the expectations and experiences of volunteering outlined in the preceding section.

The Care Landscape

In addition to the foundation of public sector care for older people in all of the countries in the O4O project, there were varying patterns of services provision by commercial organisations, voluntary organisations, community organisations and projects (Table 2.2).

As noted in the section above and reflected in Table 2.2, all countries had volunteering organisations of various sorts. Commercial providers operated in subtly different ways across the different regions as well. In Scotland and Northern Ireland, the private sector mainly acted as a provider of residential care facilities in rural areas, whilst in Finland and Greenland the private sector provided community-based care such as cleaning, laundry and food provision services through contracts with the Municipality or with individuals. Timebanks, where people register services they would give in exchange for receipt of useful services that others might provide, were present only in North Karelia's provision model, although mentioned as part of a wider service provision landscape, beyond older people's care, in Greenland and Scotland.

It was important to consider the extent to which it would be 'in the culture' of each country to consider that community social enterprises might be a provider of services for older people. As has been shown, social enterprise means different things in Scotland/Northern Ireland and Sweden/Finland/Greenland. In the O4O study, project partners were asked to consider both definitions of social enterprise and record

*Table 2.2   The variety of service providers in the O4O partner countries/
regions*

Service providers	Finland (N. Karelia)	Sweden (Luleå)	Greenland	Northern Ireland	Scotland
Council/state	√	√	√	√	√
Voluntary organisations	√		√	√	√
Commercial organisations	√		√	√	√
Seniors, religious & sports organisations		√	√	√	
Timebanks	√				

the extent to which these types of organisations were active in the older people's service provision sector.

Findings showed that in Finland (North Karelia) and Greenland social enterprises were not evident in the older people's services sector and they were not seen as a strong alternative for producing enhanced social and health services. In Greenland it was noted that general policy is targeted at children and younger people, encouraging them to remain in Greenland; therefore older people's policy, in general, is neglected. In Sweden, in the Luleå region, there were no social enterprises focused on older people's services. However, this was widespread in Sweden as a whole. In the neighbouring Municipality of Umeå, for example, there were social enterprises that focused on older people's care. In Northern Ireland, information sourced from the Social Economy Network was unable to identify any social enterprises providing services targeted at older people in rural areas. Similarly in Scotland, such enterprises were uncommon. One example from the Highland region was *Highland Home Carers*, an employee-owned business providing nursing support and home care services to frail or disabled people across the north of Scotland so they could continue to live independently in their own homes (www.highland-home-carers. co.uk).

Therefore, it can be seen that the public services provided for older people tend to be of the technical, illness or care-oriented type and whilst a variety of payment models are in place, the public sector is still either the major provider or takes responsibility for organisation. Ideas of enhanced services aimed at improving quality of life for older people or keeping less frail people maintained healthily at home remain largely unaddressed, except perhaps in Finland, and the current range of providers remains traditional: public sector, commercial sector or various types of voluntary organisations, with little current breakthrough of different models of social enterprises into service provision.

DISCUSSION AND CONCLUSIONS

Social Enterprises, the Role of Context and Implications for the Future

Each region participating in the O4O project shared a set of common challenges: peripherality and rurality; ageing populations with increasingly larger proportions of older people in their rural populations compared with urban places in the same country; a neo-liberal policy turn demanding state retrenchment with increasing responsibility for service provision and payment left to communities and citizens; and budgetary constraints or cutbacks.

In the face of these challenges, each region was considering how to keep older people out of expensive institutional care, living at home in their community. Simultaneously, each participant region was interested in increasing the role of 'volunteers' as both a free workforce and to build social participation and networks, thereby increasing social capital and wellbeing. As has been shown, each country participating in O4O came into the project from 'a different place'. Table 2.3 summarises the situation of each country.

By examining context alone we might expect that community social enterprises would develop according to the dominant models operating in each country. Thus, in Scotland and Northern Ireland, the types of community social enterprises would comprise a significant component of volunteer input, benefit to local community-of-place (focused on the specific sector of older people), and receive support (advice and funding) from a range of tailored and generic sources. In Sweden, Finland and Greenland, we might expect community social enterprises to be primarily operating according to a standard, commercial business model, with a proportion of the paid, subsidised workforce being made up of the otherwise hard to employ. This would suggest context as determinant. However, although there was significant evidence of this, in that structural support (including relationships with municipalities' regional development agencies, for example) continued to perpetuate the models that currently exist, there was also evidence of evolution and flexibility towards hybrid models of provision. Thus, context remains a significant, but not absolutely sole, determinant.

Table 2.3 Social enterprise factors and older people's services in O4O partner countries/regions

	Scotland	Northern Ireland	Greenland	Sweden (Luleå)	Finland (N Karelia)
Social enterprise (SE) factors					
Definition	Not-for- profit business	Not-for-profit business	Employs hard-to-employ	Employs hard-to-employ	Employs hard-to-employ
SE specific funding	Multiple state sources	Some state sources	No specific focus	Council match-funds EU social projects	Focus on commercial business
SE specific support agencies	State supported	Little tailored to SE	Potential access to business consultant	Commercially oriented	Commercially oriented
Volunteering	Well-developed voluntary sector	Many small voluntary organisations	Pensioners associations,etc.	Pensioners associations, etc., some municipality	Aiming to enhance municipality support for volunteer development
Older people's services sector					
Service focus	Technical, sickness-oriented	Technical, sickness-oriented	Technical, sickness-oriented	Technical, sickness-oriented, some social	Most socially/health maintenance-oriented
Payment	Largely free	Largely free	Mix	Largely self-paying	Mix
Role of voluntary sector/SE	Some voluntary, occasional SE	Some voluntary	Little voluntary sector input	Little voluntary sector input	Little voluntary sector input

As indicated in Farmer, Hill and Muñoz's Introduction to this book, as the O4O projects developed in each partner country/region, it became possible to see a variety of community social enterprise outputs or products/ service offerings. It could be argued that these illustrate an evolving approach towards the role of volunteers and volunteering and hybridisation of provision models according to local resources, mindsets and opportunities. In Scotland (Highland Region) O4O community social enterprise production led to the formation of three community social enterprise organisations providing enhanced services after gaining Council (Local Authority) grants or regional development agency (Highlands and Islands Enterprise) funding. Context Mapping interviews showed the investment of time and effort required by the O4O Project Manager in encouraging and supporting social entrepreneurs and other community volunteers. This was done in a stage-by-stage process which built trust and shared understanding rather than allowing fears of volunteering and service withdrawal to stifle effort and enterprise. In Northern Ireland, O4O led to two projects having their current social enterprise extended, a lunch club and a meeting place, and one community project, a radio station, drawing on government initiative funding. The O4O Project Manager emphasised that in these projects the solution already lay with people in the community – the evidence was already there of their enterprise, commitment and achievement. O4O then enhanced confidence and self-belief in being able to make meaningful provision for older clients.

In Luleå in Sweden, one might have expected – given the context described above and the lack of a tradition or culture of volunteering – to see only commercial social enterprises in operation under O4O. However, whilst the three O4O social enterprises operated with a business model and governance approach that were due in large part to the steer given by the O4O Project Manager who had a background in working in business, two of the three did in fact incorporate extensive volunteer input. The O4O social enterprises were the Healthgalleria (a voluntary-type initiative in a local school, bringing together older and younger people); a supported employment initiative (a village helper employed through the local shop) through a more traditional Swedish social enterprise model; and an information technology training programme with older people training one another. Each project gained finance through a mix of Municipality and regional development agency sources. The O4O Project Manager stated that, at village level *and* at Municipality/regional development agency level, he could not use the language of volunteering to encourage involvement or financial support. Rather, he had to couch all O4O discussions in terms of creating a safe place for older people to live in their community. The focus was thus on how safe, welcoming and warm *their* community was and could be, thus generating a sense of community pride. The Project Manager believed that this would generate participation, and his evidence of engagement in the three projects showed this to be the case.

In Finland, the O4O project outputs were much slower in being realised due to three main factors. First, confusion persisted over what a social enterprise meant in the O4O region; as discussed above, the dominant model led to uncertainties over what could be produced on the ground. Secondly, there was a different mindset in the partner region as the regional development agency that was the local lead agency for O4O had a greater focus on commercial business, within which the volunteering approach was a poor fit. Thirdly, services for older people were already extremely well established within the state infrastructure and there was thus little room for manoeuvre with new, social enterprise-based provision. The O4O Project Manager stated that in Finland, there was a cultural sense of responsibility for older people that underpinned state and Municipality commitment. Here, we saw greater influence of context leading to persistence of current approaches, with little scope for the integration of what are seen as alternative models.

In Greenland, informal volunteering through social networks was evidenced as significant. However, as with Sweden and Finland there was almost no history of public, formalised volunteering in service provision. This was coupled with a greater state emphasis on children and a paternalistic approach towards older people's care, such that older people themselves do not need to think about how they would be cared for in their old age, with more able retirees migrating to Denmark. Much of the work of the O4O Project Managers therefore involved educating and informing people about volunteering, reducing the fear that volunteering was associated with state service withdrawal, and explicitly building on what people were already doing. This they achieved through repeated radio broadcasts, social events, newspaper articles and lobbying of government. In addition, the extreme rurality of Greenland was highlighted by the O4O Project Managers as being a significant component of whether and how such social enterprises could operate. Consequently, they focused their O4O efforts on bringing people together for the first time and enhancing communication through monthly phone calls and regular newsletters such that people in different parts of the expanse of Greenland were informed of each others' efforts and achievements. The following quote emphasises the crucial aspect of rural context and how it led to an emphasis on networking, and on inclusive, sustained communication for mutual support:

> The scale of Greenland is enormous, and there are no roads outside the main area. For example, it takes one week to get from the capital to East Greenland

... We have to fly to Denmark, then Iceland, then take a helicopter to the town in E. Greenland ... But O4O is very exciting because it is giving the opportunity for us to find out what elderly people think about elderly care in the east of Greenland, and also to give people in the east of the country an opportunity to give their views – they have never been asked before. (Project Manager, Greenland, May 2009)

Thus, within the O4O community social enterprise experiences we see a picture both of working *within* context and adaptation and evolution *beyond* context. We see evidence of the ongoing significance of structure – government support, norms of delivery – which directly affects what is perceived to be possible and what is actually possible in terms of scope for innovative community social enterprise development *per se*, and specifically in the domain of older people's care. Given the push within Scotland and Northern Ireland towards social enterprise, and development through and by communities and neighbourhoods, it is likely that O4O-type community social enterprises, dependent on extensive volunteer input, will continue to be contextually viable. In Finland and Greenland, this seems to be less likely, due to the contextual aspects outlined above. In Luleå in Sweden we see, through O4O, some hybridisation of social enterprise and of the space within which care for older people is being operationalised.

However, this prediction may in itself be simplistic since there are additional challenges or elements to consider. In Northern Ireland and Scotland, social enterprise start-ups generally have to locate their funding requirements within a standard business development agency programme whilst remaining non-mainstream themselves. At regional level in Sweden and Finland the social enterprise model is encompassed within standard business support activities of development agencies. Thus, ongoing support and consequent sustainability may be more feasible, even where a hybrid approach is generated, as in Luleå.

Returning to the key points made in this chapter's introduction we can see that the findings from the Context Mapping echo those in the wider literature. First, we see that the O4O Project Managers were operating within their contexts, navigating both local and extra-local connections, and developing and operationalising their bridging and political social capital. They are connected both with the communities and with municipalities, and with funding agencies and other stakeholders important to the establishment and survival of community social enterprises. They are also encouraging networking and building of capital in those communities where O4O is taking place, particularly in Greenland.

Secondly, the formation and delivery of the community social enterprises in the O4O partner countries add further evidence of the tension that exists – in the literature and on the ground – between what should be provided by the state and what could and should be provided by the community. We see different expectations, most notably between Scotland and Northern Ireland on the one hand, and Finland (particularly), Sweden and Greenland on the other. Through O4O, therefore, there is further evidence of how these normative expectations are played out on the ground.

Thirdly, the research points to the fact that knowing the cultural norms and what is considered appropriate and acceptable is critical. The O4O project exemplifies this consistently, through: how volunteering is perceived and therefore how O4O Project Managers had to operate; how older people's care is perceived, and thus what becomes possible and practicable in communities; and how the role of the state is perceived by a range of actors and agents, and how this translates into what 'becomes possible' on the ground. Also, and central to the Context Mapping, are the perceptions of what a social enterprise is, should and could be. This directly affected the types of activities on the ground, largely perpetuating established norms, but in the case of Luleå also leading to an adoption of volunteering in two community social enterprises, thus giving a hybrid approach. Through the example of O4O we see further evidence of the centrality of cultural context.

REFLECTIONS ON THE CONTEXT MAPPING METHODOLOGY

Context Mapping through questionnaires, interviews and participant validation generated insightful findings from different regions on the backdrop influencing current approaches to community social enterprise development for older people's enhanced service provision. The evidence provided a perspective for considering the ways social enterprises develop (or not). The mapping allowed researchers to see similarities and differences across partner countries which would otherwise be lost in the typical focus on tasks and on-the-ground delivery, and provided an interesting analytical framework for reflecting on what actually happened in the international project to build community social enterprises.

The first component of Context Mapping, questionnaires, generated extremely useful data on the policy, funding and political norms and systems surrounding and underpinning health and social care, and the care of older people. It also began to generate in the Project Managers and other team members some curiosity as to why researchers regarded these as important parts of 'their world', and led to discussions at the international project partners' meetings that were unlikely to have taken place otherwise. The second component, six-monthly telephone interviews, focused on what the O4O Project Managers were doing and why, and how and why things were, or were not, progressing in each of the O4O projects for which they were responsible. This allowed for a focus on *why* things were being done in a certain way, what rationale underpinned the approaches and activities, and what might be the reasons for certain developments. Project Managers were asked a core set of questions every time so that a picture could be built of how circumstances changed during the lifetime of O4O. This allowed the significance of context to be prominent as project teams sought to establish initial interest in volunteering, set up community social enterprises, and sought to enhance the performance of those social enterprises. It also led to a sense amongst O4O Project Managers that their perspectives were valid and important in gaining a better understanding of process and that they had expertise to offer to the international project team.

The third component of Context Mapping, workshop sessions at each of the internal project partners' meetings, led to significant shared learning that would not have taken place otherwise. It also allowed for critical validation of findings by the Project Managers which were extremely useful to the researchers in the partnership. Summaries of the questionnaire findings and telephone interviews were circulated prior to meetings to allow project partners to see what was happening in other countries or regions, and why. The variation in social enterprise models and perspectives on volunteering was viewed as instructive and important for seeing and understanding how and why things are 'done differently' in different regions and countries. Thus, the in-country norms, rules and systems were examined and compared, and doing this deliberately within Context Mapping helped reflection on possibilities and how challenges might be variously addressed. In the case of Luleå, this led to the development of alternative approaches. In all other cases O4O Project Managers reported enhanced understanding which led to an appreciation of their situation within a wider context. Further, the Context Mapping enabled O4O Project Managers to examine what influences in the macro environment may be helping or hindering the development of local social enterprises.

Thus, in addition to researchers benefiting from an enhanced understanding of the significance of context to the establishment and sustainability of O4O community social enterprises, the O4O Project Managers reported greater shared understanding of these aspects and, where appropriate, fed these into the development of O4O project activities in their countries and regions. Context Mapping therefore deliberately created the opportunity for reflection beyond the minutiae and pressures of project delivery, towards discussions on current and future adaptations for enhanced sustainability of social enterprises for older people's care.

REFERENCES

Brennan M.A. & Luloff A.E. (2007), 'Exploring Rural Community Agency Differences in Ireland and Pennsylvania', *Journal of Rural Studies*, 23, pp. 52–61.

Bridger J.C. & Luloff A.E. (1999), 'Towards an Interactional Approach to Sustainable Community Development', *Journal of Rural Studies*, 15, pp. 377–387.

Cleaver F. (2001), 'Institutions, Agency and the Limitations of Participatory Approaches to Development' in Cooke B. & Kothari U. (Eds.), *Participation: The new tyranny?*, London: Zed Books, pp. 36–55.

Cleaver F. (2004), 'The Social Embeddedness of Agency and Decision-Making' in Hickey S. & Mohan G. (Eds.), *Participation: From tyranny to transformation? Exploring new approaches to participation in development*, London: Zed Books, pp. 271–277.

Cohen A.P. (Ed.) (1982), *Belonging: Identity and social organization in British rural cultures*, Manchester: University of Manchester Press.

Davies A. (2007), 'Organic or Orchestrated: The nature of leadership in rural Australia', *Rural Society*, 17(2), pp. 139–154.

Davies A. (2009), 'Understanding Local Leadership in Building the Capacity of Rural Communities in Australia', *Geographical Research*, 47(4), pp. 380–389.

Department of Trade and Industry (2002), *Social Enterprise: A strategy for success,* London: DTI.

Edwards M. (2009), *Civil Society*, Cambridge: Polity Press.

Flora C.B., Emery M., Fey S. & Bregendhal C. (n.d.), *Community Capitals: A tool for evaluating strategic interventions and projects*, Ames, Iowa: Iowa State University, North Regional Centre for Rural Development.

Gray I. & Sinclair P. (2005), 'Local Leaders in a Global Setting: Dependency and resistance in regional New South Wales and Newfoundland', *Sociologia Ruralis*, 45(1/2), pp. 7–52.

Hailey J. (2001), 'Beyond the Formulaic: Process and practice in South Asian NGOs' in Cooke B. & Kothari U. (Eds.), *Participation: The new tyranny?*, London: Zed Books, pp. 88–101.

Henderson P. & Vercseg I. (2010), *Community Development and Civil Society. Making connections in a European context*, Bristol: Policy Press.

Huotari T., Pyykkönen M. & Pättiniemi P. (2008), 'Sosiaalisen ja taloudellisen välimaastossa. Tutkimusnäkökulmia suomalaiseen sosiaaliseen yritykseen', *Sosiaali- ja terveysturvan keskusliitto ry*, 8.

Khotari U. (2001), 'Power, Knowledge and Social Control in Participatory Development' in Cooke B. & Kothari U. (Eds.), *Participation: The new tyranny?*, London: Zed Books, pp. 139–152.

Mackleworth P.C. & Caric H. (2010), 'Gatekeepers of Island Communities: Exploring the pillars of sustainable development', *Journal of Environmental Development and Sustainability*, 12, pp. 463–480.

O'Brien D.J., Hassinger E.W. & Brown R.B. (1991), 'The Social Networks of Leaders in More and Less Viable Communities', *Rural Sociology*, 56(4), pp. 699–716.

O'Brien D.J., Raedeke A. & Hassinger E.W. (1998), 'The Social Networks of Leaders in More and Less Viable Communities Six Years Later: A research note', *Rural Sociology*, 63(1), pp. 109–127.

46   *Community Co-Production*

Oldenburg R. (1999), *The Great Good Place: Cafes, coffee shops, bookstores, bars, hair salons, and other hangouts at the heart of a community*, Cambridge, Massachusetts: Da Capo Press.

Oldenburg R. (2002), *Celebrating the Third Place: Inspiring stories about the 'great good places' at the heart of our communities*, Cambridge, Massachusetts: Da Capo Press.

Patton M.Q. (1990), *Qualitative Evaluation and Research Methods*, Thousand Oaks, California: Sage Publications, 2nd edition.

Putnam R. (2000), *Bowling Alone: The collapse and revival of American community*, New York: Simon & Schuster.

Skerratt S. (2010a), 'How are Scotland's Rural Communities Taking Ownership of their Own Future?' in Skerratt S., Hall C., Lamprinopoulou C., McCracken D., Midgley A., Price M., Renwick A., Revoredo C., Thomson S., Williams F. & Wreford A. (Eds.), *Rural Scotland in Focus 2010*, Edinburgh: Rural Policy Centre, Scottish Agricultural College, pp. 42–51.

Skerratt S. (2010b), 'Hot Spots and Not Spots: Addressing infrastructure and service provision through combined approaches in rural Scotland', special edition of *Sustainability:* Human populations in remote areas, 2(6), pp. 1719–1741. Available at: www.mdpi.com/2071-1050/2/6/1719/ (accessed 17 February 2012).

Skerratt S. (2011), 'A Critical Analysis of Rural Community Leadership: Towards systematised understanding and dialogue across leadership domains', *Journal of Contemporary Issues in Business and Government*, 17(1), pp. 87–107.

Sorensen T. & Epps R. (1996), 'Leadership and Local Development: Dimensions of leadership in four Central Queensland towns', *Journal of Rural Studies*, 12(2), pp. 113–125.

Volunteer Development Agency (2007), *It's All About Time*, Belfast: VDA.

3. Socially entrepreneurial skills and capabilities in a rural community context

Sarah-Anne Muñoz and Artur Steinerowski

INTRODUCTION

Over recent decades the promotion of the Third Sector and, most recently, social enterprise has become much more visible within UK policy and the terms 'social entrepreneurship' and 'social enterprise' increasingly used to refer to the development of sustainable trading activities conducted for social benefit (Jones & Keogh, 2006; Weerawardena & Mort, 2006). As detailed by Farmer, Hill and Muñoz in the Introduction to this book, social enterprise is promoted as a mechanism through which both economic development and social goals can be met. The public sector is encouraged to 'procure' from social enterprises, there is state support for social enterprise start-up and development, and citizens are encouraged to participate in socially entrepreneurial activities. The UK policy agenda surrounding community empowerment, community ownership of assets and service delivery accesses ideas of social business and local entrepreneurialism. Several authors in this volume make reference to the 'Big Society' policy agenda which is led by the current UK coalition government and translates notions surrounding community empowerment into support for the co-development and co-production of services by citizens.

As Hill indicates in Chapter 1, the current context of public sector cuts implies continuing retraction of the state from service delivery and greater involvement of non-state (e.g. voluntary sector and social enterprise) players, including citizens themselves, in the design, development and delivery of services while Skerratt, in Chapter 2, shows that these issues are relevant beyond the UK. All this suggests that greater attention should be paid to what communities and citizens can realistically achieve in terms of service delivery and a need to interrogate which skills and capabilities (that policy suggests are necessary) are available or latent within communities. Existing entrepreneurship and social enterprise literature points towards certain characteristics of the social entrepreneur, with the most distinguishing factor being the ability to apply an entrepreneurial/business approach to create social value. Social entrepreneurs are often portrayed as visionary leaders who engage in risky behaviour in order to derive social innovation. They look for opportunities to add social impact throughout their entire value chain; set up and develop new social organisations, inspire people around them to take action and turn their visions into realities that generate social rather than personal profit (Leadbeater, 1997; Peredo & McLean, 2006; Shaw & Carter, 2007). If citizens and existing community groups are to take a bigger role in service provision through the type of community social enterprise (CSE) response that is promoted by contemporary policy, there is a need to understand the extent to which community actors possess the necessary skills and are willing and able to harness those skills within socially enterprising service solutions.

These issues have particular implications for rural areas where populations are often smaller, older and more dispersed, yet rural contexts have been little explored in social enterprise research. Williams (2007) has suggested that those living in rural areas display a greater propensity to engage in social rather than commercial entrepreneurship when compared with those living in urban areas, but the number of people in rural communities with the appropriate skills, willingness and the capability to participate is unclear and may be limited (Organisation for Economic Co-operation and Development (OECD), 2008). Social enterprises could benefit rural areas by using a bottom-up approach to develop services that more appropriately meet local needs and, by doing so, satisfy local communities (Osborne et al, 2002; Department of Trade and Industry, 2005; OECD, 2008). Accordingly, this chapter draws on entrepreneurship and social entrepreneurship literature to discuss policymakers' demands of remote and rural communities in terms of their involvement in service provision.

The role of older people within entrepreneurialism, and social entrepreneurialism in particular, is relatively unexplored although initiatives such as the Silver Economy Network[1] have highlighted an increasingly pan-European research and policy interest in issues around both the role of older people in economic activity and social enterprise as a provider of jobs, for those who are under-employed, unemployed or retire early. Drawing on evidence from the O4O: Older People for Older People project (O4O) this chapter adds to knowledge of socially entrepreneurial skills and capabilities within two under-researched areas: the rural context and older entrepreneurs. The types of skills and capabilities associated with social entrepreneurship within current literature and research are first highlighted and then analysed in relation to issues about their application in remote and rural areas. Examples from O4O are used to show how entrepreneurial skills and capabilities may need to be developed and used within rural communities to generate and sustain CSEs for service provision.

METHODOLOGY

The O4O project tested the generation of rural CSEs through a particular type of action research that involved what the project researchers termed a 'facilitated' model of community entrepreneurship wherein an action researcher, or O4O Project Manager (PM), worked with community members to *facilitate* socially entrepreneurial approaches to the provision of services for older people within particular localities.

In this chapter we highlight the types of socially entrepreneurial behaviour, skills and capabilities that PMs were required to employ when working with communities, and the implications of this for the development of social enterprises in other rural communities. Through interrogation of the PM's role, we highlight the endogenous skills and capabilities communities need to find within themselves, and then employ, in order to complement O4O's 'facilitated' model. This is followed by reflections on how rural communities may be able to work together entrepreneurially to design, develop and sustain services for their own locale, and on how examples from O4O demonstrate that members of remote and rural communities may be reluctant to engage with what they perceive as 'business orientated' concepts such as social enterprise. The implications for developing the social enterprise agenda are subsequently analysed and questions raised about the types of support offered to communities and the ways in which 'entrepreneurialism' is conceptualised. This is achieved using data collected from six O4O PMs in their weekly and monthly project activity reports, from 2007 to 2010. This activity used standard templates which were completed by PMs in each of the O4O partner countries (Scotland, Northern Ireland, Greenland, Finland and Sweden). It captured activities carried out in each of the 16 participant communities in 5 countries; the timescales of progress; and the PMs' perceptions of, and reflections on, their own roles within the process of creating social enterprises and the perceived risks and challenges of the process. The activity reports were collated by a researcher and subject to thematic analysis. This analysis, along with the PMs' interviews detailed by Skerratt in Chapter 2, form the basis of the discussion presented here.

SOCIAL ENTERPRISE, SOCIAL ENTREPRENEURSHIP AND SOCIAL ENTREPRENEURIAL SKILLS AND CAPABILITIES

Despite increasing academic and policy interest in *social entrepreneurs* and *social entrepreneurship*, commentators remain perplexed by the poorly defined nature of these concepts (Mair & Marti, 2006; Peredo & McLean, 2006). In the following sections we expand on the definitions of 'social enterprise', 'social entrepreneur' and 'social entrepreneurship' offered by Farmer, Hill and Muñoz in the Introduction, in order to facilitate identification of the skills associated with socially entrepreneurial behaviour within existing studies, and allow comparison with current policy expectations around service co-production and learning from the O4O project in relation to rural CSE.

Defining Social Enterprise

The UK government has defined a social enterprise as a business that provides services, goods and trade for a social purpose, operates independently of the state and is specifically concerned with investment and surplus reinvestment for social objectives (Department of Trade and Industry, 2002, 2005). Thus, social enterprises are organisations that attempt to generate a profit, but operate on a 'not for personal profit basis', and apply any surplus they create to furthering their social objectives and delivering community benefits (Allen, 2005). Defourney and Nyssens (2008) highlight that social enterprise is conceptualised differently throughout Europe. There is, for example, a longer history of workers' co-operatives in Mediterranean countries and, as Skerratt emphasises in Chapter 2, a strong focus on work integration enterprises within Scandinavia. It is also evident that the concept has more cachet and relevance in certain countries, such as the UK, but that social enterprise-type activities – that is, trading for social purpose – occur throughout, and are increasing in, the European Union (Defourney & Nyssens, 2008). Taking an overall perspective on the European position it can be summarised that social enterprise is viewed as a form within the category of social organisation/ social business/community enterprise.

Social enterprises may not always introduce new products or services but may produce existing types of services or products in settings previously considered uneconomical, or with staff groups previously considered unemployable, and it might be argued that producing under a social banner utilising commercial tools is innovative in itself. Casson (2005) differentiates two types of entrepreneurship: 'high entrepreneurship', which involves a substantial degree of innovation, and 'low entrepreneurship', which is concerned with creating new enterprises to replace an existing model with no significant innovation. Viewed through this lens, community social entrepreneurship might represent a 'low' type of entrepreneurship because it involves the utilisation of existing service delivery models by different actors (CSEs). Also, following Skerratt in Chapter 2 and Radford and Shortall in Chapter 5, it is evident that diverse environments and their consequent challenges can shape the characteristics of a social entrepreneur or social enterprise and that studies of CSE development need to consider the context and influences of communities. CSE development such as that carried out within O4O may also draw on skills and capabilities traditionally associated with community development work, such as empowering individuals and groups (Barron & Taylor, 2010), facilitating local leadership (Davies, 2009), and negotiating between community and state institutions (Mendes, 2009).

Defining Social Entrepreneurship

The complexity of attempts to define 'social entrepreneurship' is recognised by Farmer, Hill and Muñoz in the Introduction, but essentially, if a social enterprise is defined as an organisation that trades for social purpose, it can be considered an output of the processes of social entrepreneurship. To understand how entrepreneurship produces enterprises within the rural context it is necessary to draw on existing literature identifying the processes of social entrepreneurship which is essentially concerned with the 'discovery and exploitation of profitable opportunities' (Shane & Venkataraman, 2000:217), involving innovation, change, creativity, discovery, development, risk and uncertainty (Berglund & Johansson, 2007).

In the late 1990s 'social entrepreneurship' emerged as a new label to describe the process of working for social rather than personal profit objectives (Dees, 1998; Johnson, 2000; Thompson, 2002). With the advent of this social turn within 'traditional' commercial entrepreneurship (Burchell & Cook, 2006), consumers, business people, policymakers and researchers began to take greater interest in the positive societal development produced by the process, for example through employment and innovation (Sarason et al, 2006). However, the process of social entrepreneurship encompasses more than the establishment of social businesses (Haugh, 2005; Mair & Marti, 2006; Birch & Whittam, 2008) since it includes a range of activities underpinned by the principles of utilising opportunities to create social value (Nicholls & Cho, 2008). Thus, social entrepreneurship is about applying principles from 'for-profit' business to meet a core social mission (Pomerantz, 2003). Consequently, within the context of service provision in rural areas, social entrepreneurship should involve the utilisation of a business-like approach to the mission of delivering community-based services. This approach would engage actors in 'finding new and better ways to create and sustain social value' while simultaneously pursuing financial returns on investment (Peredo & McLean, 2006). As 'social entrepreneurship', this would be 'an innovative approach for dealing with complex social needs' (Johnson, 2000:1).

Those involved in social entrepreneurship are often described as possessing a range of individual characteristics including leadership, vision and risk-taking (Leadbeater, 1997; Peredo & McLean, 2006), and this individualistic foundation to social entrepreneurship can be observed in many definitions (e.g. Mair & Marti, 2006; Dees et al, 2001) that derive from consideration of the extent to which individuals and/or organisations can engage in social entrepreneurship, and how. Later in this chapter we consider this focus on individual action in relation to the generation of community-led social enterprises and how conceptualisations of social entrepreneurship need to be opened up to collective action.

Social Entrepreneurial Skills and Capabilities

Identifying the skills and capabilities associated with the processes of social entrepreneurship and social enterprise development illuminates understanding of what is required of community members in the development of CSE. Through narratives from the O4O project, we are able to map how social entrepreneurial skills can be used in the development of social organisations; how communities can be better supported to harness and develop these skills; and how existing understandings of individual entrepreneurship need to be opened up to show how the processes of entrepreneurship/enterprise development unfold in a community setting.

Social entrepreneurs may be seen as the 'primary definer[s]' of social entrepreneurship (Allan, 1999): as one species in the genus entrepreneur (Dees, 1998) but with particular facets and talents (Cools & Vermeulen, 2008). Within existing typologies of social entrepreneurship it is possible to pinpoint certain key capability domains, characteristics and skills. Tables 3.1–3.3 show three overarching entrepreneurial capability domains that have been identified from existing literature – opportunism, leadership and networking – highlight the characteristics and skills associated with each of these domains and suggest how these are employed in social enterprise development. The typology of social entrepreneurship developed by Zahra et al (2009) has been used to show how these skills may be employed differently at different geographical scales of operation. CSE development of the kind discussed in this book occurs primarily at the local level although, as Hill's discussion of policy context in Chapter 1 shows, the action of CSE at the local level may be aligned to macro-level social aims and objectives that are played out at regional and national levels.

One key social entrepreneurial capability can be referred to as 'opportunism' (Nicholls, 2008:20). Dees (1998), for example, tells us how social entrepreneurs are able to perceive opportunities to meet a social need and use this knowledge to define a social mission to pursue. They are characterised by a *socio-moral* motivation or *social-mission* focus to their entrepreneurial ambition and activities and address social problems utilising techniques from business (Austin et al, 2006; Harris et al, 2009) through the pursuit of new opportunities to achieve their mission, with continual 'innovation, adaptation and learning' (Dees, 1998:4). In some cases, social entrepreneurs develop and spread innovative approaches that differ significantly from existing methods of service delivery (Nicholls & Cho, 2008) and see places for businesses where others do not, because of their life and work experiences, beliefs and attitudes. As Shane (2000) and Shane and Venkataraman (2000) argue, opportunities are not objective phenomena separated and distinct from the entrepreneur. They are individually idiosyncratic conceptualisations of an instantiated social and economic system (Sarason et al, 2006). Thus, individual backgrounds, experiences and beliefs allow social entrepreneurs to set up new organisations, develop and implement innovative programmes and organise or distribute new services.

As Tables 3.1–3.3 also illustrate, entrepreneurs operating at different geographical scales may find 'opportunity' in different ways (Zahra et al, 2009). Some identify worldwide social challenges and mobilise forces to tackle them while others focus on local issues. Some social entrepreneurs build collaborative relationships to introduce social initiatives (Pearce & Doh, 2005) and others are adept at creating organisations to tackle social issues. Thus, a social entrepreneur is a key force in forming the character of a social enterprise:

> Social Bricoleurs usually focus on discovering and addressing small-scale local social needs. Social Constructionists typically exploit opportunities and market failures by filling gaps to underserved clients in order to introduce reforms and innovation to the broader social system. Finally, Social Engineers recognize systemic problems within existing social structures and address them by introducing revolutionary change. (Zahra et al, 2009:519)

Social entrepreneurs also employ a range of skills around leadership (Nicholls, 2006, 2008). Dees (1998:2) describes them as individuals who act as 'change agent[s] in the social sector' because they have the necessary

Table 3.1   Socially entrepreneurial domains showing key skills and capabilities – opportunism

Entrepreneurial capability domain	Social entrepreneurial characteristics	Social entrepreneurial skills	Associated social entrepreneurship processes	Functioning at different scales (after Zahra et al, 2009)
Opportunism.	Creativity.	Opportunity perception.	Identification of social needs and establishment of a social mission.	LOCAL: local knowledge.
	Innovative thinking.	Generation of new ideas.	Identification of ways to meet social needs through enterprising (often innovative) solutions that the public and private sectors cannot or will not deliver.	REGIONAL to NATIONAL: knowledge of wider gaps in public and private service provision.
	Risk-taking and experimentation.	Ability to overcome problems and challenges.		NATIONAL to INTERNATIONAL: wider vision of social systems.

Table 3.2 *Socially entrepreneurial domains showing key skills and capabilities – leadership*

Entrepreneurial capability domain	Social entrepreneurial characteristics	Social entrepreneurial skills	Associated social entrepreneurship processes	Functioning at different scales (after Zahra et al, 2009)
Leadership.	Vision.	Vision for combining social and economic goals within organisational model.	Effective combining of social and economic goals.	LOCAL: catalyses local change agents.
	Drive.	Ability to mobilise resources.	Bring in staff and volunteers.	REGIONAL to NATIONAL: professional volunteers and employees are needed.
	Charisma.	Catalyse action of others.	Catalyse others to act in aid of the social mission.	NATIONAL to INTERNATIONAL: works to change existing social systems and requires popular support.

Table 3.3 Socially entrepreneurial domains showing key skills and capabilities – networking

Entrepreneurial capability domain	Social entrepreneurial characteristics	Social entrepreneurial skills	Associated social entrepreneurship processes	Functioning at different scales (after Zahra et al, 2009)
Networking.	Effective communicator.	Building of discursive legitimacy.	Building discursive legitimacy through support for the social mission.	LOCAL: negotiates local laws and regulations.
	Collaborator.	Drawing in of resources.	Builds relationships that bring resources to the enterprise.	REGIONAL to NATIONAL: works to institutionalise alternative service delivery structures.
		Knowledge arbitration.		
		Utilising and strengthening social capital.		NATIONAL to INTERNATIONAL: needs significant financial and human resources.

skills to catalyse action in others to aid the progress of their social mission (Pearce, 2003). They instigate this action in a way that combines social and economic objectives or, as Zahra et al (2009:523) put it, 'one of the greatest skills of many social entrepreneurs is their ability to inspire, marshal and mobilise the efforts of commercial and non-commercial partners, donors, volunteers and employees in the pursuit of social wealth'.

A range of skills that can be classified as networking are also employed by social entrepreneurs. By establishing what Zahra et al (2009) define as 'strategic networks' they are able to draw in the resources required to meet their social mission and, according to Barnir and Smith (2002), avoid the limitations on current resources. Networks are thus employed for two reasons: to pull in resources and strengthen ventures, and to deliver impact and create social value. As Pearce and Doh (2005; quoted in Zahra et al 2009:523) state: 'Building collaborative relationships to implement social initiatives is often crucial for success.'

Research suggests that being socially entrepreneurial is not limited to those individuals who work to start a social business and that the associated entrepreneurial skills and capabilities can be applied outside the social business context to generate social value. For example, within the public sector socially entrepreneurial actors in relation to health will include librarians (Allison, 2007) and health professionals (Farmer & Kilpatrick, 2009). Thus, social entrepreneurial skills could be important in the context of community co-production of services even though they are not used to start a social business in the traditional sense.

In the remainder of this chapter we consider which social entrepreneurial skills are important for the generation of community service delivery organisations in rural areas by using evidence drawn from the O4O project.

USING SOCIALLY ENTREPRENEURIAL SKILLS FOR COMMUNITY SERVICE CO-PRODUCTION IN RURAL AREAS

Social Enterprise and Entrepreneurship in Rural Areas

Thus far we have painted a picture depicting what policy is asking of remote and rural communities in terms of their participation in service co-design, delivery and production. In the UK, contemporary policy focuses on promoting activity that is instigated at neighbourhood level and conducted to benefit communities. It assumes an existing level of community identity and action, such as neighbourhood groups, that can be built upon to generate co-production by inviting existing citizen groups to get involved. Policy-related documentation that discusses non-state players bidding for government contracts (The Conservative Party, 2010) implies a business-like approach that will involve the utilisation of socially entrepreneurial skills.

Communities are being asked to utilise business tools to address their social needs by combining enterprise activity with community/social goals. They are asked to consider how they would meet social needs through service provision, take innovative approaches to resolving social issues and add social value, engage others within their community, and find effective ways of dealing with social challenges. In many settings, communities must find ways of delivering services that public or private organisations will not, or cannot, provide, and this implies a need to develop and employ strategic networks, build collaborative relationships and harness wide support for their social mission. Thus, community social entrepreneurship requires catalysts for change, mobilisation of resources and other actors, leadership and inspiration, which amount to a requirement for particularly high levels of determination and drive at community level if social enterprise is to become established.

In the following section we discuss the example of O4O where the development of CSEs through an action research process affords learning on the types of skills needed and the ways in which they must be employed if rural communities are to engage with service co-production. Learning from O4O is also deployed to discuss potential barriers to asking rural communities to engage with service provision in a socially enterprising way. PMs from the participating countries are not named but given an identifier (number) when quotes from their activity reports and interviews are used.

Facilitated Community Entrepreneurship for Service Delivery in Rural Areas

Within the contexts outlined above, policy promotes widespread community social entrepreneurship. However, beyond studies of community energy (King, 2009) and community development literature that highlights the skills associated with generating community organisations, there is little evidence-based information on how contemporary communities become socially entrepreneurial and/or enact their social entrepreneurialism. We suggest that exploration of this topic requires consideration of community social entrepreneurialism as a hybrid of community development and social business principles and processes. In this context, much of the existing social enterprise literature focuses on emergent social enterprise rather than facilitated CSE development which O4O, through its action research methods, worked to test. By providing PMs to work with communities, O4O aimed to understand whether policy around community co-production of services is realisable on a scale that extends beyond those communities with existing high levels of civic action or socially entrepreneurial leaders. As a project it sought to work with rural communities to identify social need and whether a socially entrepreneurial approach could be taken to meet that need. This facilitated model had three levels of social entrepreneurship: a) the O4O project itself, with its socially entrepreneurial principles and goals; b) the O4O PMs, who were recruited because they had the potential to utilise socially entrepreneurial skills within communities; and c) the communities and community members who took part in the project activities.

In Chapter 4 Farmer and Stephen (herself a Project Manager) describe the process from a PM's perspective. In this chapter we focus on the processes by which PMs used socially entrepreneurial skills and capabilities in order to highlight the types of endogenous skills and capabilities that other communities would need to draw on to complement exogenously promoted social enterprises within a facilitated model of social enterprise development.

O4O PMs employed socially entrepreneurial skills and capabilities in different ways, to differing degrees, and with variable types of output, success and resultant social enterprise organisations. This, as Farmer and Stephen discuss in Chapter 4 and Skerratt in Chapter 2, was probably reflective of the different personal backgrounds and histories of the PMs as well as the different socio-cultural and economic contexts that they were working within, and it is not our aim to identify the degree to which these differences existed or to explore their underlying causes. Rather, we specifically identify those socially entrepreneurial skills and capabilities that were utilised by O4O PMs – although they were not always employed within the creation of a social business. This approach allows us to demonstrate the types of socially entrepreneurial skills and capabilities that are widely needed if the policy goal of ubiquitous service co-production and co-delivery is to be delivered by communities, and particularly by rural communities.

OPPORTUNISM AND COMMUNITY SOCIAL ENTERPRISE: IDENTIFYING SOCIAL NEED AND SPOTTING THE GAPS

We have already highlighted that the ability to identify social need is considered a key capability of a social entrepreneur; that is, a need must be identified that will form the *raison d'être* of the social enterprise to be developed. Within the context of CSE development this must be a genuine social need within the community which is currently unmet through other types of service provision, and for which the community is willing to accept social enterprise as an appropriate form of service delivery. Within O4O, PMs were employed to work with communities to identify social needs specifically related to the health and wellbeing of older rural residents which, due to the social entrepreneurial aims of O4O, was seen as a key starting point for the generation of socially entrepreneurial activity within each community. It is difficult to separate the role of the PM and the actions undertaken by actors within the communities since both were central to the process of needs and opportunity identification, and both the PMs and the community members they worked with were seen to draw on socially entrepreneurial skills and capabilities from within the opportunism domain (Tables 3.1 (see p. 54) and 3.4 (see p. 68)). Thus, the process of need/opportunity recognition within each of the communities can be argued socially entrepreneurial in nature because it involved identification of an unmet social need within the community and the adoption of a social mission by a community group. It also involved the use of socially entrepreneurial skills associated with opportunity identification because the actors were focused on meeting need through ways that generated social benefit, rather than personal profit.

The PMs played a key role in bringing people within the community together, facilitating discussions that included ways of identifying social need and facilitating linkage of these needs with opportunities to meet them through socially entrepreneurial activity. The nature and adoption of social enterprise organisational models varied by locality and it was often the PM who suggested that socially entrepreneurial solutions could be used to meet need. This has implications for the wider adoption of CSE since without the facilitative role of a PM, community groups may not engage in socially entrepreneurial methods. In some communities, particularly those in Scandinavian countries, there was a strong feeling that the state should provide services to meet the identified social need. PM 1, for example, said that there was no 'precedent' for social enterprise in the region and it was therefore not a 'business-model' that community members would consider, or accept, as a vehicle for meeting social need. In instances where communities were prepared to take action to meet need within their locale they often tended towards informal helping solutions or grant-funded options, even where identification of a need presented an opportunity for a socially entrepreneurial solution.

PMs had to draw on the local knowledge of community members to facilitate the creation of a social enterprise and, as they were working at the scale of a community, generally a village or collection of small settlements, this required them to employ skills that have been associated with the 'social bricoleur'; that is, to draw on local knowledge and resources to address small-scale problems through socially enterprising behaviour (Zahra et al, 2009). In addition to working with local knowledge embedded in communities to identify need, the PMs brought their own knowledge of the social, economic, demographic and physical landscapes of the communities and regions in which they worked. The importance of their interactions with community members to draw on their local knowledge to identify local social need is manifest in this quote from PM 2:

> The [local community] champions . . . tend to get things done, so we need to harness their energy. . . . But we also make sure that we get to the wider group so I've been to community council meetings, older people's centres, lunch clubs etc. Champions have a lot of influence locally and so when I'm in these communities I'm testing reactions all the time; I listen to gossip, I find out what's happened in the past. . . . (PM 2)

Different types of need were identified through this process and ranged from unmet need that emerged from rounds of community dialogue, to embedded need that had long persisted within the community but had been tackled through some form of informal help-giving. There were also crisis points where, for example, the potential removal of public service provision was identified. This meant that individual communities had diverse types of social mission.

PMs generally facilitated a process in which communities identified opportunities rather than acting in the manner of an individual entrepreneur by spotting gaps themselves. They approached this in different ways. For example, in one O4O partner region, the PM engaged in rounds of community dialogue and took part, informally, in community activities, saying: '[I have] taken a community development approach; I gave the community groups potential suggestions and then started discussing their needs' (PM 2).

This approach contrasts with that taken in other communities. PM 1, for example, took a significantly more active role by selecting the communities perceived to be most likely to engage in social entrepreneurial activities. Here, the project team shortlisted five potentially suitable villages and invited the communities in these villages to attend meetings at which the project team *explained* the concept behind O4O and *suggested* that the community might like to develop a social enterprise. The final selection of the three villages considered most suitable was based on the local O4O project team subjectively gauging communities' interest in, and capacity for, running a social enterprise. PM 1 indicated a degree of project team decision-making describing the use of criteria to select the villages, such as 'villages that are prepared to fight' and 'villages that have established previous projects'. This suggests that the project team sought communities of 'action'. PM 1 said: 'You need to find people who have the spirit for doing things. They need to have a fighting spirit. You need to have villages where "it is in the milk".'

The PMs found that although policy promotes community engagement with social entrepreneurship and co-production this was not necessarily understood by citizens. In some cases citizens were unused to *identifying* need and in others they were used to *meeting* such need through informal community helping and therefore unaccustomed to social enterprise solutions. Therefore, even though the local knowledge of citizens was central to identifying social need within communities, PMs played a significant role in facilitating consideration of socially entrepreneurial solutions to meet this need.

PMs often had to translate informal community dialogue about needs into identification of a particular way of meeting those needs through social enterprise. This was done in combination with other, more formalised methods of identifying older people's needs, including surveys and interviews. For example, following community dialogue in one community, survey methods were used to obtain a general overview of older people's transport needs as a precursor to a 'more detailed consultation . . . to identify community transport requirements' that was conducted using a set of in-depth, face-to-face interviews with people who were in particular need. In another community, interviews were used to find out about older people's residential needs, and elsewhere PMs organised informal community meetings to gather information on older people's needs and preferences, or worked with existing voluntary groups to identify unmet social need that could be addressed through social enterprise. PM 3 noted: 'The citizens' meetings will result in the setting-up of groups of volunteers and the appointment of resource persons who will be the prime movers for the volunteer groups. The idea is that the groups will operate independently [of the PM].'

In using different methods to identify needs, the PMs applied their knowledge of gaps in public/private service provision more generally, and used knowledge translation skills more often associated with social entrepreneurship at the regional or national scale (Zahra et al, 2009). This has implications for communities that are not involved in a facilitated model of CSE as they would need to ensure inclusion of people with such 'boundary-spanning' capacity. Some communities may possess an individual who can and will assume this role, but this may be a role for public sector workers if policymakers continue to encourage the proliferation of CSEs.

LEADERSHIP: CATALYSING ACTION AND BRINGING PEOPLE ON BOARD

In the preceding sections we posited the view that O4O PMs played a central role in working with communities to identify social need and stimulate thinking about the potential of a social enterprise solution as a means of meeting need. However, to take forward the development of CSEs both the PMs and the community members had to utilise leadership skills and capabilities that are often associated with social entrepreneurship. PMs, particularly in the early stages of the process, acted as champions for the idea of CSE development; a reassuring figure for community members and someone with the vision and drive to push ideas forward. As the development of CSEs progressed within communities, successful initiatives often proved to be those in which local people took on the central roles in the process. To different degrees within the O4O communities, both the PMs and local volunteers drew on their leadership skills to meet the identified social need by bringing in new people (e.g. through volunteering), agreeing to sit on an organisation's board, providing advice and taking a role within an organisational structure; as PM 1 noted of one village: 'This [CSE] is built around the spirit of three elderly people; they are very well known in the municipality. They are behind this project. One of them is the Project Manager; they "own" the project.'

However, the PMs' reports evidence the perception that they were sometimes central in catalysing others into action by supporting communities to identify and enhance their skills and by bringing staff and volunteers into proto-organisations. They employed a range of community engagement strategies to do this, including meeting community members and other stakeholders, and participating formally and informally in community/village activities. They also had a role in building trust within the community, identifying key individuals who were connected into informal social networks, and could disseminate information throughout the community and act as contact points to pull in further community resources. As such, PMs acted as both local change agents and regional/national social entrepreneurs since they utilised community engagement strategies to tap into the knowledge of 'local agents' but brought an awareness of wider 'financial and human resources' (Zahra et al, 2009:524).

Combining the Social and Economic: The Informal and Formal

Although community members were central in identifying needs and opportunities within their locale, the O4O PMs often facilitated the adoption and development of a social enterprise approach, and went on to draw on socially entrepreneurial skills in order to apply business practice to meeting those needs. They showed evidence of keeping organisational development 'focused', intentionally avoiding 'mission drift', and ensured that the social needs identified by the community remained the key driving principle for the development of local enterprises. They did this by, for example, providing assistance at first hand to community members but also, in certain instances, by bringing in external experts or organisations to provide social enterprise training or business support. PM 4 said: 'We worked with them over an eight week period on management and business training leading to Service Level Agreements, and drawing down finance, and helped them to draw up bids. . . .'

PMs were often key to facilitating applications for start-up or grant funding for initiatives within the communities, or opportunities to sell to the public sector. This involved identifying potential income sources and completing funding and grant applications, tender documents or negotiations with the public sector. An example was given by PM 1: 'I helped them with their project [funding] application. . . . They are not used to running a project; I had to give them the tools to do this. . . . We worked together with them to do the application. We identified with them the main goals and sub goals.'

In carrying out this facilitative role, the PMs drew on their own socially entrepreneurial leadership skills and encouraged these in community members. As the CSE development process progressed, tensions sometimes developed within the community group. PM 5, for example, found that 'working relationships in X and Y groups between local participants [were] becoming strained as individuals seek to play greater or lesser roles in projects'. PM 2 highlighted how the PM's role was valuable as both an *internal* part of the community development process: 'Partly it's [CSE development] about sitting alongside people and being one of them, rather than doing things to them'; and as an *external* leader who could bring objectivity and connections with external resources: 'The credibility and status of the outside O4O Project Officer [PM] . . . is . . . they are perceived as a valuable asset coming from outside [the community] and can be a potent force.'

In this role, PMs were able to bring valuable input as an 'arbitrageur of knowledge' (Zahra et al, 2009) and while individuals may emerge from within communities to take on this role, without the presence of an external facilitator like the O4O PM, capacity issues such as smaller and dispersed populations, and the existing burden on volunteers may limit the number of potential participants in social enterprise development, in rural and remote areas.

BUILDING NETWORKS: COALITIONS AND COLLABORATIVE RELATIONSHIPS

O4O PMs reported a requirement to attract the necessary resources to begin building a CSE. They noted that, even where the organisation created was not a social enterprise, they were needed to attract resources to create voluntary or grant-funded organisations. While the community was involved in network-building to harness resources, it was often the PMs who identified grant and start-up funding opportunities, sourced application information and assisted community members to complete the applications.

Maintaining relationships with community members is a delicate task and the need to show sensitivity to community dynamics was acknowledged in the PMs' reports, which also show that they were not phased by 'communication and relationship issues' and drew on personal resources to deal with issues in ways that minimised any potential damage to their relationships with the community.

Legitimising the Idea of Service Co-production (for Different Stakeholders)

A social entrepreneurial skill that lies within the networking domain is that of 'building discursive legitimacy' (Nicholls, 2010). This is a process in which social entrepreneurs are adept at embedding the knowledge that their organisation is a viable and reliable provider of goods or services. For community service provision to succeed through the social business model, social enterprises must be seen as 'legitimate service providers' in the eyes of those designing, running, commissioning and receiving services. Data from the PMs' reports demonstrate that the 'legitimising' process occurred at different scales and changed over time as individual enterprises developed.

At the start of the process PMs had to engage with 'legitimisation' at local level, with communities, by discussing the idea of CSE development with them. PM 3 stated:

> [Citizens] . . . are increasingly being encouraged to take care of their problems. It is a very big challenge to get older people to understand to do things for themselves. This generation is used to things being provided for them.

Co-production is not necessarily something that communities are aware of, or confident they could be involved with, and the hesitancy of community members to engage with co-production through social entrepreneurship can be ascribed to a variety of factors that vary between communities and countries. For example, the different cultural and political contexts within the O4O case study communities (Skerratt, Chapter 2) contributed to a more 'paternalistic' attitude within regions where community members expressed a preference for a public sector response to need. Throughout the O4O partner countries, PMs reported reluctance within some communities to engage in training activities related to 'social business'. PM 2, for example, suggested that facilitation of CSE must sometimes involve 'stealth', saying: 'I am very careful what words I use. For example, I very rarely say "social enterprise"; it can be very off-putting for people.'

Evidence from O4O indicates that engaging citizens with the notion of service co-production is a precursor to community social entrepreneurship and that where community members are unfamiliar with the concepts of identifying social need, and of meeting them through social enterprise, acceptance of the social enterprise model as a legitimate provider of services is essential. Within O4O, breaking down suspicions around social enterprise so that the approach became viable and legitimate in the eyes of their communities became a key task for PMs. As PM 2 said: 'People can be very reluctant at the first meeting, they are suspicious and then they start to get energy and work on it.'

Once the idea of CSE service co-production is legitimised within a community and its citizens take on roles in its development, it becomes necessary to engage with legitimisation at another level; that of the Local Authority/state. Although CSE development is grounded in the local, several factors mean that it is also necessary to build wider public support for service delivery through a CSE. Within O4O, PMs took on the role of building discursive legitimacy more widely through, for instance, informal meetings, forming committees and disseminating project information to stakeholders, including politicians. From PM 1's perspective, there is a need to 'convince' the public sector that CSE development is not a 'wholesale takeover of social care' and, for a CSE to contract with the public sector, public sector representatives must view such organisations as legitimate service providers. In the O4O process, PMs took on the roles of identifying key public sector representatives to engage with and promoting the concept of CSE provision as a viable option. The evidence from O4O thus suggests that, where legitimacy is not embedded with key individuals within the public sector, the viability of the CSE idea could be jeopardised.

The O4O process has shown that leaders in remote and rural communities are required if this type of social innovation for service delivery is to be legitimised with the wider community, including potential service users, and the public sector, including potential commissioners. This suggests the importance of figures that possess the socially entrepreneurial capability of building discursive legitimacy (Nicholls, 2010). Such people need to be competent in both the civic discourse of the community, with awareness of local needs, cultures and social value, and the public discourse of the state, with awareness of co-production, procurement and budgeting. They must be competent and confident in shifting between the two and in reconciling their sometimes divergent foci. Often, the PM acted as a key manager of the relationship between the community and the public sector but as, or if, CSE becomes embedded as a concept and legitimised as a service provider within the public sector, the need for explicit promotion and translation of the idea is likely to fade.

THE SKILLS AND CAPABILITIES OF THE RURAL COMMUNITY SOCIAL ENTREPRENEUR

Throughout this chapter we have outlined ways in which O4O PMs and community members drew on their skills and capabilities of social entrepreneurship in order to create CSEs of various types. We have also highlighted skills and capabilities that other communities and citizens would need to use to create a social enterprise for service provision. This, as Tables 3.4–3.6 show, has allowed us to identify a set of socially entre-preneurial skills that are needed in order to catalyse and sustain CSE for service provision in rural areas.

1. *Facilitates community 'consensus' over social need and mission:* Community social entrepreneurship requires a group to come together to identify social need. This can be driven by an individual or group of citizens. Understanding the nature of local need involves under-standing local context and the human and financial resources that can initially be drawn upon to start the process of social enterprise devel-opment. Particular skills related to informal and formal processes of information-gathering may be needed. The social entrepreneur(s) must be able to relate community identification of need with gaps in current public and private service provision with the type of service that could potentially be developed through a social enterprise.

   This has implications for the social enterprise policy agenda, as it suggests that the public sector and social enterprise support agencies need to provide assistance for bringing communities together, rather than assuming that this process will spontaneously emerge. The evi-dence from the O4O project discussed in this chapter also suggests that while this consensus-building activity takes place on the local scale and requires in-depth knowledge of local context, the design of

Table 3.4 Socially entrepreneurial domains showing key skills and capabilities and relevance for rural areas – opportunism

Entrepreneurial capability domain	Social entrepreneurial characteristics	Social entrepreneurial skills	Associated social entrepreneurship processes	Functioning at different scales (after Zahra et al, 2009)	Community social entrepreneurship
Opportunism.	Creativity.	Opportunity perception.	Identification of social needs and establishment of a social mission.	LOCAL: local knowledge.	Group comes together to identify need within the community.
	Innovative thinking.	Generation of new ideas.	Identification of ways to meet social needs through enterprising (often innovative) solutions that the public and private sectors cannot or will not deliver.	REGIONAL to NATIONAL: knowledge of wider gaps in public and private service provision.	Group agrees on social mission.
	Risk-taking and experimentation.	Ability to overcome problems and challenges.		NATIONAL to INTERNATIONAL: wider vision of social systems.	Consensus achieved on 'new' idea to take forward.

Table 3.5 Socially entrepreneurial domains showing key skills and capabilities and relevance for rural areas – leadership

Entrepreneurial capability domain	Social entrepreneurial characteristics	Social entrepreneurial skills	Associated social entrepreneurship processes	Functioning at different scales (after Zahra et al, 2009)	Community social entrepreneurship
Leadership.	Vision.	Vision for combining social and economic goals within organisational model.	Effective combining of social and economic goals.	LOCAL: catalyses local change agents.	Understanding of local informal helping and voluntarism.
	Drive.	Ability to mobilise resources.	Bring in staff and volunteers.	REGIONAL to NATIONAL: professional volunteers and employees are needed.	Sensitive negotiation of community dynamics.
	Charisma.	Catalyse action of others.	Catalyse others to act in aid of the social mission.	NATIONAL to INTERNATIONAL: works to change existing social systems and requires popular support.	

Table 3.6 *Socially entrepreneurial domains showing key skills and capabilities and relevance for rural areas – networking*

Entrepreneurial capability domain	Social entrepreneurial characteristics	Social entrepreneurial skills	Associated social entrepreneurship processes	Functioning at different scales (after Zahra et al, 2009)	Community social entrepreneurship
Networking.	Effective communicator.	Building of discursive legitimacy.	Building discursive legitimacy through support for the social mission.	LOCAL: negotiates local laws and regulations.	Bridging the community and the public sector.
	Collaborator.	Drawing in of resources. Knowledge arbitration. Utilising and strengthening social capital.	Builds relationships that bring resources to the enterprise.	REGIONAL to NATIONAL: works to institutionalise alternative service delivery structures. NATIONAL to INTERNATIONAL: needs significant financial and human resources.	De-mystifying the 'social enterprise'.

service delivery models requires PMs to introduce knowledge of wider public and private service provision contexts.

2. *Provides leadership but also facilitates this in others:* The rural community entrepreneur must be able to bring others into the process of social enterprise creation in a way that is sensitive to how needs have been traditionally, and are currently, met through informal help-giving within the community. They will act as a figure to draw other community members into the process of organisational development and do so in a way that is sensitive to local community dynamics and issues of representativeness and inclusion.

3. *Builds legitimacy at different levels:* In current policy and community contexts the rural community social entrepreneur must be able to promote the concept of service co-production and delivery by CSE to audiences ranging from community members to the public sector. They must have the capacity to communicate with different stakeholders and take on a role in negotiating and building coalitions between the community and the public sector.

The idea of community social enterprise as a model for service provision may become embedded within all layers of the public sector, from national government to local purchasing managers, but until that happens social entrepreneurs will be required to transition back and forth between the community and the public sector and where they are not comfortable in this role, social enterprise development within rural communities may be stifled.

CONCLUSIONS

In promoting a social enterprise agenda, policymakers need to be aware of the types of skills they are assuming that communities have and are capable of applying. There are particular difficulties in finding and applying these skills in small, dispersed remote and rural communities, often with ageing populations. Evidence from the O4O project shows that community members can be entrepreneurial but this action tends to be motivated by a desire to help others within their community, to help sustain their community into the future, and is often built on existing altruistic activities. None of these motivations are associated with interest in business-like activities or in assuming provision of services previously supplied directly by the state.

Data from O4O PMs' reports highlight the importance of socially entrepreneurial skills beyond the concept of running a social business; that is, their importance to the wider processes of the co-design and co-production of services. Therefore, the skills of social entrepreneurship might be beneficially, and delicately, built in rural communities if they are to engage fully in service co-production. Entrepreneurial skills are needed to make these types of organisation 'work'. Harnessing and generating entrepreneurial skills within communities may mean moving away from traditional business-focused training and support structures towards those that build skills organically and in locally sensitive ways. The complex set of skills needed to negotiate CSE development, such as opportunism, leadership and networking, will be challenging to foster at a local level and there is a need for further development and testing of locally appropriate forms of social entrepreneurship training, for example with particular consideration of the language, method and timing of delivery.

If communities are unable or unwilling to engage with entrepreneurship then it is unlikely that they will become involved with the types of service delivery that co-production policy currently promotes. Thus, if a government-generated social enterprise agenda is to be successful it needs to be supported by structures and funding for building collective action and collective entrepreneurialism and to move away from concepts that assume or favour individual, naturally occurring leaders. Currently, communities without appropriate leaders are unlikely to be involved in emergent CSE development. However, the evidence from O4O also shows that the presence of a community leader or facilitator, such as the O4O PMs, needs to be supported in various ways – and not least by other community members. Opening up typologies of social entrepreneurship from a focus on individual visionaries to collective forms of action would help develop understanding of CSE development to inform agendas of policy, procurement and community/business support.

NOTE

1.   http://www.silvereconomy-europe.org/ (accessed 1 July 2011).

REFERENCES

Allan S. (1999), *News Culture*, Buckingham: Open University Press.
Allen B. (2005), 'Social Enterprise: Through the eyes of the consumer', *Social Enterprise Journal*, 1, pp. 57–77.
Allison M.M. (2007), 'Women's Health: Librarian as social entrepreneur', *Library Trends*, 56(2), pp. 423–448.
Austin J.E., Stevenson H. & Wei-Skillern J. (2006), 'Social and Commercial

Entrepreneurship: Same, different, or both?', *Entrepreneurship Theory and Practice*, 30(1), pp. 1–22.

Barnir A. & Smith K.A. (2002), 'Interfirm Alliances in the Small Business: The role of social networks', *Journal of Small Business Management*, 40(3), pp. 219–233.

Barron C. & Taylor B.J. (2010), 'The Right Tools for the Right Job: Social work students learning community development', *Social Work Education*, 29(4), pp. 372–385.

Berglund K. & Johansson A.W. (2007), 'Constructions of Entrepreneurship: A discourse analysis of academic publications', *Journal of Enterprising Communities*, 1(1), pp. 77–102.

Birch K. & Whittam G. (2008), 'Critical Survey: The third sector and the regional development of social capital', *Regional Studies*, 42(3), pp. 437–450.

Burchell J. & Cook J. (2006), 'Confronting the "Corporate Citizen": Shaping the discourse of corporate social responsibility', *International Journal of Sociology and Social Policy*, 26(3/4), pp. 121–137.

Casson M. (2005), 'Entrepreneurship' in Henderson D. (Ed.), *The Concise Encyclopedia of Economics*, Liberty Fund: Library of Economics and Liberty. Retrieved from: http://www.econlib.orh/library/Enc/Entrepreneurship.html (accessed 1 June 2011).

Cools E. & Vermeulen S. (2008), *What's in a Name? An inquiry on the cognitive and entrepreneurial profile of the social entrepreneur* [online]. Vlerick Leuven Gent Management School. Retrieved from: http://www.vlerick.be (accessed 1 June 2011).

Davies A. (2009), 'Understanding Local Leadership in Building the Capacity of Rural Communities in Australia', *Geographical Research*, 47(4), pp. 380–389.

Dees J.G. (1998), *The Meaning of Social Entrepreneurship*, Stanford University. Retrieved from: http://www.fuqua.duke.edu (accessed 1 June 2011).

Dees J.G., Emerson J. & Economy P. (2001), *Enterprising Nonprofits: A toolkit for social entrepreneurs*, New York: John Wiley & Sons.

Defourney J. & Nyssens M. (2008), *Social Enterprise in Europe: Recent trends and developments*, Working Paper, 08:01, EMES European Research Network Working Paper.

Department of Trade and Industry (2002), *Social Enterprise: A strategy for success*, London: Department of Trade and Industry.

Department of Trade and Industry (2005), *A Survey of Social Enterprises Across the UK*, London: Department of Trade and Industry.

Farmer J. & Kilpatrick S. (2009), 'Are Rural Health Professionals also Social Entrepreneurs?', *Social Science and Medicine*, 69(11), pp. 1651–1658.

Harris J.D., Sapienza H.J. & Bowie N.E. (2009), 'Ethics and Entrepreneurship', *Journal of Business Venturing*, 24(2009), pp. 407–418.

Haugh H. (2005), 'A Research Agenda for Social Entrepreneurship', *Social Enterprise Journal*, 1, pp. 1–11.

Johnson S. (2000), *Literature Review on Social Entrepreneurship*, Canadian Centre for Social Entrepreneurship, Alberta: University of Alberta School of Business.

Jones D. & Keogh W. (2006), 'Social Enterprise: A case of terminological ambiguity and complexity', *Social Enterprise Journal*, 2(1), pp. 11–26.

King A. (2009), 'Local Energy, Owned by Local People', *Petroleum Review*, 63(748, supplement), pp. S4–S5.

Leadbeater C. (1997), *The Rise of the Social Entrepreneur*, London: Demos.

Mair J. & Marti I. (2006), 'Social Entrepreneurship Research: A source of explanation, prediction, and delight', *Journal of World Business*, 41, pp. 36–44.

Mendes P. (2009), 'Teaching Community Development to Social Work Students: A critical reflection', *Community Development Journal*, 44(2), pp. 248–262.

Nicholls A. (2006), *Social Entrepreneurship: New paradigms of sustainable social change*, Oxford: Oxford University Press.

Nicholls A. (2008), *New Models of Sustainable Social Change*, Oxford: Oxford University Press.

Nicholls A. (2010), 'The Legitimacy of Social Entrepreneurship: Reflexive isomorphism in a pre-paradigmatic field', *Entrepreneurship Theory and Practice*, 34(4), pp. 611–633.

Nicholls A. & Cho H. (2008), 'Social Entrepreneurship: The structuration of a field' in Nicholls A. (Ed.), *New Models of Sustainable Social Change*, Oxford: Oxford University Press, pp. 99–119.

OECD (2008), *OECD Rural Policy Reviews: Scotland, UK: Assessment and recommendations*, Edinburgh: Scottish Government.

Osborne S.P., Beattie R.S. & Williamson A.P. (2002), *Community Involvement in Rural Regeneration Partnerships in the UK: Evidence from England, Northern Ireland and Scotland*, London: Policy Press.

Pearce J. (2003), *Social Enterprise in Anytown*, London: Calouste Gulbenkian Foundation.

Pearce J.A. & Doh J.P. (2005), 'The High Impact of Collaborative Social Initiatives', *Sloan Management Review*, 46(3), pp. 30–39.

Peredo A.M. & McLean M. (2006), 'Social Entrepreneurship: A critical review of the concept', *Journal of World Business*, 41, pp. 56–65.

Pomerantz M. (2003), 'The Business of Social Entrepreneurship in a "Down Economy"', *Business*, 25(3), pp. 25–30.

Sarason Y., Dean T. & Dillard J.F. (2006), 'Entrepreneurship as the Nexus of Individual and Opportunity: A structuration view', *Journal of Business Venturing*, 21(3), pp. 286–305.

Shane S. (2000), 'Prior Knowledge and the Discovery of Entrepreneurial Opportunities', *Organization Science*, 11, pp. 448–469.

Shane, S. & Venkataraman S. (2000), 'The Promise of Entrepreneurship as a Field of Research', *Academy of Management Review*, 25(1), pp. 217–226.

Shaw E. & Carter S. (2007), 'Social Entrepreneurship: Theoretical antecedents and empirical analysis of entrepreneurial processes and outcomes', *Journal of Small Business and Enterprise Development*, 14(3), pp. 418–434.

The Conservative Party (2010), *Invitation to Join the Government of Britain. The Conservative Manifesto*, London: Conservative Party.

Thompson J.L. (2002), 'The World of the Social Entrepreneur', *International Journal of Public Sector Management*, 15(2), pp. 412–431.

Weerawardena J. & Mort G.S. (2006), 'Investigating Social Entrepreneurship: A multidimensional model', *Journal of World Business*, 41, pp. 21–35.

Williams C.C. (2007), 'Socio-spatial Variations in the Nature of Entrepreneurship', *Journal of Enterprising Communities*, 1(1), pp. 27–37.

Zahra S.A., Gedajlovic E., Neubaum D.O. & Shulman J.M. (2009), 'A Typology of Social Entrepreneurs: Motives, search processes and ethical challenges', *Journal of Business Venturing*, 24, pp. 519–532

4. Organisational processes and the policy–practice gap

Jane Farmer and Kate Stephen

INTRODUCTION

In this chapter we consider how community social enterprises form and factors that influence their development. We also reflect on the early stages of the process of enterprise development in the specific locale of the Scottish Highlands.

As Muñoz and Steinerowski discuss in Chapter 3, there is a stereotype of the (social) entrepreneur as an individual 'person of action' and, as Hill argues in Chapter 1, government policy depicts a desire for ubiquitous community social enterprise as an alternative service and product provider; alternative, that is, to public sector or commercial sector provision. Policy analysis reveals a gap between the desire for community social enterprise and its ubiquitous spontaneous emergence. This may be because there are many challenges for community members in designing and driving the development of local social enterprise. Recently, government policy has acknowledged the need for community activists to catalyse, mentor and give confidence to communities (Conservative Party, 2010), and in this chapter we also reflect on the mediating role of an appointed community social enterprise leader; that is, one appointed by the public sector, a project or agency, with a remit to act as both a mentor and catalyst for change; indeed, what current policy jargon refers to as a 'community activist'.

In the O4O: Older People for Older People project (O4O), which is the underlying and ongoing case study that informs practical aspects of this book, these community activists were the O4O Project Managers. By looking through the lens of one such Project Manager's story (Kate Stephen, who worked with four rural communities in the Scottish Highlands), and by reflecting on her experience, we analyse the process of organisational development of O4O-type community social enterprises and draw wider lessons about the community social enterprise process development. Following the O4O Project Manager's story, as told in her own words,[1] we consider what it tells us about:

- the engagement of communities in the social enterprise concept;
- identification of service gaps;
- the role of an appointed community activist in delivering community social enterprises;
- the types of organisational models that emerge and why;
- how communities and the local context interact with social enterprise development processes; and
- the feasibility of a 'bottom-up' approach to community social enterprise development.

THE O4O CONCEPT AND THE ROLE AND REMIT OF O4O PROJECT MANAGERS

Because the O4O project involved testing the idea that communities could and would build social enterprises for service delivery and assessing whether this would deliver benefits, it required communities to engage in trying to build social enterprises so that the whole process could be observed. In effect, O4O entered into an endeavour to 'nurture' the development of social enterprises in communities. This can be justified in terms of the goal of evaluating the feasibility of government policy regarding community social enterprise. Further, since government seeks the growth of social enterprise, it needs to take either an encouraging, but essentially 'hands off' stance (i.e. waiting for communities themselves to generate the desire to build social enterprise and seek out resources and help); or actively 'force' the development of social enterprise. O4O was a way of understanding and evaluating the notion of 'forcing' community social enterprise.

The role of the O4O Project Managers was crucial to making social enterprise 'happen' in communities. They spanned the boundary between O4O's 'big idea' of nurturing community social enterprise to provide basic local services such as 'lift-giving' and 'neighbourly helping', and making it happen on the ground. The Project Manager's job was to link with communities, repeatedly visit them, form relationships with existing groups or formulate new groups, and mentor community groups to start social enterprises for service provision. In this context 'mentoring' is difficult to define but essentially the Project Manager's role was to subtly 'push' social enterprise as an outcome, give confidence to communities through providing a resource, and provide a conduit between communities and external resources and networks whilst adhering to O4O's key principles. Specifically, in order to mimic real-life situations and avoid project dependency there was to be no direct provision of money from O4O to communities. It was useful to assess how and where communities might find resources and by what processes. The Project Manager was intended to guide the process of establishing social enterprises, but not to explicitly lead or do all of the work. Project Managers were intended to be a resource for communities, but not paternalistically telling communities what to do. They were required to understand the context and empathise with 'community feeling', but be resilient and sufficiently distanced to force the process.

At the start of the O4O project an archetype of the process that Project Managers were to undertake with communities (Figure. 4.1) was drawn by the O4O Project Management Group in consultation with leaders of community agencies and groups, including representatives of a Housing Association, Highlands & Islands Enterprise and the Highland Social Enterprise Zone. Its purpose was to help to identify between two and four participant communities in each international partner's region; 'ask' communities if they would participate in O4O; discuss opportunities for social enterprise development with community members and groups; and help communities bring their ideas to fruition by linking with external resources of various types, including politicians, education providers and regional development agencies. The latter were intended to be sources of 'free' training, help and finance, and it was envisaged that 'business' and 'enterprise development' principles and techniques would be embedded into the development of the community enterprises. O4O Project Managers were thus required to 'bridge' the paradigms of rural community development and small business/social enterprise development. The skills and attitudes required were reflected in international recruitment of Project Managers in the five participating regions that sought to implement social enterprises, of which two (Scotland and Northern Ireland) had previously worked in community development; one (Sweden) had a business development/project management background; one (Finland) was from a social work/volunteer organisation background; and one was a local government manager (Greenland).

Whilst, as reflected in Chapters 3 and 5, there is extensive literature on the idea of 'social enterprise', it remains a contested concept, a 'mixed bag' of organisational ideas lacking robust analysis and evaluation. Developing different types of socially oriented organisations quite possibly requires different skills commensurate with developing different types of businesses, services or voluntary organisations, but there is a dearth of evidence that addresses the skills and knowledge sets required by agents whose purpose is to develop social enterprises of different types and in different contexts, and perhaps at the behest of the state. O4O's context was particularly specialised, encompassing a combination of factors, as follows. First, it involved developing social enterprises but whilst social enterprise was the 'ideal type' communities were 'free' to develop different

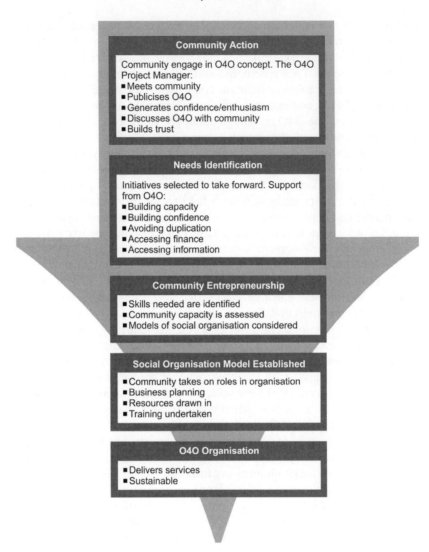

Figure 4.1   Archetype of the O4O social enterprise development process

types of organisational forms; for example, co-operatives, time-banks, voluntary organisations, social enterprises or hybrids. Secondly, this was to be done in a rural context, with the complications of sparse population, embedded relations and a very constrained market. Thirdly, O4O focused on those aged 55 years and over, an amorphous grouping encompassing relatively active/inactive, healthy/frail and socially diverse people.

Apart from studies of volunteering there is little European research that addresses the capacity and desire of older age groups to establish businesses or assume responsibility for developing and running social enterprises but, as noted, the O4O project 'forced' social enterprise development, with that agenda. That, in itself, potentially required a specialised set of skills and aptitudes including marketing, persistence and negotiation.

To record activities and facilitate reflection, O4O Project Managers kept reflective diaries throughout the three years of O4O. They were involved in six-monthly international forums where face to face discussion allowed comparison of O4O development processes across the international partners. Reflective interviews were also conducted with an external evaluator, and the Project Managers held bi-monthly international video-conferences to share their experiences. Reflective text drawn from the personal project diaries of Kate Stephen (KS), the O4O Project Manager for the Scottish Highlands, is reproduced here in order to convey the real-life experiences and pressures of being an O4O Project Manager working with communities to try to develop social enterprises. Following Kate's reflections we discuss the lessons for processes of developing community social enterprise.

THE SOCIAL ENTERPRISE PROCESS: AN O4O PROJECT MANAGER'S PERSPECTIVE

A cursory visit to most rural areas in the Scottish Highlands is likely to give the impression of tranquillity with few visible signs of modern living. There may not be many people visible, especially if the weather is bad (as it often is). Anyone who can be seen is most likely to be over the age of 55. In many coastal villages, remnants of the accoutrements of the fishing industry lie neglected and rusting. There is little evidence of employment and industry. The same impression would be given on similar visits to rural areas elsewhere in the Northern Periphery of Europe. The word enterprising does not spring to mind; indeed, the term 'socially enterprising community' might appear an oxymoron when applied in a rural context. Simultaneously, however, there are high levels of formal and informal volunteering in Highland, indicating a motivation to help each other. The O4O project set out to test whether this might translate into willingness to produce services. I was employed, from 2007–2010 as Project Manager to mentor four communities in this process. [KS: Personal Project Diary, February 2009]

Reflections on the Role of an O4O Project Manager

O4O had guiding principles: to maintain older people living in their own homes and communities for as long as possible; to promote older people as a positive force; and to bring generations together to support older people. In addition, I tried to follow the National Standards for Community Engagement [Scottish Community Development Centre, 2005a) and to maintain a person-centred approach (McCormack, 2004). The advice note for using the Standards in rural communities (Scottish Community Development Centre, 2005b) describes some specific issues and responses for rural communities for many of the Standards. I tried to avoid making assumptions about who 'older people' were and what their needs might be. To help, I thought about my own relatives, neighbours and volunteers I'd met in previous jobs. My job description described the Project Manager as an 'animateur and facilitator'. The aim was to engage with older people in communities and establish what needs they could meet by developing a local service. This would involve injecting ideas from elsewhere and giving examples from other communities as well as getting local suggestions and ideas. The Project Manager was to support the community to design and set up the service. In reality, due to pressure to deliver results and in an effort to support the community, my role transpired to be much more proactive; 'doing' as well as supporting others to do. The situation needed a high level of reflexivity because I knew I needed to provide sufficient help to support the community while avoiding doing so much that they lost ownership.

At the start, I had numerous discussions with individuals and agencies active in the communities selected for inclusion. This helped to build a picture of each community including its history, previous community development and general characteristics. The information gathered helped to ensure the projects were relevant to the local context.

As a child I lived in an area in the Highlands where two villages, separated in geographical terms only by a river, were quite distinct and occasionally hostile to each other. Where there is no 'river' such lines of distinction are not so easy to identify but villagers can find divisions based on history, civic boundaries determining service delivery, socio-economic or religious groupings [as illustrated by Radford and Shortall in Chapter 5]. There was insufficient time in O4O to research each community in depth, but my knowledge from growing up in the Highlands made me alert to potential sensitivities and divides.

This shared cultural heritage also contributed to a degree of 'insider status' that was useful in 'opening doors' and initiating relationships in communities and also with service providers, although this couldn't always be assumed even when I regarded myself as a local due to my historical family connections and the amount of time I spent in the area. Insider status is ambiguous and pertains differently depending on specific social situations. I took the approach of working shoulder-to-shoulder with local people and my approach was to commit to working with/in each community as if it were my home community. The level of emotional investment involved in this approach can be difficult to sustain and some might argue this approach is too personal and lacks objectivity.

People's perception of my role, based on aspects of representing a large European-funded project and a university research centre, brought another dynamic to relationships. Depending on the attitudes and previous experience of individuals, I was either given more credibility or less! I had to reflect on the power implications of this 'external expert' status, both when it was viewed positively and negatively, on the collaborative relationships I had with volunteers and community representatives. Generally, my approach was that the community was the 'expert'. Despite this, where communities had a history of so-called-experts dropping in to offer solutions which were locally inappropriate, I could be treated with suspicion. Simultaneously, where communities felt privileged to benefit from the involvement, I had to avoid exerting undue influence unconsciously.

Straddling the lines of insider–outsider status and of perceptions of ignorance–expertise are challenges I have faced previously as a community development worker. It was more challenging to balance the project-driven imperative of developing community social enterprise with the ethical assessment of risks and benefits to participants. Key local actors contributed vast amounts of time, effort and commitment, affecting their personal relationships, sense of well-being, work and social life. No-one expressed regret at participating and I am aware of benefits received by individuals, but I was very conscious of the risks they were taking by being involved.

I was the conduit for project development, gathering and filtering individual comments and ideas and using them, iteratively, to inform future actions and discussions. Speaking one-to-one was helpful for individuals who were reluctant to speak up in a group setting, but the approach was problematic as I was afraid that personal bias might influence which views I took forward and which I disregarded plus others might not know where the view had come from and attribute it to my own thinking. The function of conduit was critical at first, but as initiatives established, I decreased that function and shifted to a more supportive, external, role. Otherwise projects would have been overly dependent and lacked local ownership. There was pressure from funders to achieve social enterprises. At the same time, I wanted to 'make a difference' and have a positive effect in the communities. There was a constant tension in the development process between impatience to get enterprises started and respect for the pace and autonomy of the community. [KS: Project Manager's Personal Notes from Presentation and Discussion at International Project Meeting, September 2010]

REFLECTIONS ON O4O COMMUNITIES AND SOCIAL ENTERPRISE DEVELOPMENT

In Highland, it was my privilege to work with the communities of Ardersier, Assynt, South West (SW) Ross and Tongue. The word 'community' is an inaccurate shorthand for these four places as each could be said to be multiple communities; some encompassed several townships and all questioned their geographical boundaries; each contained a multiplicity of different individuals, with their ideas and motivations. The communities were picked from a short-list drawn up for the project which was collected through discussion with local agencies and funders. There was a lack of consensus from these agencies as to the final selection which was inevitably a compromise. It was originally thought it would be good to pick communities with a positive history of community action. Ultimately, the selection was a mix of active and more disadvantaged communities that funders wanted to help. [KS: Project Manager's Personal Project Diaries, 2009–2011]

Tongue

The Kyle of Tongue is on the north coast of North West Sutherland in the Scottish Highlands. The village of Tongue is the largest settlement, with Melness to the west and Skerray to the east. This area was particularly poorly served by public transport and so transport was identified as a priority for helping local older people maintain independent living. The process was dictated by the timing of a funding opportunity, applying for a community transport grant. A hastily prepared application was assembled (largely by me) after discussions with two key locals who agreed that the opportunity to get funding shouldn't be missed. A steering group was gathered, including representatives from Melness, Skerray and Tongue. This was organised by local people who persuaded others to join. Thereafter, I met regularly with the steering group and invited a range of experts from community transport and social enterprise to community meetings. A key milestone in this enterprise was winning funding. While this was initially greeted with excitement, there was a significant delay in activities as the group grew in confidence, became organised, and undertook the necessary bureaucracy, e.g. opening a new bank account. Each new stage made group members stop and think about the level of responsibility they were assuming and decide who in the group should take on the responsibility; my role was to encourage but also to respect the pace of the group. Half way through the project, funding allowed for local people to be employed or contracted to develop the enterprise. This meant a wider range of support could be provided locally.

The service 'T4T: Transport for Tongue, Melness and Skerray' was initially established as a sub-enterprise of a local community development company and is now (in 2011) developing into a community company in its own right. The service comprised: (1) informal lift sharing co-ordination; (2) a community car scheme; (3) a community owned car and minibus scheme designed to generate income. This organisation constitutes a far more ambitious project than was originally planned. The scale and nature of the development were influenced by external advisors and catalysed by the removal of the local post bus service, a last vestige of local public transport. Local events and fund raising activities helped to advertise the service and generate support.

Within the community group, one volunteer stood out as a catalyst for development. Many of the other volunteers found themselves in the group, after a conversation with this woman, not quite sure how they'd got there or when they'd actually agreed to be involved. The success of T4T owes much to her enthusiasm, powers of persuasion and dedication. The future sustainability of the group depends on continued commitment from existing and new volunteer drivers, community transport grants, and income from fares. It will be challenging to charge sufficient fares to cover costs. [KS: Project Manager's Personal Project Diaries, 2009–2011]

Assynt

While the process for development was essentially the same in all communities, elements were affected by local circumstances. In Assynt, the local group who assembled to steer the project identified a gap in residential care for older people and wanted to establish a service. The first stage for me, therefore, was to research models of residential care and supported housing appropriate for rural communities. I advised the community that it can take years to move from a vision to the opening of a care service, with huge commitment and hard work required, and although the project would help to kick start the process, it would inevitably end before a service could be started.

One of the essential elements was to gear the community up to run a social enterprise and I obtained prospectuses for social enterprise courses. Initially there was some confusion around the term 'social enterprise' and a reluctance to undertake a course of training (saying they were too busy and didn't want the commitment of something that sounded so formal). Eventually, through discussions with the social enterprise trainers, a solution was found where the timing, title and content of their course were tweaked to be more appealing and relevant. This was essentially similar to the previous proposal, but it used the community's language and met their specific needs.

In early 2010, the local council accelerated previous plans to close local older people's care facilities. After many meetings with community members and the local council, the outcome was a shift in thinking for the local steering group which moved to consider the feasibility of a community takeover to run the current council care service as a community social enterprise. I spent some time investigating costs and efficiencies that could be made if the community were to take over. There was a mix of nervousness and reluctance with the idea that the community should approach the council with a proposal.

When the council said it was going to close the local residential care home, negotiations to start a community social enterprise began in earnest. The process was eased by willingness of council leaders to enter into a frank dialogue with the community and by a culture change within the community from resistance to determination to make it work for themselves. The council voted to pay the community to run a local service. A community interest company was established and I supported the group in formal business planning and additional fundraising. The new service, 'Community Care Assynt', started in September 2010 and in the first months there was an incredible response in the form of volunteer hours. The service is for all who have need within the community and not just older people – as many people didn't identify themselves as being old enough to come along in the past – despite being aged in their 70s or 80s. Older people are now encouraged to contribute and help out as well as to receive services.

As with T4T, one individual stands out as being integral to the development of the service. Although support from the wider community was forthcoming at the crucial start-up phase, there had been many months of behind-the-scenes dedication and many hours of preparatory work. [KS: Project Manager's Personal Project Diaries, 2009–2011]

South West Ross

The aim in SW Ross was to establish a neighbourly helping service that would engage local volunteers in doing small household tasks for frail people. Ultimately, the process failed and no social enterprise was established through O4O in SW Ross. A series of independent evaluation interviews was held with community members and the following emerged as problematical: (1)

the dispersed local population made it difficult to gather people and gain consensus (citizens did not regard themselves as comprising one community); (2) groups of people conflicted over the need for a helping service (there were different ideas); (3) there was a lack of key local individuals who emerged to drive the initiative; (4) I was regarded as having inflicted the enterprise idea on the community and there was discussion of how community initiatives should be 'bottom-up'; (5) a neighbouring area had a free, council run service and there was resentment in SW Ross that citizens were being asked to do it for themselves; (6) lack of acceptance that the public sector could no longer afford to provide.

Data from the O4O community survey showed high informal helping in SW Ross. The formalisation of neighbourly helping may act as a disincentive as, instead of just doing the act of helping, individuals have to complete forms, stick to policies, and undergo a disclosure check. In terms of scaling-up success-ful community social enterprises, the SW Ross experience is a salutary reminder that what works in one area will not necessarily work in another.

There were high levels of negativity and criticism about the O4O project, EU projects in general, and about my role in the failure to start up a service. After reflection on what I did differently in SW Ross compared to the other com-munities, I realise that my enthusiasm for the project and reluctance to give up on the idea may have blinded me from being objective about the level of buy-in from the community. Where that same enthusiasm may have supported service development in one community, it resulted in a lack of ownership in SW Ross. [KS: Project Manager's Personal Project Diaries, 2009– 2011]

Ardersier

Ardersier has a recent history of decline and disadvantage. Local people were sceptical of involvement with the O4O project, stating that one thing they could commit to was interviewing each other about the past and establishing an archive of the history of the village. This presented a dilemma because O4O was meant to be establishing social enterprises and Ardersier people were not interested. On discussion, we decided to support the village to establish an oral history DVD project which involved a group of older participants filming interviews with local older people about aspects of the past. We thought this might help groups of older people to meet and discuss their needs and wants for services. The group obtained free training from a BBC reporter and an oral history expert. They learned skills in filming, interviewing, editing and production and they met other local older people, previously somewhat iso-lated. From looking an unpromising prospect for social enterprise, the group gained confidence and began to work with other groups in the village to look at the potential to develop a café and heritage centre. A local enterprise company has been established and, with support from Highlands and Islands Enterprise (the regional development agency), a consultant was recruited to investigate the feasibility of developing these and other ideas for the village. The oral history DVD project has made a positive contribution to the village as a whole as well as to the lives of the older people who participated. [KS: Project Manager's Personal Notes from Presentation at International Project Meeting, June 2010]

THE COMMUNITY SOCIAL ENTERPRISE DEVELOPMENT PROCESS DISSECTED

Having presented excerpts from an O4O Project Manager's reflective diaries and presentations we now give consideration to the wider lessons regarding aspects of the community social enterprise development process that can be taken from this discourse.

Engaging Communities

As exemplified by South West Ross, the idea of 'a community' is intuitive but difficult to enact and activate. As well as the contested geographical borders of the communities involved in the O4O project, we found communities divided by historical differences and 'incomer'/local status. Whilst the idea of community is 'warm and fluffy', the fact that cohesive communities generally don't exist makes it difficult to harness the often meagre human capacity of rural communities and provide focused energy to build social enterprise. In the O4O project there were contested ideas from funders and local stakeholders about which communities should be targeted for inclusion; that is, those that were disadvantaged or those already 'successful' in terms of community development. Dilemmas around how to select communities and how to explain the basis for selection to community members and other stakeholders suggest that support for community social enterprise must be ubiquitous if inclusion is a goal. However, resources to support enterprise development are finite and therefore choices as to which communities to prioritise for support must be made. However, the fact that progress was made with both Ardersier and Assynt illustrates that both 'disadvantaged' and 'successful' communities can be engaged in building enterprise, although they will be at different stages of readiness for social enterprise development.

As has been illustrated, it is difficult to engage the whole of a community. Most people do not want to be involved for various reasons or do not affiliate with a culture where they could volunteer to be involved. This means that action falls on a small number of already over-worked, heavily involved individuals. Succession planning and generating sufficient volunteers for sustainability become challenging. Those who speak loudest may influence which initiatives are chosen for progression but they, and their choices, may be unpopular with others in the community and tensions between ideas and groups can erode the viability of community social enterprise development. Engagement was best where ideas gained consensus by appealing to community members' desires for their community's sustainability, sense of social justice or for improving local quality of life. This was seen in the development of older people's services in Assynt which was widely popular due to the desire to keep older people 'at home' in their locale, although there was dissent regarding the involvement of community 'factions' in taking initiatives forward.

Identifying Gaps in Services

The O4O Project Manager's story highlights how community needs and service gaps are diversely perceived by different people and groups. In each of the communities a range of service gaps was suggested and in some communities the focus of the O4O initiatives evolved. Getting a group of individuals to cohere around one idea, and progressing this, can be difficult and unrealistic from many perspectives. Perhaps, as in the cases of Ardersier, Tongue and Assynt, different ideas need to be tried before a consensus-building and feasible idea emerges. In each of the Highland communities, an original idea – that is, making a DVD of interviews about local history, developing a lift-sharing scheme and providing residential care – evolved into a different, arguably more feasible local initiative that was able to attract support from funders and other authorities: respectively, work to provide a meeting place and heritage centre supported by Highlands and Islands Enterprise; a diversified community transport scheme supported by the local authority; and community ownership of a local facility where carers could provide social care supported by the local authority. A frustration may be that a service provider or, in the case of O4O, the Project Manager, may have an idea of what they think the community needs but has to allow community members autonomy to decide its direction, mould their own solution and develop a sense of ownership of the process. A particular challenge with O4O was the need to develop community social enterprises quickly (i.e. within the relatively short timescale of the project) and, as the Assynt example of developing viable housing for older people shows, initiatives can take many years to evolve.

The Role of the O4O Project Manager

Project Managers as community activists have a key role in the emergence of community social enterprises and are particularly important at critical junctures where their ability to 'push subtly' prevents enterprise developments from floundering. We saw this in Tongue, for example, where the community group had to be 'prompted' to open a bank account for its local transport scheme.

In light of Project Manager KS's reflections, certain skills, knowledge and approaches are clearly important in achieving the emergence of community social enterprise. These include: contextual awareness and sensitivity; understanding of the imperative to 'push' development at the fastest possible pace whilst recognising that people need time to accrue information, deal with local disputes and negotiation, and catch up with the policy agenda; understanding of the role of business techniques such as business planning; attitudes such as confidence, persistence and endurance; and a capacity for long hours of work. Such skills and attitudes may well exist, or emerge, within communities but here we are specifically reviewing the potential role of an externally appointed 'catalyst' with the role of 'forcing' growth of community social enterprise service provision.

A number of theoretical 'concepts' informed the original idea of O4O Project Managers and their role, including Simmel's concept of 'the stranger' and his discussion of how the stranger has both presence and distance (Wolff, 1950). The Project Manager was conceived as an individual from outside the immediate community but with an understanding of the underpinning community culture, its acceptable norms of behaviour and its value system. They were intended as a catalytic force with connections to networks, policy ideas and resources and given an explicit remit to 'stir up' new perspectives and approaches in the community. Whether the stranger was perceived as 'good' or 'bad', the ultimate outcome was a point of change. Coming from outside the immediate community the 'stranger' both connects to, and brings, new ideas and assumptions from elsewhere. Kilpatrick's idea of the 'boundary spanner', or agent, who connects community-based resources with outside networks, resources and influences was also pertinent. Kilpatrick et al (2009) draw on the notion of 'bridging' social capital as a theoretical underpinning to the idea of boundary-spanning. Thus, the O4O Project Manager was an agent linked with useful external resources who could function as an active bridge for bringing those 'knowledge and influence resources' into the local community. Similarly, O4O Project Managers could link the community's thoughts, desires and perceptions with planning processes for, for example, local authority and health services and regional development agencies. Through their boundary-spanning, Project Managers presented community issues in the language and frameworks of services and policy, and vice versa.

Emergent Models

Over time, the communities illustrated in the reflective descriptions above and where social enterprises were developed, transpired to institute a formal social enterprise, 'community company' model. In some ways this was an intriguing outcome as the study had originally envisaged the emergence of a range of socially oriented organisational models including time-banks, co-operatives and/or voluntary organisations. It is unsurprising that social enterprise models emerged, as communities were heavily steered in that direction by the Project Manager's identification of social enterprise as an 'ideal' outcome and outside agencies harnessed by the O4O project to advise tended to promote the social enterprise model. Whilst community members were initially interested in models such as time-banks, in practice these were complex to produce in rural communities. A particular challenge was that some people wanted 'helping each other' to remain informal, whilst others were more enthusiastic to formalise reciprocity. This issue was a barrier when considering development of time-banks that require investment of discrete aspects of service in exchange for receipt of discrete withdrawals. The incongruence between informal traditional helping and formalising helping through an exchange permeated discussions for other enterprises. For example, there was an ongoing dispute over informal lift-giving versus formal arrangements in Tongue's T4T initiative.

Effects of the Local Context

The local context in terms of history, geography, residents and their past arguments or agreements served to influence the choices made and the processes of community social enterprise development. In SW Ross the Project Manager encountered resentments between communities and groups/individuals in different settlements that caused disagreement around the choice of initiative to progress. In Ardersier, community members were able to harness the interesting and varied history of the village to reinvigorate a sense of identity and pride, eventually involving school children and many local older people and generating interest in a larger local heritage initiative. Similarly, Assynt's history of community land buyout and the development of a community-owned sports centre gave citizens and local leaders the confidence and experience to think that they could take responsibility for operating older people's care.

The Feasibility of a 'Bottom-Up' Approach

It is sometimes suggested that community development and social enterprise should be a bottom-up, grounded process, with organisations that emerge from recognition of local needs by local people most likely to succeed and be sustainable. Whilst this may be true in many cases, our evidence suggests that the particular social circumstances of small, remote communities may align with an alternative model that acknowledges the complementary role of external and internal resources. Those involved in the O4O project encountered evidence of local disagreement impeding the establishment and growth of local social enterprise, but, as highlighted by the Project Manager's reflections reproduced in this chapter, distanced but legitimate and credible catalytic actors can play a useful role in some circumstances. The Highland Project Manager was viewed as having the authority of working for a local university, which gave her moral credibility, and as having embedded knowledge of 'how things work around here' from her family connections and many visits to the area during her life – although, conversely, these were, at times, viewed as disadvantages by local citizens. Similarly, the Project Manager was able to leave the rural communities where she was working, whilst local residents had to stay and often received ongoing pressure to conform to local norms.

The Policy–Practice Gap

Social enterprise development and communities co-producing services with the public sector are models currently promoted in the policy and rhetoric of political parties. These movements suggest a shift in power from public service providers towards 'an equal and reciprocal relationship between professionals, people using services, their families and their neighbours' and from provider status to facilitator and catalyst (Boyle and Harris, 2009:11). O4O sought to build co-production, with the outputs of providing transport, social activities, and social and practical support for older people; services which the public sector has grown to provide, if in increasingly unstandardised ways in recent years, to many of Europe's rural areas. One of the striking things about engaging with rural communities was the extent to which citizens were unaware of the general but gradual movement to replace public service provision with community social enterprise and volunteering initiatives. Whilst aware of the decline of their local services (OECD, 2010), citizens appear not to associate this with overall policy and political trends. In supporting communities to identify service gaps, part of the function of O4O was to enter into a dialogue about what levels of service provision could and should be expected from the public sector. Although the general population is potentially well versed in the state of the economy at macro level, through its heavy exposure in national media sources, there appears to be a gap in awareness about how this could affect local services, with some individuals maintaining a 'head-in-the-sand' attitude. In speaking with people in rural communities across the countries involved in O4O about pressures on social care budgets, researchers generally met with an incongruous mix of complaint about inadequate levels of current services and optimism that the public sector would continue to provide for truly needy people (Farmer et al, 2010b). A challenge for policymakers is to bring the macro-level concept of fiscal constraint to the local level in order to discuss what individuals and communities are expected to do through social enterprise and co-production. However, where people perceive unequal treatment they appear unwilling to participate in 'service co-production'; that is, working with local authorities to provide and support basic local services. This was demonstrated in our SW Ross example where residents in one area said they would not develop volunteering to help older people if the council was providing such a service in a neighbouring area.

The discourse around the real or mythical stoicism of rural people and how this affects help-seeking behaviour is useful in attempting to understand the context of developing co-production in the Scottish Highlands. The personality type evoked by Jim Hunter's (1995:24–25) description of his Highlander father is that of resigned indifference, fatalistically accepting whatever hardship life throws up. There is a significant distance between this type of individual and the social entrepreneur who will rise to the opportunity of co-production. At community level there is a need for community members to advance from viewing themselves as passive victims of remote forces to committing, confidently, to proactive service design and delivery. In the story above, Assynt has a history of empowerment through community ownership of assets and this is likely to have added to collective confidence that ambitions to co-produce services could be achieved.

CONCLUSION

Policy purports that it is both possible to produce social enterprise and that it brings social advantages (Alcock, 2011). Publishing on social enterprise tends to focus on large enterprises that produce products or services and run much like viable commercial enterprises except that they re-invest profit for social objectives. In this book we are considering a different type of social enterprise; one that is conceivable as the foundation of a 'Big Society' where communities of citizens contribute to helping each other, thereby producing social capital for their communities, new skills and connections, and emotional wellbeing for themselves. Even then, we must consider that community social enterprise will be more or less viable in particular conditions; for example, conditions where community members agree on focused initiatives or can harness the requisite internal and external resources for development.

In this chapter, we have used the direct discourse of an O4O Project Manager as a framework to consider the dilemmas and practical challenges of establishing social enterprise in a specific set of rural geographical, demographic and economic conditions. We show that the process is practically and politically difficult and argue that in order for ubiquitous community social enterprise to occur, as opposed to relying on spontaneous sporadic emergence, there is relevance in deploying a 'pushing' force from agencies in the form of community activists to 'force' enterprise production. As evidenced above, O4O Project Managers were able to 'push' projects at a pace that maximised development and community buy-in, and to link the capacity of communities to help themselves with the policy drive for communities to co-produce services. In this way, they represent a force for bridging the gap between policy and implementation; between what government wants and the day-to-day priorities, lived realities and future aspirations of community members. Coupled with this force – that is external yet bridges communities and external resources – communities need their own entrepreneurs to take initiatives forward. Setting up a new service is generally not an instinctive response when communities consider the challenge of ageing populations in rural areas. To overcome apathy, identify solutions and be socially entrepreneurial took individuals with characteristics that differentiated them from their more passive neighbours. These key people were the drivers of development who took their communities with them. Externally appointed community activists and socially enterprising community leaders represent a partnership. In addition, and crucially, communities need the resource of volunteers and focused implementable ideas.

NOTE

1. The Project Manager's story is reflective text written by her at the completion of the O4O project, drawing on her personal diaries kept for the duration of the project and other sources such as project meeting discussion notes. The sources consulted for each reflective piece are given in square brackets.

REFERENCES

Alcock P. (2011), *Big Society or Civil Society? A new policy environment for the third sector*, Third Sector Research Centre, http://tinyurl.com/3hka4ha (accessed 1 July 2011).

Boyle D. & Harris M. (2009), *The Challenge of Co-production: How equal partnerships between professionals and the public are crucial to improving services*, London: NESTA.

Conservative Party (2010), *Cameron Unveils Big Society Plan*. Retrieved from: http://www.conservatives.com/News/News_stories/2010/03/Plans_announced_to_help_build_a_Big_Society.aspx (accessed 5 January 2011).

Farmer J., Muñoz S., Steinerowski A. & Bradley S. (2010a), 'Health, Wellbeing and Community Involvement of Older People in Rural Scotland' in Le Q. (Ed.), *Health and Wellbeing: A social and cultural perspective*, New York: Nova Science, pp. 128–144.

Farmer J., Philip L., King G., Farrington J. & MacLeod M. (2010b), 'Territorial Tensions: Misaligned management and community perspectives on health services for older people in remote rural areas', *Health and Place*, 16, pp. 275–283.

Hunter J. (1995), *On the Other Side of Sorrow: Nature and people in the Scottish Highlands*, Edinburgh: Mainstream Publishing.

Kilpatrick S., Cheers B., Gillies M. & Taylor J. (2009), 'Boundary Crossers, Communities and Health: Exploring the role of rural health professionals', *Health & Place*, 15, pp. 284–290.

McCormack B. (2004), 'Person-centredness in Gerontological Nursing: An overview of the literature', *Journal of Clinical Nursing*, 13(Supplement 1, March), pp. 31–38.

OECD Rural Policy Reviews (2010), *Strategies to Improve Rural Service Delivery*, Paris: OECD Publishing, pp. 13–54.

Scottish Community Development Centre (2005a), *National Standards for Community Engagement*. Retrieved from: http://www.scdc.org.uk/what/national-standards/10-national-standards/ (accessed 12 November 2010).

Scottish Community Development Centre (2005b), *National Standards for Community Engagement Advice Note: Remote rural practice*. Retrieved from: http://www.scdc.org.uk/media/resources/what-we-do/national-standards/using_the_standards_in_rural_communities.pdf (accessed 12 November 2010).

Wolff K. (Trans.) (1950), *The Sociology of Georg Simmel*, New York: Free Press, pp. 402–408.

5. Socially enterprising communities: their dynamics and readiness for service innovation

Katy Radford and Sally Shortall

INTRODUCTION

Much of the literature suggests that social enterprises developed by communities continue to have a local focus, either through the provision of local trading and retail operations or of locally based social and welfare services. This mirrors our experience in Northern Ireland where we have been involved in the development of three different types of social enterprise which have remained rooted in diverse rural communities through the O4O: Older People for Older People project (O4O). What is not always included in this literature is a focus on how reliance on local volunteer support can act as a barrier, as well as an enabler, to the success of such enterprises. As we explore this, it is pertinent to also consider the circumstances in which people over the age of 55 have grown older in Northern Ireland; namely, with a legacy of societal conflict and social segregation providing the frame of reference in which people feel able to support themselves and their peers.

In this chapter, illustrations from two of the developed O4O community initiatives contribute insights into the gaps in the literature on social enterprise and problematise the premise that social economy businesses by typology are necessarily democratic initiatives. We begin with a brief, critical consideration of the social enterprise literature and note that there remains a considerable lack of data and unresolved definitional issues.

Research on social enterprises has moved beyond the business and management disciplines to give more attention to both sociological and anthropological understandings. Pursuing this new direction enables us to apply academic attention to both the communities and the contexts in which they exist in Northern Ireland and, *de facto*, the drivers and obstacles that create the environment in which they can thrive. We thus consider here, the specific circumstances in which community initiatives in

Northern Ireland develop. In so doing, we add a particular dimension to those considering the historical social and political divisions within society as well as the structural inequalities which, from the late 1960s, resulted in violence perpetrated by, and against, both state and non-state armed groups.

We follow this section with one outlining the methodology used and present a short sketch of two geographical areas in which we worked and on which we later drew for ethnographic examples. Finally, we identify three research areas that the experience of O4O-type social enterprises in Northern Ireland can inform, in terms of communities' readiness to benefit from not-for-profit enterprises. We call these sections:

- social enterprise and the heroic individual;
- biography and institutional environment;
- the political environment and the social enterprise;

and we conclude this chapter on communities' readiness to innovate new service delivery models by reviewing our explorations in light of our experiences of the tension between the social and the economic objectives of social enterprises.

CRITICAL OVERVIEW OF SOCIAL ENTERPRISE LITERATURE

There has been a considerable increase in the policy commitment to social enterprises in the UK and Ireland over the last decade, including a pledge to increase the number of older people engaged in them (Curran & Blackburn, 2001; Rural Lifelines, 2004; Peattie & Morley, 2008), and in many respects O4O could be considered an agent in forwarding that objective. In 2002, the UK government's Social Enterprise Unit described a social enterprise as a business with primary social objectives whose surpluses are principally reinvested for that purpose in the business or in the community, rather than being driven by the need to maximise profit for shareholders and owners.

Despite this, there continue to be wide-ranging debates in the academic literature as to what constitutes a social enterprise. Following Peattie and Morley (2008), we see the defining characteristics of social enterprises as, first, the primacy of social aims and, secondly, activity that involves trading goods and services. The first distinguishes social enterprises from the private sector; the second from the voluntary and community sector (Peattie & Morley, 2008:8). The complexities of trying to encourage the community and voluntary sector to undertake social enterprises, subsequent attempts to disentangle social enterprises from the voluntary and community sector, and the inherent tensions in this endeavour is a theme that has been explored by Bridge et al (2009). We explore this further, with particular reference to how rurality and the political and social climate, amongst other factors, create both physical and symbolic divisions between communities that can also impact on their success as well as a readiness to engage in their development. Furthermore, in the vein of arguments proposed by Curran and Blackburn (2001) we suggest that whilst, as Hill discusses in Chapter 1, the pan-European notion of policy supporting an emerging 'third age entrepreneurship' is politically, economically and ideologically appealing, there is little reason to presume a desire for self-employment by older people.

The O4O project's aim was to assist older people in rural areas to establish sustainable social enterprises for the benefit of their peers. This is reflective of the view that older people in rural areas can be both major beneficiaries of, and significant participants in, social enterprises (Rural Lifelines, 2004). In train with this hypothesis there is also a view that participating in social enterprises helps combat social exclusion. Applying this premise specifically to older people, it is possible to contest the disengagement theories of the mid twentieth century, that perpetuated negative stereotypes of biological ageing and privileged a gerontological perspective (Lupien & Wan, 2004) that subordinates models of successful psychosocial ageing. Whilst older people can find themselves categorised as a disadvantaged group in rural areas, they are also seen as a group that can lead and participate in positive change processes (Rural Lifelines, 2004). This has been drawn on to suggest that older people have the characteristics favourable to social enterprise as a result of life experience, and assets for business ownership.

Other research presents a less universalist view. It has been suggested that a good deal of this is conjecture based on sparse empirical evidence. Curran and Blackburn (2001), for example, suggest that older people do not necessarily believe they have the business skills to undertake social enterprises; that there is little evidence to support a hypothesis that they have a desire to start their own businesses, and more indicating interest in non-economic pursuits. It has also been suggested that older people in rural areas tend to focus on meeting social need, co-operation and democratic management, rather than on profit (Rural Lifelines, 2004). The application of the social capital theoretical perspective outlined by Putnam (2000) and Rothstein (2005) might be used to argue that the benefits of engagement and participation in socially driven activities lead to both the improved health and wellbeing of individuals as well as to the bridging and bonding of socially disadvantaged communities. Others question both the conceptual and practical effectiveness of using a social enterprise paradigm to reach disadvantaged or marginalised groups (Parkinson & Howorth, 2007; Amin, 2009).

Roginsky and Shortall (2009) have argued that there are difficulties in the very concept of social enterprise as it seeks to marry the market with civil society, even though both spheres have different ideological positions and different objectives. An overview of the social enterprise literature shows that it is mired in disagreement and contradiction, yet it is generally agreed that there is a lack of critical and conceptual research (Curran & Blackburn, 2001; Parkinson & Howorth, 2007; Peattie & Morley, 2008; Amin, 2009). Consequently, what we do not attempt here is any exploration of the wider societal benefits of the social enterprise sector as a whole, comprising, as it does, large-scale and long-term initiatives (i.e. housing associations and regional charities with trading arms) where the resources and infrastructures are reliant on the visionary entrepreneurship of paid and professional employees. Rather, what we do attempt is a nuanced discussion based on nascent and recently established businesses as to the specific direct and indirect benefits to individuals of locally based small-scale single-issue enterprises that are heavily dependent on the benevolent altruism of volunteer participants in low-level welfare services areas (such as social and befriending activities, retail, transport and catering); questioning, as part of that process, what are the over-arching dynamics that influence each group's readiness to develop and sustain the enterprise.

METHODOLOGY

Over an 18 month period, the authors worked with groups in three counties in Northern Ireland. The objective was to work with groups who wished to provide services to older people and establish social enterprises. One group was identified by Age Concern, partners in the project, and the others by a steering committee representing senior statutory service policy shapers and makers and other corporate stakeholders from within the age sector.[1] The overall programme had a series of general principles: to engage with older people's existing skills, knowledge and experience; to nurture engagement and proactivity with older people; and to build on their capacity for innovation, action, enterprise and voluntary activity.

The specific purpose of O4O was to explore the hypothesis that developing social economy initiatives in rural areas with, by and for older people, was beneficial to the physical and emotional health and wellbeing of active volunteer participants and the less active recipient participants.

The research undertaken was principally qualitative with, by necessity, a community development focus that targeted organisations working with individuals aged 55 or more. After initial interest was indicated to the researchers, and as a precursor to commencing work with the groups, a series of between four and eight exploratory meetings were conducted initially with key gatekeepers and latterly with other paid and volunteer workers – where the parameters, objectives and desired outcomes of the project were both defined and refined consensually. Over several months local reference groups were established which met weekly (and often more frequently) to carry out workshops and exchange visits, as well as a variety of training programmes including business mentoring, change management, good governance and mediation, with methodologies including role play and seminars. Semi-structured interviews, focus groups and participant observation on the part of the researchers were used to record to what level the communities played a formative role in determining the progress and direction of the process as well as noting the key issues arising. By way of ongoing monitoring of the programme, 325 questionnaires considering the value of the programme were carried out during its lifespan. Confidentiality, though offered, was waived by participants who were keen to achieve as much publicity for their endeavours as was possible, and to that end they considered the development of marketing and public relations strategies, and the use of their work as case studies, to be integral to the success of the programme.

Given the time constraints in which the projects were developed and established it has not been possible, at the time of writing, to evaluate the programme in terms of any long-term socio-economic impacts, other than anecdotally. Consequently the types of indicators used to record the success were attitudinal, behavioural and processual, and these have been gauged by the use of pre and post surveys, and interviews with programme participants.

ENTERPRISING COMMUNITIES: EXAMPLES FROM NORTHERN IRELAND

The first two enterprises (in Tyrone and Armagh) are used here as case studies; chosen to exemplify different motivations and levels of achievement to sustainably address social inclusion from a social economy perspective (see Table 5.1). Given the high percentage of start-up businesses that fail to exist beyond their first two years of trading, these two projects were chosen because they were attached to already established community groups with the financial assets and capital resources in place

Table 5.1   O4O Northern Ireland outcomes

Location	Core participants in training programme	Older beneficiaries of services	Financial projection – 12 months	Self-reported evidence of participants' wellbeing
Tyrone	8	100+	Profit double	Self-esteem Self-confidence Participation New skills
Armagh	6	Participants only	Not trading	Social interaction Self-confidence
Ards Peninsula	15	1000+	Loss	New friendships New skills Cross-community contacts

to pump-prime the social enterprises. The third venture was undertaken as a pilot programme principally because it provided an opportunity to observe, from start to finish, a project reliant on a number of statutory and community sector partners but, unlike the other two projects, it was time bound and is therefore not considered in this chapter.

By way of introduction, a little background to the context of both the Tyrone and Armagh enterprises is provided.

In County Tyrone, we worked with a group of older volunteers who have been formally constituted since 1985 to address the lack of community activities and services for older people in a six mile radius of the market town of Cookstown. The group chosen had historical links with the now reconfigured regional charity Age Concern. When we began to work with this group their existing lunch club was being run from a kitchen described by the local council as 'no longer compliant with their health and safety regulations' and consequently due to be shut down. The turnover in the rather run-down charity shop attached to it was decreasing annually. The O4O project worked through a process of change management in restructuring and visioning to: extend the existing lunch club and meals on wheels service into a wider geographical area and begin to increase the income generated from the retail outlet; develop a restaurant, where the bulk of vegetables were sourced and harvested from local farms and allotments owned and managed by older people; and provide a centre for older people to obtain information on rights and entitlements.

The principal outcomes of this project were that the existing group decided to rebrand under the name *Opportunities for Older People, O4O Cookstown* and move into larger, more appropriate main street premises. This enabled it to expand its services and project a realistic doubling of its annual business turnover, increase its volunteer base and management committee, and develop a regional information drop-in centre in partnership with the charity Age NI (Northern Ireland) (the metamorphosis of former Age Concern and Help the Aged charities). Close inspection of the individual and group dynamics involved in these processes provides us with our first insight into the reliance on key 'heroic' individuals within community groups and demonstrates how micro management by some community gatekeepers can result in an over-reliance on, and perceived exploitation of, some volunteers.

Our second case study is Markethill, a County Armagh border town which is home to 1,292 people with a 79% Protestant/Unionist majority and with 22% of the population aged over 60. It is considered to be the birthplace of the Orange Order[2] and, perhaps unsurprisingly therefore, has strong connections to the security services, with many citizens, both men and women, over 50 having served as part-time armed police and army reservists. Eight bomb attacks during the height of the Northern Irish Conflict also played a part in shaping the area into a close, conservative community living very separate and segregated lives from its Catholic/ Nationalist neighbours in outlying areas.

In this rarefied and closed community, where the unknown stranger is more often feared than welcomed, we worked with a voluntary group from within the 'Victim/Survivor'[3] sector, the bulk of whom were women who had either lost a husband or child as a result of the Conflict and for whom social life outside the home was largely shaped by their activities in the 'victim–survivor' group. This group had two paid employees and was wholly grant-dependent when we began working with them. But, cognisant of a government-led initiative to encourage 'victim and survivor' groups to bid for service-level agreements with local trusts and other statutory service providers to aid their particular client-group, their aim was to become a specialist social enterprise offering a 'safe space' as a befriender-led drop-in cafe for older people. This was to be a locus for older people to meet other older people and from where they could be signposted on to some of the therapeutic services also provided by the group. O4O provided business mentoring and financial planning support and worked with the group through a series of financial exercises and grant applications. However, during our time with them, investigations were initiated by two of their core funders on the grounds of financial irregularities. This resulted in a cessation of trading prior to what has since become a formal fraud investigation (live at the time of writing).

This case study thus provides an introduction into the section 'biography and institutional environment'; examining the emotional readiness of volunteers to engage, and the need to ensure careful ongoing monitoring of enterprises and those associated with them to ensure operational and strategic readiness. This, in turn, is illustrative of the need for funding bodies and state policymakers to develop guidelines to gauge a group's readiness to undertake responsible business activities and their understanding of good governance structures and accountability prior to investment.

Social Enterprise and the 'Heroic' Individual

The term 'heroic individual' is one which we borrow from Spear (2006). It refers to the role of the social entrepreneur in the establishment of social enterprises. The literature on the rationale and circumstances that enable social entrepreneurs to emerge and motivate others with their vision, in the communities in which they exist, is as ambiguous and contested as that on social enterprises. At one end of the spectrum there is an emerging tendency to see the social entrepreneur as energetic, imaginative, persistent and a leader (Barendsen & Gardener, 2004; Peattie & Morley, 2008). There is also, however, a potential tension between the individual in entrepreneurship and the collective and community base of social enterprises (Parkinson & Howorth, 2007). We argue that this can be even more pronounced when the social enterprise develops from a community sector organisation.

In Tyrone, Mary[4] is delighted to tell me that she has been awarded an MBE (Member of the British Empire) award in the UK New Year's Honours List (an annual national award listing), which she sees as a fitting tribute to the 25 of her 73 years that she has dedicated to volunteering with older people in her home area. She sees the expansion of the business as a reflection of her good works, and has been a positive force in garnering support for the proposed move to new premises that will consolidate the group's existing work and result in some considerable public recognition and (self) publicity.

Seemingly indefatigable, Mary shuttles between the different venues out of which the group she steers operates. Today, her main aim is to show me how successfully the catering and retail schemes are being maintained by the volunteer base, all of whom she wants to show are directly accountable to her for their actions. The financial success of these ventures is core to sustaining the craft and other social activities the group is able to provide to its members and which also require a significant body of volunteers to co-ordinate. She leaves potted plants that she has grown in the shop. A few doors down we enter an open plan dining area serviced by a dilapidated kitchen. She carries in a box full of cabbages for the lunch picked from an allotment in the garden of an older woman no longer able to manage the garden but grateful for a share in the crop that Mary and other volunteers harvest there. Positioning both of us so that we stand at opposite ends of a long trestle table, she introduces me to the 30 men and women seated, waiting for lunch. Some are volunteers with large management and organisational responsibilities for particular social activities, work in the shop or in catering roles. Others are regular customers transported in on the group's minibus for lunch and an afternoon of socialising. This group is also encouraged to take on the volunteer mantle by dint of setting and clearing tables and being proactive. It is hard to distinguish between the two groups, who merge into one as a cadre of similarly dressed people in their latter years; but it is easy to see that they are all enjoying being together. Mary, however, quite literally stands out from the others despite her closeness in age and long-term relationships with many of them. She does so by continuing to address me over their heads, joking with the seated ones, pointing out who she went to school with and whose children her own would have played with 50 years ago, and benignly patting the shoulders of volunteers. She informs them of her forthcoming MBE but leaves little space for them to initiate conversation about this or matters of concern to them. She is the wife of a successful vet, owns two small farms and is a nurse by training, but it is not her affluence that marks her out from the others. Rather, it is the seemingly guileless way she negotiates her domain, simultaneously making easy connections between the others in the room and yet keeping both a physical and symbolic distance from them. A peer by age and locality, but a benevolent philanthropist and provider, as opposed to a service user or ' mere' volunteer worker-ant, Mary is able to assert authority in the group's hierarchy, intentionally and instinctively, by acquiring from others confirmation of her hero protagonist status. The MBE provides another tool to this end. A seasoned activist and advocate for older people's causes, it is clear that she is also motivated to lobby just as hard in order to retain her place as the principal voice representing older people in the area. It is this side of the hero warrior that ultimately undermines altruism embedded in the process and which can be identified as a potential threat to the long-term success of the enterprise.

We see this more clearly if we fast-forward six months to when the new premises have been launched and the use of the services has doubled. Reflecting on how that was achieved paints a darker side to the role of the persistent hero individual identified by Spear (2006) and others (Barendsen & Gardener, 2004; Peattie & Morley, 2008). For it was during this period that Mary began to feel that her 'control' of what had effectively been a small fiefdom was being threatened. A former neighbour and close friend of Mary, a younger woman by 15 years but with the same degree of drive and commitment and the added benefit of having run a successful cafe in the town, was wrongly and unintentionally perceived as being a tacit pretender to Mary's throne. With no intention of disrupting Mary's status, but understanding the need for movement and change to be grasped and acted on rather than delayed, Paula began to take the lead in a number of areas so as not to delay the move to the new premises. As part of that process she also attempted to invigorate the Board with new members. Many of the original volunteer Board members had been brought on and handpicked by Mary and were principally there to rubber stamp her ideas rather than to be proactive or offer strategic direction. With the introduction of new members the voices of previously silenced volunteers began to provide alternative options to the day to day operations which Mary had formerly played the principal lead in envisioning and designing. A series of breakdowns in relationships between the core volunteers on the Management Committee and Mary ensued, resulting in Paula and a number of others, including the vice-chair, resigning after an exchange of lawyers' letters addressing libel and slander, and a series of mediation and training workshops implemented by O4O to try and resolve the issues in the community's best interests.

Consequently, it might be argued that the individual energies and leadership identified by other academic commentators as being core to the success of a social enterprise are contingent on being managed within a process of good governance. Heroic individuals can only be seen as such when the activities of others are given the space to be heard, valued and respected. It becomes evident that without such checks and balances in place, tensions develop when the principal leader, or key gatekeeper, within a community organisation is not necessarily the most skilled individual to develop and manage the social enterprise.

Biography and Institutional Environment

Froggett and Chamberlayne (2004) suggest that we need to understand the biographies of individual lives in shaping the development of institutions and social enterprises. We concur with this and, in the previous section, have illustrated how those with dominant personalities are able to play both a positive and a negative key role in the strategic and operational development of community groups and the social enterprises that such groups develop. But a second area of consideration which can also indicate the readiness of a community to successfully innovate is to be found rooted not just in the actions of such key individuals, but rather at the intersection between personal narratives and the cultures of organisations. In addressing this, we also recognise that institutional environments and cultures, in turn, have been shaped by a variety of events and ideologies. We have already suggested that start-up businesses tend to be precarious and unstable, and will expand further, in this section, on how that is particularly so for community-based social enterprises that have additional fragilities and thus become even more vulnerable to risk.

A phone call from Sarah, a staff member in Markethill, sounds urgent and somewhat clandestine. 'Can you meet me today – I need to see you urgently but not at the office – and I'd rather you didn't tell anyone from the group – can you meet me in the coffee shop in Tesco's?'

The group have finished the training being delivered by O4O and have drawn up a business plan which they have submitted to a number of funders in order to take forward their dream to refurbish their new kitchen and dining area which has the capacity for 200 and which they have installed on the top of a converted stable. Over several months, volunteers in the group have been taking part in business management and development activities and they are now at a stage where they have drawn up an action plan which should see them commence trading within the next month. Sarah and I meet. She is distressed and anxious, wringing her hands as she talks about being unsure about how to move the O4O project forward within the organisation as she is unable to continue working due to ill-health. As the principal administrator of the organisation's activities, something is clearly worrying her about how to realise the business plan and complete the transition from aspiration to sustainable social economy business.

The group, originally formed in 2000, exists to support local victims of the Northern Ireland Conflict. Sarah, with her background in church-based social economy enterprises both in Northern Ireland and in the Congo, was employed to put some structure and bureaucratic order into the workings of the organisation. She is responsible, in theory, to the Management Board, but in practice Board business tends to be a 'rubber-stamping' of the desires of its founding member, Carol. An unpaid volunteer, Carol is a recipient of both an OBE (Order of the British Empire national award) and a 'Living Legends' award by the Help the Aged charity. Like Mary in Cookstown, her 'heroic individual' status has thus been publicly recognised and awarded, giving her rank and repute within the sector. This has resulted in a number of public appointments which enable her to act as a spokesperson, advocating for the needs of her membership, many of whom, like her, have either served in, or had families in, the Ulster Defence Regiment.[5]

The mores of the military culture familiar to the membership has had implications for the group. Its strategic and operational management is hierarchical, with trust in Carol's leadership never questioned by staff, volunteers or the membership. Equally, loyalty, camaraderie and commitment to the 'family business', with its ethos of patronage and welfare, are never doubted. The sense of family, with all the positive associations of mutual support and allegiance that brings, is used symbolically here as it is within the lexicon of the wider military family, but it is also used here to denote actual kinship connections. Having developed out of small sub-divisions of 'victims and survivors' from within a close-knit community, the organisation has attracted a membership and volunteers from backgrounds connected through birth and marriage and through attachment to the security services. Consequently, the alternative therapeutic services, counselling and social activities provided to alleviate their sufferings were originally designed, and provided by and for, extended family networks by unskilled altruistic volunteers.

The engagement of members and volunteers began with wanting to voluntarily and *gratis* make a difference within existing networks but as the membership began to grow a prerequisite of accepting grant-aid income was imposed by funding bodies as a process of their demands for a professionalisation of services. This change of circumstances began to shine a light on the sometimes limited skills of the volunteer base and the need for capacity-building and up-skilling which, in turn, began to impact on the type of community development and service delivery undertaken by groups. As opportunities for training and remuneration increased it became difficult to ensure that those best suited to changing roles were sought outside the existing volunteer base of friends, family and neighbours. Consequently, the group's culture became an unwieldy tangle of enthusiastic volunteers and organisational nepotism. It became impossible to unravel the personal, social and wellbeing benefits derived by volunteers from the associated financial recompense and access to resources they were privy to. Furthermore, it was easy to see how informal, internal supervision structures set up in good faith to support the volunteers and the membership's duty of care issues had become knotted and matted. The overarching governance and management structures enabled those with long-term association to the organisation to become the beneficiaries of partiality and preferential treatment in terms of employment and access to resources.

Only days after my meeting with Sarah my phone rang again. This time it was Carol telling me that she was unable to reach Sarah, and that their two core funding bodies had visited and removed all financial records and computers due to concern about financial inconsistencies, double funding, poor accounting and accountability, and mismanagement in terms of family connections in the awarding of contracts and subcontracts. At the time of writing, four months after the phone calls, the organisation is in limbo pending reports from the Charities Commission due after the completion of a criminal justice investigation. The phone is unanswered in the offices, the membership is in limbo needing, but unwilling to seek, services elsewhere, the kitchen equipment lies in boxes in the huge, empty and unused dining area, and the business plan is gathering dust on a shelf.

It has been argued elsewhere that presenting a coherent story of who its members are and how the organisation of any social enterprise is born is a process that helps to contain anxieties about its efficacy (Froggett & Chamberlayne, 2004). Whilst a number of examples from O4O support this thesis, the short ethnography above also provides an example of how inconsistencies and discrepancies within 'the organisational biography', and how they intersect with the values of both internal and external stakeholders, can also be not only a source of tension in community social enterprises, but a key factor in their capacity to come to fruition and grow. Whilst it is not the intention of the authors to justify any examples of financial negligence or professional misconduct, it is, however, important to consider the frameworks in which a 'cavalier' attitude to accountability and nepotism can flourish and the significance of the dynastic context in which Northern Ireland political parties and community activism operate.

The Political Environment and the Social Enterprise

Social enterprises are products of their milieu and consequently can be expected to reflect the tensions of social class, ethnicity, institutional ethos and the other ideologies of the environment in which they develop (Parkinson & Howorth, 2007). So far, we have attempted to demonstrate how communities' readiness to innovate social enterprises can be both enabled and disabled by their volunteers' ethos; including those who take on the roles of dynamic leadership. In addition to this, we have shown how they are also shaped by the ethos and frameworks of governance in which they develop, and the cultural factors and expectations of the organisation's networks of relationships in which nascent social enterprises engage in processes of reciprocal exchange (Overall et al, 2005; Peattie & Morley,

2008). In this section we add a final ingredient into this mix; namely, the essence of the political environment from which they emerge.

The political environment of Northern Ireland is a very particular one. The specificities of institutionalised segregation have been formed in a place where there is both a very strong public sector, with high-level strategies confirming government commitment to older people, and an equally powerful community and voluntary sector that drew its strength, in part, due to dissatisfaction with the state (Radford et al, 2009). In both instances, a reputation for an implicit sectarian bias has been present as a by-product of a historical Unionist-led colonialist state where hierarchies of rule and lineage set a foundation stone for how the wider political elite now operate. Similarly, within formalised community and voluntary work the influence and authority of particular networks of political association and interest groups have affected the development and employment culture of the sector. Research suggests that in both urban and rural areas, the formalised community and voluntary sector is seen as the forte of the nationalist community and that it has a Catholic – that is, nationalist – ethos (Shortall, 2004, 2008). The church has played a strong role in this but the sector has also been one that has grown out of political dissatisfaction based on state limitations on the areas of public and private sector work in which Catholics could easily find employment. Subsequently, the sector continues to be particularly supported by, and supportive of, those forwarding republican ideals of democratic change and thus successfully incorporates a political ideology into its application of business models within social enterprises. In the past, at party political level, the Unionist community were, in the main, more confident of being able to access work within state structures than Catholic workers and consequently did not seek to achieve community cohesion through innovative social business development. They predominantly tended to channel the bulk of their community welfare activities through established church structures as an extension of tithing and religious duty and obligation, rather than as a result of communal necessity.

At first glance, our two examples from Northern Ireland might be considered exceptions to this generalisation, with their formation and continuation due to the dynamic visioning and drive of two Protestant women. But the politics of conflict are beginning to give way to the politics of stabilisation and reconstruction and, increasingly, communities are forced to reconsider their survival tactics and align with others to achieve financial stability. This is no exception for the sub-division of community organisations which incorporate both the victim/survivor and the age sectors.

A closer consideration of the gendering of the political climate provides us with a lens that should allow for another, more nuanced exploration of the development of community-led social enterprises locally and universally. In other places, within the O4O project, the success or otherwise of community-led businesses also reflects the ethnic, gendered and political milieu in which they have been established. In Greenland, for example, it is not simply geographic environment and climatic changes that have disrupted traditional Inuit community life. There, traditional gendered roles see an expectation of caring and individual autonomy in the ageing process whilst the imposition of Danish administrative and economic structures can also be considered to have played a considerable role in the social circumstances and lifestyle of the indigenous people. This is of particular relevance when considering how appropriate the application of Western European notions of collective and community-run enterprises actually is for indigenous peoples outside the mainstream of European society. Furthermore, as exemplified in Sweden, the social democratic welfare state in some Scandinavian countries has proved a model of good practice in terms of collaboration between the state and major interest organisations in the development of public policies; not least those which impact on the entire spectrum in the age sector. This, in turn, has had a strong impact on the nature of volunteering and the drivers for developing social economy activities to support what is seen as the domain and responsibility of the state (Rothstein, 2005).

In this section we have explored how some social enterprises are designed to shore up the political ideologies of those initiating them, and in doing so provide a social and economic rationale for supporting a partisan political system and process. Steering groups, funders and management committees may have the protocols and policies in place to address overt and covert 'isms', in this instance ageism, nepotism and sectarianism, requiring political and cultural diversity to be respected and promoted. But, as we have shown, these can be subverted as a result of the explicit intentions of 'heroic' individuals or the tacit institutional environments, both of which rely significantly on a cadre of volunteers to uphold their ethos. We also suggest that divisions and bias emanating from the broader political environment greatly impact on the readiness of communities to engage in innovative and creative programmes of work.

CONCLUSION

By way of review, this chapter concludes by considering the tensions we experienced between the social and economic objectives of the social enterprises discussed.

One of the most evident stressors identified is the mismatch in the language between that used by government and sponsoring bodies and that of volunteers engaged in the practice of social enterprise. The former emphasises efficiency, business discipline and financial independence, whilst the latter emphasises local issues, collective action, geographical community and local power struggles, and draws legitimacy from local or social morality (Parkinson & Howorth, 2007:31). Twenty-first-century research continues to demonstrate that social enterprises, and particularly those in rural areas, are predominantly motivated to meet social need and address local issues rather than pursue financial outcomes (Curran & Blackburn, 2001; Parkinson & Howorth, 2007; Peattie & Morley, 2008; Amin, 2009). Whilst laudable, and the clarion of the current political organ 'Big Society', such motivation, as Whitelaw further discusses in Chapter 6, does not easily lend itself to sustainability. Clearly there is a tension in trying to use civil society structures to meet the needs of the market, and it seems that the promoters and funders of social enterprise and those carrying out community-based activities have different understandings of the process and objectives, as well as what levels of corporate responsibilities are required to balance economic and social performance. It is the volunteer body, in this case a vulnerable, older volunteer body, which frequently falls between the twin pillar-drivers it aims to straddle.

Many social enterprises, even when they have flagship status, find themselves in a precarious funding position whilst rural social enterprises *per se* are described as being permanently financially fragile (Rural Lifelines, 2004; Parkinson & Howorth, 2007). The need for enterprises to be perceived by both the community and public sector as legitimate and competent (Muñoz et al, 2010) is a core component in their readiness to provide and sustain innovative service provision. This legitimacy can often be jump-started by the role of 'heroic individuals' working internally or externally to ensure the organisation's ethos is synchronised with a broader political environment sympathetic to its aims. However, to force this process by grafting it on, either too quickly or at the behest of external factors, proves fatal to meeting need and can damage existing informal helping structures.

The position of the social enterprise is similar to that of many community and voluntary organisations. Our O4O projects show that an expectation of sustainability can bring both pressure and a sense of failure to bear on groups, when the prospect of developing a sustainable social enterprise is not always tenable, or even desirable, but an imposition by local or European governments to ensure the continuation of what has, in former times, been considered good neighbourliness, gap-stopping and community life.

NOTES

1. The steering group for O4O Northern Ireland comprised senior representatives from the Department of Agriculture and Rural Development; the Office of the Older Person's Advocate; the Department of Social Development; the Commission for Victims and Survivors, Northern Ireland; the Rural Development Council; the Rural Communities Network; and Age NI; and, during the latter part of the project, the Department of Health, Social Services and Public Safety. Representation was also sought from the Social Economy Network.
2. Between the 1920s and the 1970s, Northern Ireland ran as a one-party Protestant, Orange state. We argue elsewhere that the Orange Orders and the Unionist Party, churches and businesses 'connived in the subordination of Catholic to Protestant interests in particular in housing and employment' (Radford 2004:149), thereby retaining control over the social and economic foundations of Northern Ireland.
3. Between 1998 and 2011, in excess of £80 million of central government and European funding has been allocated to a variety of organisations with the aim of supporting victims and survivors of the Conflict. Many of the community groups which have availed of these funds have done so within the context of developing social economy businesses with charitable status.
4. All names have been changed.
5. The Ulster Defence Regiment, now disbanded, was a regiment in the British Army whose armed membership comprised part-time soliders from Northern Ireland serving within close proximity to their residence, and who sustained the highest number of fatalities and casualties of the Conflict.

REFERENCES

Amin A. (2009), 'Extraordinarily Ordinary: Working in the social economy', *Social Enterprise Journal*, 5(1), pp. 30–49.

Barendsen L. & Gardener H. (2004), 'Is the Social Entrepreneur a New Type of Leader?', *Leader to Leader*, 34, pp. 43–50.

Bridge S., Murtagh B. & O'Neill K. (2009), *Understanding the Social Economy and the Third Sector*, Basingstoke: Palgrave Macmillan.

Curran J. & Blackburn R. (2001), 'Older People and the Enterprise Society: Age and self-employment propensities', *Work, Employment and Society*, 15(4), pp. 889–902.

Froggett L. & Chamberlayne P. (2004), 'Narratives of Social Enterprise: From biography to practice and policy critique', *Qualitative Social Work*, 3(1), pp. 61–77.

Lupien S. & Wan N. (2004), 'Successful Ageing: From cell to self', *Philosophical Transactions of the Royal Society*, 359, pp. 1413–1426.

Muñoz S-A., Steinerowski A. & Farmer J. (2010), 'Bringing Social Innovation and Value Creation to Community Social Enterprises'. Available at: http://www.eprc.strath.ac.uk/irr/workshop/Munoz.pdf (accessed 22 November 2010).

Overall J., Tapsell P. & Woods C. (2005), 'Governance and Indigenous Social Entrepreneurship: When context counts', *Social Enterprise Journal*, 6(2), pp. 146–161.

Parkinson C. & Howorth C. (2007), *The Language of Social Entrepreneurs*, Lancaster: Lancaster University Management School Working Paper 2007/032.

Peattie K. & Morley A. (2008), *Social Enterprises: Diversity and dynamics, contexts and contributions, a research monograph*, ESRC Monograph, March.

Putnam R. (2000), *Bowling Alone: The collapse and revival of American community*, New York: Simon & Schuster.

Radford K. (2004), 'Protestant Women, Protesting Faith: Tangling secular and religious identity in Northern Ireland' in Coleman S. & Collins P. (Eds.), *Religion, Identity and Change*: *Perspective on global transformations*, Aldershot: Ashgate Press.

Radford K., Hughes J., Murphy P., Donnell N., Murphy J. & Osborne P. (2009), 'Fields, Flags and Future Sharing: An overview of the rural perspective of community relations', *Shared Space*, Issue 7, January, pp. 65–88.

Roginsky S. & Shortall S. (2009), 'Civil Society as a Contested Field of Meanings', *International Journal of Sociology and Social Policy*, 29(9), pp. 473–487.

Rothstein B. (2005), *Social Traps and the Problem of Trust*, Cambridge: Cambridge University Press.

Rural Lifelines (2004), *Older People and Rural Social Enterprises: Their role as providers and beneficiaries of service provision in rural England*, report prepared for the Plunkett Foundation, Oxfordshire: Plunkett Foundation.

Shortall S. (2004), 'Social or Economic Goals, Civic Inclusion or Exclusion? An analysis of rural development theory and practice', *Sociologia Ruralis*, 44(1), pp. 110–124.

Shortall S. (2008), 'Are Rural Development Programmes Socially Inclusive? Social inclusion, civic engagement, participation and social capital: Exploring the differences', *Journal of Rural Studies*, 24(4), pp. 450–457.

Spear R. (2006), 'Social Entrepreneurship: A different model?', *International Journal of Social Economics*, 33(5/6), pp. 399–410.

6. Sustaining social organisations in rural areas

Sandy Whitelaw

INTRODUCTION

The favouring of a broad social enterprise-based model for creating and delivering services and initiatives is to some extent based on an assumption that such a model has the potential to achieve temporal, social and economic *sustainability* in a context where this is often perceived to be difficult (Buchanan, 2010). A contention can be made that within both broad welfare provision, and specifically the nurturing of social enterprises, the concept of sustainability and the related notions of 'capacity' and 'implementation' have tended not to be given the prominence they are perhaps due (Potter & Brough, 2004; Phillips, 2006). By explicitly attending to these foundational matters in the context of social enterprises, this chapter seeks to redress such a deficit. In the context of the particular challenges of delivering services to older people in rural areas on a realistic and on-going basis that informed the O4O: Older People for Older People (O4O) project these concerns are clearly crucial, and this recognition informed the O4O approach of exploring the possibility of older people providing support for other older people as a profitable way forward. In practical terms the vast majority of O4O projects have, to varying levels, been concerned explicitly with mechanisms that might contribute to achieving a level sustainability. By drawing upon perspectives from both general and social enterprise-specific sustainability literature, this chapter primarily seeks to develop a discussion of the broad nature and prerequisites of sustainability for rural community social enterprise. Thereafter, these resources are deployed to specific experiences that arose from various O4O projects using data gleaned from a 'sustainability template' completed by each O4O social enterprise and complemented by in-depth semi-structured interviews with a range of individuals involved in these, in Sweden and Finland. Finally, I suggest that there is a relatively strong and growing evidence base that informs our understanding of how sustainability might optimally be achieved within social organisations (e.g. Coburn & Rijsdijk,

2010) and specifically conclude that such organisations are unlikely to be sustained 'spontaneously' but rather will require a complex mix of supportive inputs.

A CONTEXT FOR THE SIGNIFICANCE OF SOCIAL ORGANISATIONS AND SUSTAINABILITY

The broad 'social economy' and its associated 'social organisations', incorporating community, voluntary, not-for-profit and, of most significance to this chapter, social enterprise, have emerged over the past 20 years as prominent features of contemporary social policy (Bridge et al, 2008), with Bull, for example, seeing such organisations as 'the saviour of public and private business failure' (Bull, 2008:268). This is based on the assumption that amongst other benefits such forms of service delivery can be constructive in terms of achieving sustainability, but a number of more specific influences can also be detected. First, and in mostly reactive terms, a social organisation model is often proposed as the most appropriate and effective response to the perceived waning of state-delivered welfare (Wickham, 2006). Catford (1998:97) notes that 'traditional "welfare-state" approaches are increasingly in decline' and that the 'third' sector is emerging as a significant player in a 'mixed economy' of care. In this context, social enterprise is seen as something that will quickly and most appropriately fill a gap (Catford, 1998). Secondly, many point to the fact that mechanisms within both the statutory and private sectors have 'failed' in various respects, including, for example, to meet the needs of individuals or groups *at all*; to meet them effectively and appropriately; or in wider terms to address wider community-identified social issues or emergent 'unmet' needs (Buchanan, 2010). Thus, the re-emergence of a mixed economy of care in the late 1980s, with contributions from various potential types of social economy-based provision, including formal voluntary organisations, charities, co-operatives and mutuals, as well as general philanthropy, was seen as both principally and pragmatically constructive (Lewis, 1998). In an era of relative economic health and political consensus on social welfare policy across the 1990s and 2000s, a state-based 'mixed economy' commissioning model took hold and became the preferred approach to mixed service provision (Lewis, 1998). This mix saw increasingly significant contributions from the third sector and was considered a generally successful model (Faucher-King & Le Gales, 2010) and, as Hill discusses in Chapter 1, it is clear that with the emergence of the notion of a 'Big Society', the new coalition government in the UK is continuing on this path.

In these circumstances, the particular importance of service *sustainability* has been emphasised (Coburn & Rijsdijk, 2010) and associated with the notion that it is most likely to be achieved when a self-sufficient entrepreneurial ethic is present within a service (Lyon & Ramsden, 2006). The centrality of sustainability to social enterprise is well recognised; for example, the Department of Trade and Industry (DTI) document *Social Enterprise – A strategy for success* states that social enterprises, 'seek to create and *sustain* social not private or economic value; they are oriented to continuous improvement, looking for a long-term return and creating lasting and *sustainable* social improvements' (DTI, 2002:6 italics added). This has been complemented by a dynamic within social organisations themselves, towards being more 'professional' and possibly 'entrepreneurial' (Todres et al, 2006). Consequently, promotion of social enterprise models as a vehicle for more flexible, innovative, appropriate and sustainable service provision has been expressed within policy and academic literature (e.g. Ridley-Duff, 2007; The Scottish Government, 2008). Beyond this relatively functional rationale sustainability has also been conceptualised and favoured in more profound terms; that is, that increased non-renewable and iniquitous economic growth associated with globalisation is essentially *un*sustainable (Figge et al, 2002). These approaches are generally associated with environmental degradation and climate change that act cumulatively to compromise the needs of future generations (Commission for Rural Communities, 2007). This sentiment for all *current* social and economic activity to have an orientation towards the future, and broadly exist within environmental capacity and limits (i.e. essentially to be sustainable), was captured by the Brundtland Commission in 1987 as 'development that meets the needs of the present while not compromising the ability of future generations to meet their own needs' (The Brundtland Commission, 1987).

In terms of the association between rurality and sustainable communities, the conventional assumption is that forces such as excessive reliance on car travel, poor rural services, low levels of enterprise and the destruction of the countryside make rural communities inherently *less* sustainable than those in urban areas (Banister, 2005). Whilst many recognise the tensions that can exist between relatively 'centralised' and 'dispersed' policy approaches and the extent to which car use could and should be promoted as a means of access and inclusion (Banister, 2005), this view has been increasingly challenged. An alternative principle has been established that suggests that with effective and appropriate planning, rural areas can be 'sustainable' in various ways (Cherrett, 2007), and this potential forms a rationale for developing rural social enterprise.

In fundamental terms, 'sustainable rural communities' is associated with a range of related features. Retaining young people, promoting a vibrant economic and cultural environment, and maintaining a level of services for older people in these areas are seen as crucial (The Scottish Government, 2007), as is the need for high-quality and well-planned environments including, for example, an emphasis on air and water quality and safety in public places. Within this, the desirability of a strong and diverse economy and employment opportunities supported by fostering a skills base within such communities through the provision of accessible training and small business support is also stressed (The Scottish Government, 2007).

Health and welfare provision is also important to the sustainability of rural communities and, in this respect, the need to provide access to high-quality multi-functional primary health care that is delivered in flexible and innovative ways is essential, as are grounded service interventions that are practically sustainable *and* delivered in a way that contributes to wider sustainability. The latter is seen in the development of what Muñoz et al (2008) term 'integrated service hubs' but which, in the rural context, may conflict with the need for localised social services that avoid excessive amounts of travel to and from centralised health and social care amenities.

In more specific terms, the desire to establish robust and accessible information and communication technologies (ICTs) as a central component of sustainable rural communities is recognised (The Scottish Government, 2007). This is predicated on the belief that ICTs can be exploited by rural communities and businesses to create more localised forms of living that reduce consumption, improve access to sensitive and appropriate service provision and, consequently, raise rural quality of life (Scott, 2002). These issues are bound by a desire to establish strong integrated public transport systems including community transport schemes (The Scottish Government, 2007).

Before embarking on any substantial discussion of the specific nature of sustainability in the context of social enterprise, it is worth initially considering a counter-factual position; that is, the implicit assumption that there *is* or *should be* an inherent association between social entrepreneurialism and sustainability is one that need not comprehensively be upheld (Bennett, 1999). Some suggest that any policy preference for a social enterprise model *per se* is contradictory in a free market context, in which the basis of provision should come from 'any willing provider' (Reform, 2011). Likewise, there is a belief that delivering social services in competitive and potentially volatile and hostile contexts fundamentally threatens sustainability (Coburn & Rijsdijk, 2010) whilst at a functional level some initiatives are clearly time limited and designed to serve a relatively short-term purpose; that is, they are not *intended* to be sustained. Rather, and as will be developed later, such projects may foster some broader *social* sustainability or, more fittingly, a form of *legacy*. More profoundly and from the particular neo-liberal/free market perspective articulated by Wickham (2006), the notion that enterprises *should* somehow be innately sustainable is anathema; there is no *de facto* right to endure as an enterprise. From this perspective, the sustainability of any business stands or falls by its ability to meet market needs, provide services of a high quality and, most importantly, be entrepreneurially *competitive* (Bennett, 1999). As such, the notion that sustainability is always good and the existence of a service should be forever 'set in stone' is specious given that a key perceived advantage of emergent social enterprises is that they might eliminate *existing* problematic services; that is, make others *un*sustainable through their ability to respond quicker, better and more creatively than existing providers to emergent needs (Bennett, 1999). For example, a social enterprise transport initiative might undermine the sustainability of existing public and private transport arrangements. Thus, initiatives being unsustainable or even 'failing' might be seen as inevitable or even positive (Mason & Royce, 2007). In O4O, whilst the majority of the social enterprises that were developed explicitly considered, and indeed hoped for, sustainability, many recognised that for various reasons sustainability might not be desirable or possible. Likewise, various practical pressures should be recognised as significant in critiquing this model and acting to destabilise the policy equilibrium (Buchanan, 2010). For example, the general worsening of the economic climate has tended to undermine the core significance of a full-scale state-based commissioning model (Milligan & Fyfe, 2004). Within that scenario, there is a growing perception of the weakness of a voluntary sector model that is overly dependent on state-commissioned funding and 'non-market' resources such as grants, subsidies or 'non-monetary'-type volunteering (Westall & Chalkley, 2007). In difficult economic times the predominant perception has thus been that such ventures have a tendency to be *practically* unsustainable (Osborne, 1997).

In summary, the context in which the notion of sustainability exists is complex. The need to achieve sustainable services may not *necessarily* be essential and, even where that is perceived to be the case, sustainability, in conceptual terms, is multifaceted; ranging from the relatively simple and pragmatic notion of maintaining the existence of a service through to more profound concern for promoting a sustainable 'way of life'. This latter position suggests that sustainability can be reflected in a range of dimensions, ranging from broad environments through to specific services, which is particularly germane in the context of sustainable rural communities.

THE CORE NATURE OF SUSTAINABILITY

Despite concerns, the particular nature of social welfare provision, and the need to achieve a *degree* of stability in provision over time, suggest that sustainability is highly significant (Jones & Keogh, 2006). Yet in many models of service and initiative provision, relatively little attention has been paid to establishing an understanding of how functional sustainability might be promoted (Huckle, 1996). For example, Catford (2009:1) suggests that 'the "science of discovery" has tended to dominate the "science of delivery"' whilst St Leger (2005:317) contends that 'for too long we have paid little attention to what we mean by sustainability'. The term itself is also ambiguous (Figge et al, 2002), with Huckle noting that 'sustainability has no single or agreed meaning . . . it takes on meaning within different political ideologies and programmes underpinned by different kinds of knowledge, values and philosophy' (Huckle, 1996:3).

The most functional definition relates to simple maintenance of a form of provision – what Huckle (1996:4) calls a 'conservative' model wherein efforts are made to essentially maintain a *status quo*. Huckle also proposes a 'strong' or more 'radical' model that sees sustainability as a dynamic concept, emerging as a product of continual change and development and where social organisations exhibit resilience and ability to *adapt* in times of difficulties or threats (Huckle, 1996:4). Beyond these pragmatic concerns, the notion of entrepreneurial sustainability has taken on wider connotations that are of particular significance to *social* enterprise. Alter (2007) notes a difference between simple 'economic' sustainability associated with mainstream entrepreneurship and a wider notion of 'social' sustainability wherein the enterprise is not only economically viable but also continues to meet expressed social needs over an extended period. The relative emphasis placed on these components can vary across social enterprises in relation to the emphasis placed on commercialism, the extent to which social needs are successfully met and, ultimately, attitudes towards 'profit' and its distribution (Phillips, 2006). Thus, economic and social ends can be at odds with each other, particularly where essential social needs cannot be met within a strict free market context. In these circumstances the need to resort to grant support would appear to be inevitable (Dudman, 2011).

Irrespective of the relative expression of purely social and economic values, the notion of 'dual value creation' for social enterprise is identified and defined by Peredo and McLean as 'the art of *simultaneously* pursuing financial and social returns on investment' (Peredo & McLean, 2006:60, italics added). More specifically, Elkington (1997) has proposed the notion of a 'triple-bottom line', suggesting that a constructive and sustainable balance can be achieved between economic, environmental and social influences (e.g. Figge et al, 2002; van Marrewijk, 2003) and that various combinations can be achieved. For example, strict 'business' cases can be made with environmental or social sustainability in mind; economic and environmental sustainability can promote social sustainability; and appropriate economic and social sustainability can contribute to wider environmental sustainability (Shaw & Carter, 2007). Significantly, many have stressed that these principles should not be 'played off' against each other; for example, that improvements in environmental quality should lead to poor economic performance or social injustice (Stern, 2006).

The notion of sustainability has also been specifically expressed in relation to rurality; that is, the broad notion of *sustainable rural communities* (Affordable Rural Housing Commission (ARHC), 2006; Best & Shucksmith, 2006). Smith (2008) concludes that sustainable rural communities 'look to the environment and to economics and to social relationships and social justice', and the UK Commission for Rural Communities identifies three principal methods for achieving sustainable rural development: 'achieving a sustainable economy, which has important rural aspects; promoting good governance, which resonates with the efforts to support community; and parish planning' (Commission for Rural Communities, 2007:4). Given the possible *ideal* features associated with a social enterprise approach – that is, being entrepreneurially robust, well governed, rooted in the needs of the local community and actively deploying those local resources – the model clearly has the potential to fulfil these expectations.

In taking on these broad themes and developing a more grounded approach to sustainability, three strands of thinking are highlighted. First, the features of successful and sustainable social enterprises; secondly, expressions of some of the barriers associated with achieving these; and thirdly, normative pointers as to how social enterprises might achieve success and sustainability. These themes and principles will now be considered.

FEATURES OF SUCCESSFUL AND SUSTAINABLE SOCIAL ORGANISATIONS

A series of empirical reviews that examine the substantive features of successful and sustainable social enterprises have recently emerged (e.g. Lyon & Ramsden, 2006; Sharir & Lerner, 2006; Shaw & Carter, 2007; Spear et al, 2009; Coburn & Rijsdijk, 2010; Cox & Schmuecker, 2010) and offer insights associated with specific notions of 'critical success factors' (Coburn and Rijsdijk, 2010) or 'enablers of success' (Cox and

Schmuecker, 2010). Whilst recognising that in an entrepreneurial context success and sustainability are not necessarily sacrosanct (Wickham, 2006), the predominant position taken in these reviews is that social entrepreneurs are driven by an expectation that as well as simple economic profit they *will* be successful and that they *will* attain profound and sustainable social achievements (Sullivan Mort et al, 2003). This desire is tempered by recognition that the initiation of a social enterprise faces significant barriers and will not emerge spontaneously. Rather, they would be heavily dependent on some form of external facilitation (Miller & Millar, 2011).

In seeking sustainability, identification of the characteristics of attainment has been approached in two ways. First, in terms of a *static* model where the various 'ingredients' that are perceived to be important are identified; and, secondly, a more *dynamic* approach that views sustainability as associated with a *process* that requires specific actions at particular points of development, including how problems or threats are dealt with (Coburn & Rijsdijk, 2010). In relation to the former, many of the identified features mirror those associated with any successful and sustainable business and highlight the importance of social organisations being primarily successful enterprises (Low, 2006) with a strong orientation towards financial and economic success (Lewis et al, 2006). Cox and Schmuecker (2010) point to a series of features *within* social organisations as 'necessary' whilst Lyon and Ramsden (2006) highlight attributes centring on the need for an enterprise to identify a market need or niche related to the ability to understand the core needs of potential client groups *and* the nature of the wider 'market'. The necessity of understanding the needs of groups and/or communities, either generally or within the specific entrepreneurial context of gaining a 'consumer perspective' or doing 'market research', and being able to identify gaps in provision or possible areas for innovation, is particularly stressed (Lyon & Ramsden, 2006). This ability to develop intelligence about on-the-ground needs is also complemented by a theoretical recognition that social organisations are required to understand the needs of wider political groups within their domain, and their possible acceptance (or not) of the proposed venture (Shaw & Carter, 2007). Consequently, the ability to develop new markets delivering a service product that is of value is seen to be more likely (Baines, 2010).

From a grounded perspective, sustainable social enterprises are dependent on *internal* organisational characteristics that include a strong and coherent team with commitment and enthusiasm and an appropriate ratio of volunteers to salaried employees (Mason & Royce, 2007). Entrepreneurial organisations with a pervasive learning orientation and a culture of openness and innovation are considered preferable (Sharir

& Lerner, 2006), and effective leadership is often cited as particularly important, with successful social enterprises being seen to be driven by socially entrepreneurial leaders (Sullivan Mort at al, 2003). This leadership is associated with a range of attributes and abilities such as self-reliance, dedication, perseverance, willingness to take risks and social passion, and more specific features, such as 'business acumen', effective management and strong financial oversight. However, sustainability is not only a function of these internal features but also, and to a significant extent, dependent on various *external* contextual features (The Scottish Government, 2008). A range of 'high-level drivers' have been identified that can positively or negatively impact on social enterprise (The Scottish Social Enterprise Coalition, 2010). First, the broad political context and the extent to which it creates a framework amenable to social entrepreneurial activity (Shaw & Carter, 2007) is seen as significant. This may relate to broad support within various policy domains through to more specific factors that might foster social organisations, such as commissioning and procurement processes that are conducive to the nature of many social enterprises (The Scottish Social Enterprise Coalition, 2010). Secondly, and more pragmatically, some point to the need to either work with communities that already have relatively high levels of capacity or to develop social enterprise through a series of capacity-building mechanisms (Buchanan, 2010).

The notion that sustainability within social enterprises may be associated with resilience and the ability to negotiate critical points (shocks) within a dynamic 'business life cycle' has been highlighted by, for example, Coburn and Rijsdijk (2010). This is founded on the assumption that all organisations pass through stages: an emergent 'fledgling' phase characterised by high levels of passion and determination, yet by their potentially fragile status prone to failure (Muñoz et al, 2008); followed by a move towards maturity where the enterprise may grow and adopt more robust business-planning capacity; and, finally, maturity, where leadership, stability, professionalism and control are present (Coburn & Rijsdijk, 2010). Each stage is considered to require different forms of support; for example, in the early stages, fundamental 'start-up' educational and financial resources; and, in the middle and mature stages, the need for diversification and reinvention (Coburn & Rijsdijk, 2010).

In summary, successful social organisations are considered to be the product of a set of definable internal features within a broadly conducive external context. Internal and external barriers are accepted and there is recognition that certain obstacles may be particularly prominent in a rural context (Commission for Rural Communities, 2007). The following section considers these features.

CONSTRAINTS ASSOCIATED WITH ACHIEVING SUSTAINABLE AND SUCCESSFUL SOCIAL ORGANISATIONS

Beyond the normative aspirations embedded in policy statements, a series of significant impediments to achieving sustainability within social enterprises are recognised (Todres et al, 2006). Fundamentally, many point to the lack of social capital or cohesion within communities as a hindrance (Cox & Schmuecker, 2010) and, as Farmer and Bradley discuss in Chapter 7, the general ethic of enterprise may be viewed with suspicion by community members. This suspicion can be related to mistrust of aligning entrepreneurship with the expectation that people will care for themselves; concern that moves to services provided by social organisations will result in accompanying weakening of state welfare; and, from the perspective of the service provider or volunteer, an unwillingness to become involved in what is perceived as a relatively weightier and riskier venture compared with 'simple' volunteering. These issues are related to the often expressed difficulty of finding active volunteers and participants which, as Hill raises in Chapter 1 and Farmer and Bradley further discuss in Chapter 7, can be particularly acute within sparsely populated rural communities.

Despite notional policy support for social enterprise (e.g. The Scottish Government, 2008) and a theoretical belief that the competitive nature of tendering, as embodied in, for example, 'Best Practice' principles, should be considered constructive in favouring 'worthy organisations' (Buchanan, 2010:14), a series of external threats are recognised (Lyon & Ramsden, 2006). Essentially, the social marketplace in which social enterprises exist is viewed by some as relatively hostile. For example, Buchanan suggests that this context can often be 'cold and depersonalised and antagonistic to the values that make them work to develop *socially* valued services' (Buchanan, 2010:15, italics added). Additionally, Cox and Schmuecker (2010) have labelled current public sector spending cuts as a 'funding cliff-edge' that will significantly reduce the potential business that social organisations can access. They suggest that demand for efficiency savings in the public sector will result in large-scale 'mass' contracting that will tend not to fully cover costs. This scenario will be favourable to relatively large-scale established public and private enterprises (which Buchanan (2010) sees as possibly tending towards being 'monopolistic') that can withstand such stringency. These circumstances will be unfavourable to social organisations, particularly those that are small and/or of an emergent nature (Cox & Schmuecker, 2010). These circumstances are compounded by a tendency for the contracting process to be unnecessarily complex, with brief timescales, and shaped by restrictive, technical specifications – rather than focusing on the contribution of service users and social outcomes (Buchanan, 2010). Also, the particular rural context may be hostile: the overall size of the market is likely to be smaller, possibilities of economies of scale limited, and success by one enterprise may be at the expense of another valued service (Banister, 2005).

Finally, in terms of providing timely and appropriate support, there is a recognition that current provision is relatively weak. Coburn and Rijsdijk (2010:8) note 'a widespread view . . . that the current support available to social enterprise is not wholly geared up to identify, promote and encourage success'. As such, there is acceptance that many social organisations find it difficult to locate and access support, even when it is theoretically available (Cox & Schmuecker, 2010). Additionally, a lack of entrepreneurial ability *within* social organisations may hinder the possibility of developing basic organisational infrastructures and consequently achieving relevant business support, access to funding, and entry to public sector procurement and commissioning processes (Mason & Royce, 2007; Cox & Schmuecker, 2010). These barriers for *individual* enterprises are compounded by the fact that there are, in reality, very few successful social organisations and, as such, achieving a 'critical mass' of successful exemplars is difficult (Buchanan, 2010). Again, this issue is particularly acute within a rural context (Cherrett, 2007).

In summary, recognising and avoiding a range of potential barriers is imperative for achieving sustainable social enterprises. In the following section these points are accommodated within a practical consideration of how social enterprise might be sustained.

NORMATIVE POINTERS AS TO HOW SOCIAL ORGANISATIONS MIGHT BE MADE MORE SUSTAINABLE

Combining the positive and negative factors discussed above produces a series of normative pointers for enhancing sustainability in social enterprises. However, prior to embarking on this discussion, it should again be noted that there are varying perspectives on the extent to which (social) enterprise could and should be nurtured and supported by external actions (Phillips, 2006). For some, the idea of externally bolstering entrepreneurial activity is incongruous because thriving enterprises should be *inherently* successful due to the strength of their internal features and their ability to operate effectively within the givens that come from a relatively 'free' market (Wickham, 2006). In contrast, most suggest that such spontaneous emergence and growth in relatively hostile social and economic circumstances is unlikely and that social enterprises and social entrepreneurs will need external help (Buchanan, 2010). Given this, the concept of *capacity-building* as a precursor of sustainability has emerged (Lewis et al, 2006) and is described by Victoria Health (2005:53) in the following way: 'capacity building involves the development of sustainable skills, organisational structures, resources'. The Scottish Social Enterprise Coalition (2010) has identified the elements it associates with capacity-building, including leadership, partnership-building, organisational development, workforce development and resource allocation. The DTI document *Social Enterprise – A strategy for success* (2002) suggests that capacity-building should happen at three general levels: establishing the value of social enterprise, creating an enabling environment and making social enterprises better businesses. There is, therefore, a perception that the value of social enterprises needs to be established and promoted at national level and that the state must confirm their value by acting to create conducive legal, regulatory, tax and administrative contracting environments (Sullivan Mort et al, 2003). This might be done by, for example, developing generic company structures (Low, 2006) and establishing 'community benefit clauses' in public sector procurement processes (Lyon & Ramsden, 2006). Work to raise awareness and empower communities to become involved in social enterprise is also recommended (The Scottish Social Enterprise Coalition, 2010).

An aspect of achieving this favourable context is the need to enable social enterprises to access a critical level of finance over a suitable period of time. Obtaining appropriate and timely finance has been identified as particularly significant in promoting social enterprise, particularly at start-up (Harding, 2007) and there is a perception that many enterprises are under-funded (New Economics Foundation, 2006). Whilst various potential financial sources can be identified – including mainstream capital (e.g. commercial banks, equity finance, share issues); 'alternative' forms of capital (e.g. Alternative Investment Markets (AIM), PLUS Markets, 'venture philanthropy' and the Big Society Bank); specific funds such as the Single Regeneration Budget, Neighbourhood Renewal Fund and Regional Development Agency investment funds; and specifically targeted provision such as Future Builders and the Adventure Capital Fund (see Sullivan Mort et al, 2003; New Economics Foundation, 2006) – possible changes to taxation arrangements such as the extension of a Community Interest Tax Relief (CITR) scheme and amending the basic rate of income tax for social enterprise workers (The Community Development Finance Association, 2011) are also posited.

In relation to longer-term sustainable funding Lyon and Ramsden

(2006) reflect on the issue of raising fees for services rendered, whilst the UK DTI, on the specific basis of social enterprises being 'first and foremost, a business ... that means it is engaged in some form of trading' (DTI, 2002:13), clearly establishes the possibility, or perhaps necessity, of generating income from fees. Within a perspective of having the ability to pay and, in more general terms, achieving collective equity, such an act could clearly be problematic, undermine the fundamental status of a social enterprise model and is suggestive of the continued need for some core public funding support to be maintained (Mason & Royce, 2007). This issue has been approached in four ways. First, some have suggested that sustainability will only be achieved by on-going support from streams of income from 'the State' (Phillips, 2006). Secondly, the enterprise could seek to expand into wider markets in order to achieve a deeper critical mass – for example, to other geographical areas, client groups and types of activities (Harding, 2007). Thirdly, economic sustainability can be enhanced via a process of 'co-production', wherein one part of a social enterprise (a 'hub') subsidises another (the 'spokes') and, finally, the enterprise can open up its services to those who are able to pay (but are not necessarily the primary market) in order that revenue can be applied to subsidise services for those in greater need (Cox & Schmuecker, 2010). In more critical terms, it has been suggested that inability to access varied revenue sources has resulted in social organisations relying excessively on traditional voluntary sector grant aid which, in itself, impedes sustainability (Cox & Schmuecker, 2010).

Beyond these broad influences, the importance of establishing easy access to quality tailored business support is crucial (Lyon & Ramsden, 2006). Harding (2007) has highlighted the importance of providing enterprise training and suggested that this tends to heighten the likelihood of sustainability. Such training typically involves management and leadership, planning, marketing, finance and human resource management (Todres et al, 2006). Lyon and Ramsden (2006) emphasise the need for practical on-going support via, for example, advice, counselling and networking, and list various types of providers such as: specialist social enterprise support organisations (e.g. Co-operative Development Agencies, Councils for Voluntary Service and Rural Community Councils); mainstream business support (e.g. The Small Business Service); public sector organisations (e.g. Regional Development Agencies and local authorities, community planning, local economic forums, local social economy partnerships); the private sector (e.g. solicitors, accountants and business consultants); and banks and financial institutions.

In the preceding sections I have considered the nature and possible dynamics of processes associated with sustainability and in the following section deploy these resources in relation to the specific experiences of the various O4O social enterprises.

SUSTAINABILITY IN O4O PROJECTS

Many of the community-based social enterprises developed through O4O had the intent of sustainability woven into the core of their planning and development; that is, their fundamental aim was to create and *sustain* effective and appropriate welfare services for older people within rural communities. The Swedish project *Hälsogallerian* (Health Gallery) reported that sustainability was one of the important goals in its project plan and others identified specific examples of activity oriented towards sustainability. *Ystävänpysäkki* (Place of Friendship) in Nurmes, Finland cited the existence of 'future planning' to foster volunteering; the Assynt initiatives *Community Care Assynt* and *Assynt Community Transport* developed 'phased development plans', and the *Hälsogallerian* and *Trygga Jämtön* (Safe Jämtön) projects in Sweden deployed an explicit 'business' model for development. The notion of development towards sustainability occurring in stages was particularly prominent in O4O but, given that many of its social enterprises were in their relative infancy, these developments were considered to be emergent, with most still building early foundations during the period 2007 to 2010, when the overall project was funded by the European Union. The need to utilise the existing enthusiasm and support that tended to exist at the onset of projects, and to make relatively rapid progress in this phase, was highlighted by *Community Care Assynt* and *Assynt Community Transport O4O* whilst the *Hälsogallerian* in Niemisel, Sweden, noted that it would occur over a three year period and comprise distinct phases: developing services for older people, developing entrepreneurship for women and developing housing for elderly living.

The broad context in which O4O was being undertaken was significant. In Chapter 5 Radford and Shortall suggest that social enterprises are 'products of their milieu' and a 'reflection of ideological, political and policy environments'. There was evidence that O4O's social enterprises were context-aware and acting to achieve engagement and cohesion with the wide policy context and associated stakeholders. For example, *Ystävänpysäkki* sought active connections with their local authority colleagues, and all of the enterprises in Northern Ireland had extensive communication with public sector and charitable agencies, around housing, social inclusion and ageing. Many O4O social enterprises accepted that the emergent political context was potentially hostile and the economic future unclear. For example, the *Koli Village* enterprise in Finland saw the future of new innovations as hard to foresee and developments in Northern Ireland were considered to be hampered by a hiatus in the policy development around the victim and survivor sector. In this context, Skerratt (2008) has highlighted the existence of a gap between policy timeframes and practical work on the ground that has tended to hinder social enterprises. This gap relates to a general dislocation between overly optimistic centralised policy aspirations and the reality of nurturing social organisations on the ground – and is exacerbated by overly complex legislation (Muñoz et al, 2008).

Beyond context, effective leadership emerged as a prominent issue for achievement in O4O and many participants drew upon forms of leadership from existing project personnel or from external support introduced to them. For example, the work in both Luleå municipality and Ystävänpysäkki in Nurmes benefited from the energy provided by their respective Project Managers although, as Radford and Shortall note in Chapter 5, the potential and problemtic nature of self-appointed internal 'heroic' leaders as community gate-keepers can create a form of over-reliance, distort organisational processes and alienate other volunteers.

A further feature strongly associated with sustainability was the ability for social organisations to be simultaneously innovative and needs-led – and O4O offered various examples of this. In the context of transport solutions, *Koli Village* sought to establish 'alternative models for help to the elderly' whilst *Lieksa Vuonislahti Village*, which had a focus on transportation, shopping and home help, described the 'need for *new* models to allow the elderly to remain in their own village when getting frail'; *Transport for Tongue* found innovative ways to address specific needs in an area poorly served by public transport. The *Sundom IT* enterprise also developed innovative ways to improve communication via Information Technology. Those who led specific O4O social enterprises were conscious of the importance of being led by communities and of recognising their capacity to be innovative. And whilst this was not always easy to achieve, it is clear that strong and active relationships with communities are crucial to appraising needs, understanding obstacles to developing specific social organisation activity, developing volunteering and taking forward plans. *Cuan FM*, for example, couched self-sustainability as important only 'if that is the community desire' whilst work in Highland Scotland stressed a 'needs-led' approach which manifested as the Project Manager engaged in a consultation exercise with public sector and third sector practitioners to determine unmet needs (Farmer & Steven, Chapter 4).

The perceived need to be economically sustainable was also prominent within O4O social enterprises, various of which reached different levels of viability. For some, it was only possible with on-going support from state income streams. For example, *Trygga Jämtön* suggested that continuation of its activities was dependent on financial support from the Municipality and the *Transport for Tongue* initiative sought funding from a government community transport programme. Others recognised the potential of expanding into wider markets including other geographical areas, client groups and types of activities as a means of achieving critical mass, high levels of independence and consequent sustainability. Indeed, as Radford and Shortall discuss in Chapter 5, the Cookstown programme extended its lunch club and meals on wheels provision to a wider geographical area and was therefore able to increase the income from a retail outlet, establish a restaurant and provide an information centre for older people. In a similar vein, *Trygga Jämtön* extended the service to two adjoining villages and charged people in those villages for the service. Beyond the internal dynamics, O4O demonstrated the benefits of using existing external support and, in the context of O4O Northern Ireland's Markethill case study, established the significance of the 'emotional readiness of volunteers' and on-going monitoring of 'operational and strategic readiness' (Radford and Shortall, Chapter 5).

In practical terms the Northern Ireland initiatives were built on the desire to build capacity for specific social enterprises with existing voluntary and charitable groups whilst in Sweden the Project Manager *selected* three villages to work with based on their perceived levels of activism and track record of having delivered projects. To complement this, there was evidence within O4O projects that external 'enabling' support such as inputs to develop entrepreneurial skills, foster networks with other social enterprises and promote access to start-up capital was sought and actively used. A facilitator in Sweden cited this support as 'giving them the tools' to develop. In Sweden, the Luleå Municipality appointed an O4O Project Manager who supported and mentored communities interested in the O4O concept. In Scotland, specific training from a Social Enterprise Academy was provided for volunteers involved in establishing *Community Care Assynt*, and *Transport for Tongue* brought in a social entrepreneur who offered leadership, advice on governance and support in relation to funding, volunteer co-ordination and reporting. Likewise, in Finland, management of O4O was undertaken by a business development organisation, *Pielisen Karjalan Kehittämiskeskus Oy* (PIKES) based in Nurmes. This organisation has experience of working with the municipalities in North Karelia and employed a Project Manager to work with communities to develop O4O social enterprises.

Whilst many of the O4O social enterprises sought support, there was acceptance that this was often difficult to access, and for one project, *Transport for Tongue*, it came at a point later than would have been fully useful. Fundamentally, a lack of entrepreneurial ability within social organisations was highlighted as hindering the possibility of developing basic organisational infrastructures and subsequently achieving relevant business support, access to funding, and entry to public sector procurement and commissioning processes. As previously noted, such barriers for *individual* enterprises are exacerbated by the existence of only a few successful social enterprise role models, the lack of social capital or cohesion within communities and the suspicion with which the general ethic of 'enterprise' is viewed. All of these issues were to some extent related to the difficulty expressed by many of the enterprises of finding active volunteers and participants from the relatively small pool of people available in remote and rural communities and in communities where there was a lack of social capital and even some conflict (as was the case in *Saver Naver*). Thus, the potential to engage communities in the process that is required to initiate any broad-based enterprises was considered difficult.

Beyond these rather functional approaches to sustainability, perhaps the most significant finding to emerge from the O4O case study is the notion of sustainability being a relatively complex concept. In Chapter 7, Farmer and Bradley highlight the differing expectations that stakeholders may have about the nature of what is to be 'sustained' as a product of social entrepreneurship. Simplistically, policymakers may suggest that the straightforward sustainability of a tangible service is sufficient. However, our work has suggested the existence of more complex and relatively intangible expressions of 'sustainability'. For example, whilst the *Ardersier Family History* project was initially concerned with simply collating oral history in the village, it ultimately led to the creation of a meeting place for older people; more profound positive impacts on individual wellbeing and self-worth; improved skill sets such as interviewing, filming and editing; and, more widely, an enhanced sense of community identity and cohesion.

CONCLUSION

Perhaps one of the strongest ethics informing thinking around achieving organisational and entrepreneurial sustainability is that of promoting a relatively unhindered market in which entrepreneurs are given the freedom to develop in ways *they see fit* (Wickham, 2006). For some, the most effective way of promoting this is, in Isaiah Berlin's terms, to act negatively; that is, that positive or active means of encouraging enterprise are generally undesirable and the most significant drive should be towards removing as many impediments to entrepreneurship as possible, to allow 'spontaneous' and 'natural' enterprise to flourish (Berlin, 1969). This is colloquially couched in terms of 'cutting red tape' or 'reducing the burden on enterprise'. As such, the very *need* to actively promote enterprise would be considered paradoxical and the growth of unprompted entrepreneurial activity favoured (Wickham, 2006). In the context of responding most appropriately and effectively to felt or expressed needs within communities some of the policy assumptions of social enterprise appear to favour such spontaneity. For example, the DTI Document *Social Enterprise – A strategy for success* (2002) suggests the significance of 'creativity' and 'innovation' in initiating social enterprises. Whilst this may be principally sound and, perhaps more significantly, politically and practically an expedient way forward, our experiences with O4O have suggested that this 'light touch' approach has the potential to be problematic in two ways. First, in relation to achieving an appropriately planned and thus balanced range of services in a rural context that are sensitive to local need, an unfettered market mechanism could offer a free market into which a range of large-scale, though not necessarily optimal or appropriate, social entrepreneurs enter. Worse, the development of a relatively de-regulated system of social organisations has the potential to act as a 'Trojan horse' that could ultimately be taken up by private interests. Harris (2011:27), for example, notes that social enterprises could 'quickly be bought out by private-sector sharks'.

In more specific and practical terms such a circumstance will tend not, in itself, to foster social organisations on the ground, particularly in rural contexts. In keeping with Miller and Millar's (2011) perspective on the likelihood of mutual 'spin-outs' within the English health service, the predominant perspective from O4O has been that achieving sustainability in rural social organisations is a relatively onerous and complex task, the fulfilment of which will generally require significant amounts of nurturing and support. The characteristics of rural places suggest that social enterprise will not easily become established and sustained with existing low levels of community coherence and capacity. This realism is founded on the identification of what appear to be genuine barriers to sustainability. Fundamentally, the entrepreneurial ethic of the social enterprise models does not sit easily with many (older) rural participants. Those who simply wanted to 'volunteer' did not want to take on what was perceived to be the risk involved in setting up a social enterprise and, whilst there may be a belief that 'younger' older people, particularly 'incomers' to rural communities with prior entrepreneurial experience, may fulfil this role, this expectation was by no means considered to be strong. Suspicion of enterprise was expressed, with communities indicating concern that the state was looking for a cheap option to statutory provision; that is, one that is not established on a 'fully costed model' but partly dependent on 'free' volunteering – and as such potentially unsustainable. Ideally, the need to ensure that social organisations should be based on a 'full costing model' could therefore be stressed.

In addition to possible deficiencies around supply, there was concern that rural communities may not have a critical mass of demand to sustain on-going social enterprise provision; that is, rural communities do not offer a 'true market' and as such may need additional subsidised state support to allow services to be delivered that would not be strictly 'viable' in a simple market. Whilst some suggest that social enterprises should form partnerships with other providers in an area, and indeed there was evidence within O4O of this type of co-productive partnership working,[1] there was also recognition that such co-operation in a market context has the potential to be paradoxical; that is, the sustainability of one social enterprise might be achieved at the expense of another local service, such as, for example, another social enterprise, voluntary organisation or small local private enterprise. Whilst the need to mitigate against such an outcome could come from moderation through good communication and managing the market via community planning mechanisms, the potential for competition and conflict remains – with the possibility that the sustainability of individual projects, and more significantly whole systems of provision, could be threatened. This more balanced understanding and holistic perspective on service provision and sustainability was reflected in a shift in orientation towards sustainability within O4O; away from the early stage emphasis which was largely on the economic sustainability of individual projects to a broader vision of sustainable social benefit.

A series of practical barriers have been identified through O4O. Existing governance and regulatory schemes are not considered to be conducive to rural social enterprise development and many rural participants were not aware of the support available for enterprise and felt a need for better signposting of resources and contacts. More positively, and in contrast to the tendency towards the negative associations between rurality and enterprise suggested earlier, some within O4O felt that the relative dearth of provision in rural settings has the potential to motivate voluntary and social enterprise work. As such, there was a view that sustainability was possible, but crucially would need to be based on the existence of a series of significant prerequisites. In practical terms, various forms of capacity-building training, support, mentoring and information-sharing are clearly required but beyond these pragmatic actions a set of profound conceptual developments and realignments are required.

First, there must be a repositioning of expectations through which some parts of communities come to expect less from the state, and to complement this the state must give up control of decision-making and provide real support for social entrepreneurship in rural communities. Secondly, for enterprise to flourish it has to be acknowledged that this cannot be achieved by 'quick fixes' (Skerratt, 2008) and that what is required is the establishment of a series of longer-term prerequisites, particularly the nurturing of basic capacity within communities and developing an understanding of the nature and basis of social enterprises; that is, to 'sell' the notion. Thirdly, to complement this there needs to be strong and genuine contextual support from the state in order to foster social entrepreneurs and social enterprises. This should include a generally conducive policy context, and access to 'start-up' funding and public procurement processes. And finally, all of these issues may be bound up in the perceived need for a (relatively) 'managed' rather than 'free' market approach (Flynn & Williams, 1997).

These latter themes suggest the opening up of a relatively new and more nuanced conceptualisation of the relationship between social enterprises, community capacity and sustainability. In contrast to a relatively instrumental view of seeing self-standing social enterprises as inherently self-sustaining, usually in economic terms, our experiences within O4O suggest a series of more complex insights. First, the need for practical support and, more profoundly, strong community cohesion or capital as likely *precursors* to the possibility of enterprise is clear. Secondly, there is evidence that the establishment of social enterprise can, in turn, foster enhanced community cohesion, as occurred in *Is IT Sundom* and *Ardersier Oral History* where sustainability in its strictest sense was *not* the prime driver. In these cases, developments out of the initial enterprises acted as stimuli for subsequent, sustained community volunteering and activism where the sustainability did not necessarily rest on economic grounds but on the more profound basis of social and community capacity. In this sense, the notion of simple temporal or economic sustainability can perhaps be replaced by the more multifaceted notion of entrepreneurial *legacy* wherein potential sustainability is reflected in varied social terms.

NOTE

1. In Finland, for example, Lieksa Municipality worked with existing voluntary and community organisations and the Social Services department of North Karelia University of Applied Sciences, and met with members of the community, local council administration and other service providers and stakeholders.

BIBLIOGRAPHY

Alcock P. (2010), 'Building the Big Society: A new policy environment for the third sector in England', *Voluntary Sector Review*, 1(3), pp. 379–389.

Alter K. (2007), *Social Enterprise Typology*, Seattle: Virtue Ventures LLC.

ARHC (2006), *Affordable Rural Housing Commission: Final Report*, London: ARHC.

Baines D. (2010), 'Neoliberal Restructuring, Activism/Participation, and Social Unionism in the Nonprofit Social Services', *Nonprofit and Voluntary Sector Quarterly*, 39(1), pp. 10–28.

Banister D. (2005), *What are Sustainable Rural Communities? Thought piece for the Commission for Rural Communities.* Retrieved from: http://www.ruralcommunities.gov.uk/files/Sustainable%20Communities%20Thinkpieces.pdf (accessed 21 February 2012).

Bennett R. (1999), *Corporate Strategy*, Harlow: Pearson Education.

Berlin I. (1969), *Four Essays on Liberty*, Oxford: Oxford University Press.

Best R. & Shucksmith M. (2006), *Homes for Rural Communities*, York: Joseph Rowntree Foundation.

Bridge S., Murtagh B. & O'Neill K. (2008), *Understanding the Social Economy and the Third Sector*, London: Palgrave Macmillan.

Buchanan I. (2010), 'The Place of Social Enterprise in UK Contemporary Policy' in Gunn R. & Durkin C. (Eds.) *Social Enterprise: A skills approach*, Bristol: The Policy Press.

Bull M. (2008), 'Challenging Tensions: Critical, theoretical and empirical perspectives on social enterprise', *International Journal of Entrepreneurial Behaviour & Research*, 14 (5), pp. 268–275.

Catford J. (1998), 'Social Entrepreneurs are Vital for Health Promotion – but they need supportive environments too', *Health Promotion International*, 13(2), pp. 95–97.

Catford J. (2009), 'Advancing the "Science of Delivery" of Health Promotion: Not just the "science of discovery"', *Health Promotion International*, 24(1), pp. 1–5.

Cherrett T. (2007), *How Can we Plan for Sustainable Rural Communities?*, Cheltenham: Commission for Rural Communities.

Coburn J. & Rijsdijk R. (2010), *Evaluating the Success Factors for Establishing a Thriving Social Enterprise in Scotland*, Edinburgh: Scottish Government Social Research.

Commission for Rural Communities (2007), *Planning for Sustainable Rural Communities: A new agenda?*, Cheltenham: The Commission for Rural Communities.

Cox E. & Schmuecker K. (2010), *Growing the Big Society: Encouraging success in social and community enterprise in deprived communities*, London: Institute for Public Policy Research.

DTI (2002), *Social Enterprise – A strategy for success*, London: DTI.

Dudman J. (2011), 'Is the Partnership Model Right for Public Services?', *The Guardian*, 16 February, p. 3.

Elkington J. (1997), *Cannibals with Forks: The triple bottom line of 21st century business*, Oxford: Capstone.

Faucher-King F. & Le Gales P. (2010), *The New Labour Experiment: Change and reform under Blair and Brown*, London: Stanford University Press.

Figge F., Hahn T., Schaltegger S. & Wagner M. (2002), 'The Sustainability Balanced Scorecard – Linking sustainability management to business strategy', *Business Strategy and the Environment*, 11, pp. 269–284.

Flynn R. & Williams G. (Eds.)(1997), *Contracting for Health: Quasi-markets and the National Health Service*, Oxford: Open University Press.

Harding R. (2007), 'Understanding Social Entrepreneurship', *Industry & Higher Education*, 21(1), pp. 73–84.

Harris J. (2011), 'From John Lewis to Workers' Co-ops: These Tories love wrong-footing the left', *The Guardian*, 19 April, p. 27.

Huckle J. (1996), 'Realizing Sustainability in Changing Times' in Huckle J. & Sterling S. (Eds.), *Education for Sustainability*, London: Earthscan.

Jones D. & Keogh W. (2006), 'Social Enterprise: A case of terminological ambiguity and complexity', *Social Enterprise Journal*, 2(1), pp. 11–26.

Lewis G. (1998), 'Coming Apart at the Seams: The crises of the welfare state' in Hughes G. & Lewis G. (Eds.) *Unsettling Welfare: The reconstruction of social policy*, London: Routledge/Open University Press.

Lewis R., Hunt P. & Carson D. (2006), *Social Enterprise and Community Based Care: Is there a future for mutually owned organisations in community and primary care?*, London: The King's Fund.

Light D. (1998), *Effective Commissioning: Lessons from purchasing in American managed care,* London: OHE.

Low C. (2006), 'A Framework for the Governance of Social Enterprise', *International Journal of Social Economics*, 33(5/6), pp. 376–385.

Lyon F. & Ramsden M. (2006), 'Developing Fledgling Social Enterprises? A study of the support required and means of delivering it', *Social Enterprise Journal*, 2(1), pp. 27–41.

Mason C. & Royce M. (2007), 'Fit for Purpose – Board development for social enterprise', *Journal of Finance and Management in Public Services*, 6(3), pp. 57–67.

Miller R. & Millar R. (2011), *Social Enterprise Spin-outs From the English Health Service: A right to request but was anyone listening?*, Third Sector Research Centre Working Paper 52, Health Services Management Centre, Birmingham: University of Birmingham.

Milligan C. & Fyfe N. (2004), 'Putting the Voluntary Sector in its Place: Geographical perspectives on voluntarism and social welfare', *Journal of Social Policy*, 33(1), pp. 73–93.

Muñoz S-A., Farmer J. & Stephen K. (2008), *Achieving Social Enterprise Development in Rural Communities O4O Policy Briefing No. 2*, Inverness: Centre for Rural Health.

New Economics Foundation (2006), *Developing a Social Equity Capital Market*, London: New Economics Foundation.

Osborne S. (1997), 'Managing the Coordination of Social Services in the Mixed Economy of Welfare: Competition, cooperation or common cause?', *British Journal of Management*, 8(4), pp. 317–328.

Peredo A. & McLean M. (2006), 'Social entrepreneurship: A critical review of the concept', *Journal of the World of Business*, 41, pp. 56–65.

Phillips M. (2006), 'Growing Pains: The sustainability of social enterprises', *International Journal of Entrepreneurship and Innovation*, 7(4), pp. 221–230.

Potter C. & Brough R. (2004), 'Systemic Capacity Building: A hierarchy of needs', *Health Policy and Planning*, 19, pp. 336–345.

Ramesh R. (2011), 'Big Society Bank Aims to Boost Social Enterprise: Will the "big society" bank help social enterprises do bigger business, in the face of cuts?', *The Guardian*, 22 February, p. 4.

Reform (2011), *Reform Scorecard*, London: Reform.

Ridley-Duff R. (2007), 'Communitarian Perspectives on Social Enterprise', *Corporate Governance*, 15(2), pp. 382–392.

Scott M. (2002), 'Delivering Integrated Rural Development: Insights from Northern Ireland', *European Planning Studies*, 10(8), pp. 1013–1025.

Sharir M. & Lerner M. (2006), 'Gauging the Success of Social Ventures Initiated by Individual Social Entrepreneurs', *Journal of World Business*, 41, pp. 6–20.

Shaw E. & Carter S. (2007), 'Social Entrepreneurship: Theoretical antecedents and empirical analysis of entrepreneurial processes and outcomes', *Journal of Small Business and Enterprise Development*, 14(3), pp. 418–434.

Skerratt S. (2008), *Culture and Policies: Helping or hindering rural social enterprises in service provision?*, O4O Policy Briefing No. 1, Inverness: Centre for Rural Health.

Smith M. (2008), 'Sustainable communities and neighbourhoods: Theory, policy and practice' (*The encyclopedia of informal education*). Retrieved from: www.infed.org/communities/sustainable_communities_and_neighbourhoods.htm

Spear S., Cornforth C. & Aiken M. (2009), 'The Governance Challenges of Social Enterprises: Evidence from a UK empirical study', *Annals of Public and Cooperative Economics*, 80(2), pp. 247–273.

St Leger L. (2005), 'Questioning Sustainability in Health Promotion Projects and Programs', *Health Promotion International*, 20(4), pp. 317–319.

Stern N. (2006), *The Economics of Climate Change*, London: HM Treasury/ Cabinet Office.

Sullivan Mort G., Weerawardena J. & Carnegie K. (2003), 'Social Entrepreneurship: Towards conceptualization', *International Journal of Nonprofit and Voluntary Sector Marketing*, 8(1), pp. 76–88.

The Brundtland Commission (1987), *Report of the World Commission on Environment and Development: Our common future*, New York: United Nations World Commission on Environment and Development.

The Community Development Finance Association (2011), *Community Investment Tax Relief (CITR): Towards an improved tax relief scheme from 2012*, London: CDFA.

The Office of the Deputy Prime Minister (2004), *Skills for Sustainable Communities: The Egan review*, London: The Office of the Deputy Prime Minister.

The Scottish Government (2007), *Scotland Rural Development Programme 2007–2013*, Edinburgh: The Scottish Government.

The Scottish Government (2008), *Enterprising Third Sector Action Plan*, Edinburgh: The Scottish Government.

The Scottish Social Enterprise Coalition (2010), *In Business to Change Lives: A manifesto for social enterprise in Scotland*, Edinburgh: The Scottish Social Enterprise Coalition.

Todres M., Cornelius N., Janjuha-Jivraj S. & Woods A. (2006), 'Developing Emerging Social Enterprise Through Capacity Building', *Social Enterprise Journal*, 2(1), pp. 61–72.

van Marrewijk M. (2003), 'Concepts and Definitions of CSR and Corporate Sustainability: Between agency and communion', *Journal of Business Ethics*, 44, pp. 95–105.

Victoria Health (2005), *Integrated Health Promotion: A practice guide for service providers*, Melbourne: State Government of Victoria.

Westall A. & Chalkley D. (2007), *Social Enterprise Futures*, London: The Smith Institute.

Wickham P. (2006), *Strategic Entrepreneurship*, Harlow: Prentice Hall.

7. Measuring the value of social organisations as rural service providers

Jane Farmer and Sara Bradley

INTRODUCTION

As Hill discusses in Chapter 1, policy has been incrementally turning in favour of promoting the benefits of providing, supporting and enhancing aspects of public services using social enterprises (H.M. Treasury, 2002, 2004, 2005; Department of Health, 2007; Cabinet Office, 2010). This is purported to improve accessibility to appropriate services, provide 'added-value' social capacity by, for example, providing work experience and developing community initiatives, and enhance wellbeing through volunteering and feelings of contributing to community (Home Office, 2003; H.M. Treasury & Cabinet Office, 2006; Scottish Social Enterprise Coalition, 2007). A 2010 *Economist* article stated that, 'In Britain and America governments hope that a partnership with social entrepreneurs can solve some of society's most intractable problems' (p. 55). The economic crisis ensuing in the late 2000s and corresponding sound-bite policy notions like the 'Big Society' (Conservative Party, 2010) produced a context in which the public could perhaps be convinced of their role, indeed duty, to participate in co-producing services in partnership with the state. The 2010 *Economist* article proceeded to highlight that social enterprise-type innovations remained 'small scale' and fragmented as service providers, partly due to the challenge of identifying an indicator of success: 'businesses have profit: the social sector lacks a similarly simple yardstick' (p. 56).

In this chapter, the potential for evaluating the impacts of social enterprises is considered and approaches to evaluation are critiqued through the lens of the O4O: Older People for Older People project (O4O) that worked with communities to establish social enterprises in five Northern European countries. It is hard to argue with the concept of evaluation, but in the context of evaluating a policy initiative aimed at generating multiple social and health outcomes evaluation is complex. Within O4O, evaluation could be viewed as operating within two frames of reference. One was 'internal' and processual, involving iterations of formal and informal feedback that fed the process of developing O4O organisations by Project Managers, communities and other stakeholders in line with a participatory action research approach (Minkler & Wallerstein, 2008). The second sought to take an 'external', more technical, outcomes-based perspective asking to what extent O4O produced impacts for individuals, communities and service providers; in essence, attempting to measure whether the beneficial outcomes purported by policy were feasible. Outcomes to be measured were constructed based on a theory derived from research evidence. This chapter focuses on this external stream of evaluation.

To produce data on the impacts of the O4O project a framework for evaluation was designed to consider the health and social outcomes of community social enterprises involving older people in rural areas to provide services. The framework was designed as a test because it was known at the outset that some data, such as service activity data at individual community level, would be difficult or impossible to collect (Nimegeer et al, 2010).

Policymakers urge evaluation but frequently provide impractical conditions for evidence-gathering. For example, evaluations may be required to measure impacts over a very short timescale, such as one to five years. In the O4O project, an evaluation framework was tested with the purpose of assessing the feasibility, acceptability and value of different methods of data collection to investigate impacts on wellbeing and social capital, service demand and costs. This was done in the context of small, dispersed communities, at a distance from service centres and focused on the role of, and value for, people aged 55 years and over.

In this chapter we consider approaches to social enterprise impact evaluation such as 'social return on investment' (Nicholls et al, 2009) and briefly consider the ethics of 'implementation research', whereby researchers may be viewed as promoting government policy, albeit in the interests of 'testing' its validity. The chapter concludes by turning to evidence from O4O to suggest that there is more to the identification of success by various stakeholders than objective measurement approaches. Perceptions of successful outcomes can be time-dependent, influenced by political desires and through promotion. Tipping points, influencers, dissemination routes and fashion all affect the value ascribed to an initiative, particularly when outcomes are hard to define and produced longitudinally. In this, the O4O project and the production of services by community social enterprise align with the introduction of other policy initiatives; that is, their acceptability and embedding is often related to their 'fit' with the direction of policy ideology, adaptation to context and champions – rather than linked to robust summative evidence of impacts (Greenhalgh et al, 2004). This is partly due to the length of time it takes to realise outcomes, the costs of conducting robust evaluation, and the fact that structures, policies and society are simultaneously changing and adapting (Pommier et al, 2010). Achieving realistic measurements of difference and understanding potential wider impacts of social enterprise policy initiatives on social and health outcomes require a reflective long-term multi-stakeholder perspective.

THE RELEVANCE OF EVALUATION

A 2010 Demos review (Wood & Leighton, 2010) highlighted that many third sector organisations are poorly equipped to conduct evaluation; that is, lack skills, resources and time. The review says focus must move from measuring outputs such as the numbers of hours of volunteering or number of clients assisted, to measuring outcomes (e.g. people helped to find work, health gain or social participation built). The reviewers also suggest that funders and grantees are simultaneously culpable within a culture of non-standardised and sporadic evaluation. Yet, as Wood and Leighton (2010) argue, if social entrepreneurs cannot prove they are making change as they wish, why should potential supporters and investors choose to provide funding or award contracts? Clearly, evaluating the impact of social enterprises is required from several perspectives:

1. *The state*: Given that increasing production of services by social enterprises and voluntary organisations is a strong thrust of current policy, it is important to establish the extent to which social enterprise produces the benefits governments suggest or to which they aspire. Social enterprise could be viewed as a government tactic to produce services more cheaply within a retrenching welfare state. In this scenario, the benefits promoted should be seen as a 'sweetener' to the public to accept greater responsibility for self-help. Drawing attention to this perspective Draper et al (2010:1103) note that there are two perspectives on policymakers' enthusiasm to involve citizens: *optimistically*, citizen involvement might be viewed as nurturing empowerment whilst *cynically* it might be viewed as 'a technocratic solution to political problems'. Perez et al (2009) draw on Rifkin (1996), noting there are dichotomous 'frames of reference' for enlisting communities: *target-oriented* – that is, using participation from the top-down

to engage communities in the state's bidding – and *empowering* – that is, a nurturing, bottom-up, approach to facilitate communities to help themselves. Government needs evaluation evidence showing positive impacts from increased public service production by social economy organisations in order to help promote community involvement in service-delivering activity.

2. *Public service providers/commissioners*: Given the considerable culture change and consequent effort to change processes and staff attitudes that social enterprise provision of services demands for the public sector, public service producers such as councils and health authorities also want evidence that 'it works'. They need evidence that services will be of satisfactory quality and cost compared with direct public sector provision. If a goal is to convince public sector managers that they should contract with community social organisations, then best value, dependability and sustainability over the longer term must be identifiable. The reasons for the public sector contracting with social enterprises could be expectations of the following types of benefit:

    a) in a traditional sense, social enterprises might start up that produce services more cheaply, that are more locally attuned or with additional social and environmental benefits when compared with previous public service and/or commercial providers; and,

    b) social enterprises might start up that alter demand. For example, a good neighbour, lift-giving or domestic help initiative might help to keep older people living healthily at home and out of hospital or residential care.

In the latter case, robust evidence would be required to convince commissioners to divert resources from an established service, such as a residential care home with buildings and staff, to a new, community-based service. The concepts of additionality and displacement are pertinent here (Lyon, 2009). The former refers to how a social enterprise might provide something additional to existing public services. The latter refers to effects on other services caused by the establishment of a new social initiative; for example, as noted above, other service inputs might decrease in response to new patterns of demand generated by the actions of a new social enterprise. As Wilson (2009:51) suggests, new social enterprises 'are often responding to niches in their "market", addressing needs that they feel are not being met by other means in their community . . . . The kind of solutions developed by social entrepreneurs will usually be complementary to "normal" public services, providing greater user involvement, greater innovation and the ability to take more risks.'

3. *People and communities*: The public wants to be reassured that the benefits of service production by local social enterprises outweigh the burden placed on the community to produce them. At issue is whether there is human capacity in communities to develop and run social enterprises and provide a volunteer workforce, particularly in rural communities where there is already a high level of volunteering (SQW Ltd., 2002) and, consequently, less scope for increasing capacity for more voluntary work (Farmer et al, 2008). Whilst benefits from volunteering are proven, if a small number of people are over-committed their health and the social capital of the community may be adversely affected (Morrow-Howell et al, 2003).

4. *Additions to knowledge*: From an academic perspective it is important to develop the evidence base about the outcomes of social enterprise so that knowledge and theory are extended. However, this can be controversial: witness the recent outcry over the UK Arts and Humanities Research Council's proposal to study 'The Big Society' in its research strategy (Jump, 2011). Protesters stated that a research council should not be promoting elements of government policy by blatantly naming the policy as a theme.

THEORY-BASED EVALUATION

An approach to social enterprise evaluation is to define the causal theory or change model that links inputs, intervening stages and variables, and outcomes (Chen, 2005). Theory-based approaches to evaluation help to identify and situate the key outcomes of interest within the overall 'project' of what is to be achieved (Cole, 1999; Birckmayer & Weiss, 2000) and help to define steps between an intervention and an outcome that facilitate choice of measures and measurement methods. Theory-based evaluation approaches have been developed by the Aspen Institute, whose 'theory of change' approach was developed to evaluate complex community-based change interventions (Weiss, 1995), and by Pawson and Tilley (1997) whose 'realistic evaluation' approach is widely used. Realistic evaluation seeks to identify mechanisms that produce change, contextual conditions that trigger these, and outcomes that might pertain given the conditions; and looks at 'context–mechanism–outcome' patterns. Mapping the theory of outcomes production and including different stakeholders' routes to outcomes are principles of the *Social Return On Investment* (SROI) method of evaluation which is the current 'gold standard' for measuring the outcomes of social organisations (Cabinet Office, 2009). SROI is considered later in this chapter.

Within O4O, the case study that is used to illustrate this chapter, a theory of processes and outcomes production supported by research evidence (Berkman et al, 2000; Fernandez-Ballesteros, 2002; Luoh & Herzog, 2002; Lum & Lightfoot, 2005), was used to guide evidence-gathering. Figure 7.1 shows how, theoretically, individuals who engage in community action to develop social enterprises will: a) extend their social contacts and networks; b) gain new skills, experience and confidence; and c) in time, provide services to help others in the community. Extending this, individuals will: d) gain wellbeing benefits from improved physical and psychological health through more social contact; and e) generate human capital that may be expended for their own or community benefit. Considering benefits at the community level, hypothetically involvement in social enterprise will: f) generate social participation and network extensions to produce community social capital; and g) collate individuals' wellbeing benefits to produce greater *community* physical and psychological health. And finally, for health and social services, this will result in lower demand, especially for 'crisis' types of services such as General Practice out-of-hours calls and emergency ambulance calls, because people will be happier and healthier, more socially connected and, as a consequence, will help each other; local community members will be formally involved in providing services that will maintain people's health and social care in the community; and the services that are provided (i.e. by local community members) will be locally appropriate. This theory was used to identify outcome measures to evaluate the success of the O4O project.

Policy influenced by currently prevalent biomedical and managerial paradigms demands outcomes measurement but researchers from community development, health planning and health promotion suggest that community involvement is a process and that policymakers should be interested in how community involvement affects processes of production (Rifkin, 1996; Minkler & Wallerstein, 2008). Draper et al (2010) argue that participative processes require to be studied, rather than treating community involvement as an intervention.

THE O4O EVALUATION

Regarding the theory-based evaluation of the O4O project shown in Figure 7.1, it is next necessary to show how the theory translated into decisions about what to 'measure' and how. Pommier et al (2010) suggest

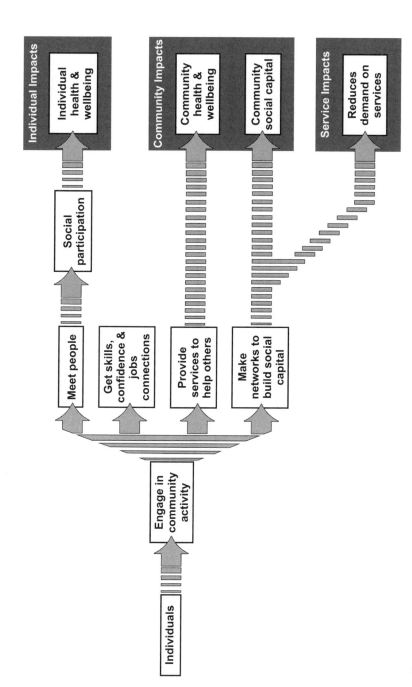

Figure 7.1   A theory of social enterprise processes and outcomes production

measurement and methods should be guided by the complexity of the intervention or programme to be measured and the likely availability of data:

1. *Open programme* – the scenario requires broad development of understanding; there is a need for intensive information and there is low availability = a qualitative approach.
2. *Closed programme* – the scenario requires extensive, precise information which is readily available = a quantitative approach.
3. *Complex programme* – the scenario requires intensive and extensive information and there is variable information accessibility = mixed methods approach.

Taking this framework, together with an appreciation of the stakeholders for whom it was important to provide evaluative findings – that is, individuals, communities, service providers, policymakers and academics – it was decided that data should be sought to consider the impacts on individuals (health status and social participation), communities (community health status and social capital) and service providers (demand and costs). To an extent, the precise indicators explored were selected due to the health and social services focus of our research interests, pragmatics, likely availability of data, and likely capacity to be able to collect data. In other words, there was an interaction between thinking about methods, what data might be gathered, what these data might indicate and the stakeholders that it was important to influence.

Measuring Individual-Level Outcomes

The impacts of developing community social enterprises on individuals' health and social participation were of interest. This was addressed using two iterations of qualitative interviews in communities in the Highland region of Scotland. Using this method limited findings to individuals' perceptions of impacts rather than objective measurements (e.g. physiological measurements for health). Two main themes were explored: individuals' perceptions of direct effects of O4O involvement on their own and other individuals' health, and impacts on social participation which individuals might associate, indirectly, with health effects.

Interviews were conducted in the four participating communities in Highland towards the start of the O4O project (summer 2008) and with the three remaining Highland communities involved towards O4O's end (summer 2010). In 2008, 27 semi-structured interviews were conducted with individuals aged 55 and over. Most interviewees were selected as people living in the communities who had volunteered to participate in aspects of the O4O project; that is, helping to build social organisations in communities to provide basic-level services, such as lift-giving or domestic support. Additional interviewees were suggested by these O4O volunteers. An aspect of interest was to capture change for potential O4O service users. A challenge with first-round interviewing was identifying potential future O4O service users since it was unknown at that stage what services the communities would want to produce.

In 2010, interviews were conducted with 14 individuals aged 55 and over. At this stage the idea was to include those who had remained working with O4O over the period of the project, those who had been attracted in as volunteers to work on O4O, and service recipients. Fewer interviewees in 2010, compared with the number in 2008, were accounted for by the drop-out from the project of the South West Ross community, which did not, ultimately, develop a social organisation, and the fact that in two of the communities no services had actually been started at the time of follow-up interviews. The qualitative interviews focused on broad outcome areas: health and social participation. Interviewees were encouraged to discuss what was important to them, with the focus being their perceptions of health and social participation impacts. At both stages interviews lasted up to 40 minutes, were conducted by the same researcher and were recorded and transcribed. Transcriptions were coded by theme and managed using NVivo software. Some issues around the methodology and findings are now discussed.

First, the process of 'before' and 'after' interviewing that had seemed straightforward when writing the evaluation proposal proved to be complex. The individuals working with O4O changed and some were 'lost' to the process of interviewing for various reasons, including lack of interest in participating, illness, and their community no longer being involved with the project. Secondly, it was difficult to follow service users as it was unknown, at the start, who these would be, and even by project end only one community had actually developed a service that was being used. Despite these complications and despite the lack of objective meas-urement, 'before' and 'after' interviews were useful in gathering evidence about health and social participation impacts and how people perceived and evaluated these. The approach allowed comparison at different stages; and at the second stage interviewees also showed an element of reflec-tion and description of the processes of their involvement and how they thought that had affected their health. Findings highlighted how people categorised health and wellbeing benefits. They differentiated between outcomes clearly linked to health service accessibility, and outcomes that might be perceived to link with health, but indirectly. Tangible, clearly health-related outcomes were keeping older people living in their communities and out of hospitals or residential care in distant towns. At stage two interviewing, interviewees identified health benefits from people getting transport to hospital, General Practitioner (GP) or dental appointments and older people's care in their community.

In relation to the health and wellbeing benefits for themselves and others linked to the social participation elements of developing and providing O4O services, there was ambivalence about potential benefits. In 2008, several said they thought volunteering had good effects on mental outlook and in 2010 interviewees spoke in a general way about participation having good effects, noting, for example, that they had met new people; there was integration between generations and between incomers and locals; and that they felt a sense of pride and fulfilment at what had been achieved. For many, the potential health and wellbeing benefits of participation were only tacitly acknowledged and understood.

Strikingly, in the 2010 interviews, some individuals reflected on the worry and stress that involvement in the O4O process had caused them. Various reasons were given: it was additional volunteering to that already undertaken; it involved very long hours of volunteering; and the type of volunteering (establishing and running community social enterprises) required a high level of responsibility. With regard to impacts on participation, reflections indicated that only a very small number of 'new' volunteers had been brought into participating through the O4O project's activities. Thus, rather than extending health benefits, for some O4O was thought to disadvantage health due to increasing their volunteering work. O4O also had different impacts in different communities, and this depended on the previous state of the community (e.g. apathetic or active) and the relatively 'stressful' nature of the project. For example, in Ardersier people got involved in meeting each other to conduct interviews about history whilst in Assynt the community were considering organising local residential care. To illustrate the journey for the different communities, the findings for each are summarised.

O4O Ardersier: an oral history project that led to the development of a community meeting place

Overall, interviewees' comments expressed a sense of enjoyment and satisfaction. There was a perception of positive impacts, insight into other people's experiences, involvement in the community and acquisition of skills such as interviewing, filming and editing. Being interviewed helped appreciation of self-worth, renewed a sense of identity and history and gained respect from others in the community. The project was thought to have been good for intergenerational understanding; helped community cohesion; reduced the resentment of 'disadvantaged area status'; and helped community pride through gaining publicity for the community.

O4O Assynt: developing community-owned social care for older people

The uncertainty surrounding the existing Local Council-run residential care home and its planned closure had caused anger, fear and anxiety in the community. Interviewees thought that older people were anxious about the future and fearful that a new service delivered through O4O represented a public service cut. The consequences and chances of long-term success of community social enterprise provision were considered uncertain. Two interviewees said involvement in O4O had been detrimental to their health and personal lives because of the heavy workload and commitment. One interviewee sometimes felt resentful that O4O had 'taken over her life', though looked forward to a sense of achievement when the service was operational. Another interviewee thought involvement had been 'a tie' and what she had anticipated as a six month commitment had turned into twelve months; there had been 'no escape'. Another interviewee described involvement as 'great fun', saying he was a people person who liked getting out and about.

O4O Tongue: a community transport scheme (T4T)

T4T was said to have given older people more independence, opened up choices and made a difference to the lives of older people in the community. People were said to be no longer 'beholden' to friends and neighbours for transport. This was perceived to benefit individuals' wellbeing. Combating isolation was said to have positive health and social impacts on older people. In terms of generating participation in volunteering, one person said it helped more people to get involved whilst another said the social enterprise had not increased the amount or the spirit of participation outside T4T. A further interviewee believed another year needed to pass before impact could usefully be evaluated and thought it had been 'a struggle' to get volunteers.

Measuring Community-Level Outcomes

Whilst interviews allowed consideration of the impact of developing social enterprises on individuals, a survey was used to consider impacts for communities. For the survey, communities were selected as the unit of analysis, with the outcomes of interest being changes to health status and social participation. The impact on communities was considered important as community benefits, including social capital and wellbeing, are promoted in government policy on social enterprise. The idea in O4O was to measure community health and social participation as a proxy for social capital 'before' and 'after' the O4O project. Community is a contested concept; we defined it as a geographical and social entity – that is, the people living within a distinct geographical 'boundary'. GP list data were used to identify people aged 55 and over; thus the boundaries of an individual practice's coverage defined community. A quick-to-complete, self-reporting, acceptable and widely used measure of health status was desired, so the SF12 (Ware et al, 1996) short form of standard questions was selected. As a measure of social capital, the 'social capital module' of questions from the UK General Household survey was selected (Office for National Statistics, 2003). This includes measures of informal social participation (e.g. giving and receiving 'favours' from a neighbour) and formal social participation (e.g. being on the management board of a local voluntary organisation). Demographic variables were also included in the questionnaire.

Ethical approval was received from the relevant National Health Service committee. The ethical committee was accepting of the basis of the survey; that is, that it was considering community-, not individual-, level differences and was therefore satisfied that it was not necessary to identify individuals and that the survey would not involve matching individuals' status at different timepoints. This helped to gain ethical committee approval. Some communities had small populations. To avoid differences in sampling for larger and smaller communities the whole population aged 55 and over at the participating general practices was included. Both of these issues transpired to have impacts on the feasibility, usefulness and acceptability of the 'before and after' survey method of data collection for measuring community impacts.

A 58% (1428/2462) response rate was achieved following one reminder. The reminder had to be sent to the entire population group, as individuals were not identifiable to the researchers. Forty-six per cent of respondents were male and 54% female. Most (75%) were between 55 and 75 years old and 79% described their health as good, very good or excellent. Seventy-eight per cent were not born in the local area; 31% were employed full-time or part-time, 40% had a university degree and/or professional qualification, and 88% had access to a vehicle. We know that the 58% who responded did not include duplicate responses as testing was conducted and any possible duplicates removed. The survey provided statistical evidence of differences between the Highland communities involved in the O4O project, involving self-reported health status (P=0.003), origin of residents (P=0.014), their access to a vehicle (P=0.007) and their level of education (P=0.001). Thus, communities differed on several characteristics.

The community survey produced a data set that could be analysed to consider which variables were most closely associated with social capital. When chi-square tests were conducted (depending on the data type, continuity correction, linear by linear or Pearson's chi-squared tests were used), better health, younger age and individual community of residence were variables found to be independently associated with indicators of social capital. '*Doing a favour for a neighbour*' was additionally associated with being in employment, higher education levels, having access to a vehicle and higher income. '*Attending a community meeting*' was associated with being female, higher education, having access to a vehicle, community of residence, higher income and not being born locally. Additional demographic variables were associated with other particular social capital variables.

Such findings are useful for informing policymakers about which types of people aged 55 and over are most likely to participate and thereby build community social capital. Similarly, data showed which groups were least associated with social capital variables. These data could be used to consider which characteristics related to social exclusion may be addressed. Survey data also showed that individual communities had different levels of social capital that were independently associated with 'community' rather than related to the characteristics of people living there. This indicates that there are elements of social capital that are related to place and the complex features that constitute it. Such elements might include local leadership and governance arrangements (Kilpatrick & Abbott-Chapman, 2005). A question is why these come about in particular places.

The proposal within O4O had been to repeat the community survey at O4O 'end' in order to measure changes to health status and social capital. After much deliberation a decision was made not to do this as it was considered unrealistic to think that O4O could have made a measurable impact on community-level health and social capital between 2007 and 2010. Given start-up administration and the need to survey within the three year period, the timeframe for O4O to run and to make any impact was short. Originally it was thought that O4O social enterprises would be more directly and obviously related to health services and to bringing people together in social participation (e.g. Good Neighbour Schemes were one of the ideas originally envisaged) but they transpired to be indirect: transport, developing a place for social care and developing a DVD based on interviews about community heritage. A limited number of people were thus likely to have been affected by O4O and it would be impossible to identify them due to the anonymity of the survey.

In addition, the first survey elicited complaints from some recipients. These included comments about wasting paper by sending out a reminder questionnaire to the whole population and that a sample, rather than the whole population, should have been used for the survey. Given the importance of maintaining good relationships with the participating rural communities the decision was taken not to risk further annoying community members by distributing another survey. The first survey had produced a large amount of data with scope for analysis; a second survey would have produced an equivalent amount of data that would likely be similar to the first survey. For these reasons it was considered both unethical, in putting participants to further trouble for little extra gain, and inefficient to repeat the community survey.

It is interesting how these methodological restrictions are obvious in retrospect but lost in the heady enthusiasm of proposal-writing and eagerness to meet the policymakers' desire for measurable outcomes. Pommier et al (2010) categorise the challenges of measuring community-based health/social change 'interventions' as: a) methodological (choosing the appropriate and measurable unit of analysis); b) differentiating programme effects from other trends; c) identifying very small effects from community-level programmes; d) the time it takes for any level of community penetration of effect; and e) the limitations of linking theory to the complexity of interventions and levels of influence.

Measuring Outcomes for Service Providers

Impacts on individuals and communities are important, but to consider changing methods of service provision and types of services it is also necessary to show service providers whether they will experience benefits:

> In the absence of good information about other kinds of value, narrow cost considerations can become the primary basis on which decisions are made. This can lead to false economies – savings being achieved in the short term at the expense of more significant costs over the longer term, or at the expense of negative consequences in other public policy domains. (New Economics Foundation, 2009a:5)

Despite the sentiment expressed in this quote, cost reduction is arguably the prime motivator for public service commissioners' interest in social enterprises as service providers. Improving quality by providing more locally attuned services, sustaining provision and developing better relationships between citizens and public service providers are other justifications used for introducing co-production. In rural areas, developing community social enterprises that harness local people to co-produce services may also be viewed positively as a way of moving on 'standoff' situations. In O4O, for example, service providers were interested in involving the local community in managing a day care facility as they had, for some years, been battling with community protests around closing a residential care home. The O4O evaluation framework sought to identify potential areas of cost saving for service providers and assess whether data on cost changes could be captured. From other studies considering service costs to small rural communities there was a suspicion that it would be difficult to obtain data at local area level (West et al, 2004; Nimegeer et al, 2010). Health and council services do not generally apply budgeting processes by area, but rather by service type, and in rural areas postcodes often cover large areas so even drill-down using that method can be difficult.

Considering overall issues of measurement, as with the community-level survey considered above, the time for change to occur within the O4O project was rather short. The O4O social organisations chosen by communities to develop were less directly related to health services than had originally been envisaged, making quick and distinct impacts on services unlikely, and confounding factors, such as new data collection systems or models of service delivery, might actually be wholly or partly responsible for any discernible changes.

Considering impact from the public sector's health and social services perspectives was important because we wanted both to inform them of impacts to their services and influence the way these services were delivered. We were interested to see whether different organisations were better able to provide data; and council and health services are increasingly involved in joint working around older people's services. From previous study, an initial list of potential service impacts was identified, including:

- emergency ambulance call-outs;
- calls to the out-of-hours primary care help-line;
- calls to the local GP for out-of-hours visits;
- actual local GP out-of-hours visits;
- emergency hospital admissions;
- length of stay in hospital for emergency and elective admissions;
- falls;
- receipt of local authority home care packages;
- numbers of local people entering residential care.

The topics for which data were available are now considered below.

Primary care out-of-hours services
We wanted to establish which data were available to measure potential change to out-of-hours call-outs to GPs and other primary health care providers for those aged 55 and over. Since the 2004/5 new General Medical Services (GMS) Contract a picture of variable provision of

first contact with services out of hours has arisen across rural Scotland (Pollock, 2008). Some communities can contact local health professionals out of hours through local arrangements between GPs and Health Boards but most people are obliged to call the national out-of-hours telephone triage line 'NHS 24'. Of the six GP practices aligned with communities in O4O, four could contact their local GP directly. Interestingly, only one GP practice shared its data on GP out-of-hours calls whilst the other three said they did not hold these data. When we asked the health authority, they said there was no requirement to collect these data because 'the important thing was that the community might need a GP, not how many times the community actually called the GP'. Two communities were obliged to use NHS 24 out of hours and these data were retrievable by GP practices from NHS 24.

Ambulance service call-outs
The ambulance service was able to provide data on numbers of phone calls and numbers of actual call-outs categorised by age and GP practice.

Hospital emergency admissions
Data on emergency hospital admissions and length of stay for both emergency and elective admissions were retrievable from hospital data, by GP practice.

Home care and personal care recipients
Despite lengthy negotiations with the local authority it was impossible to discern from routinely gathered data the numbers of people in communities who were receiving types of social care services. Data were only available by postcode areas, and in the Highlands a postcode can cover a wide area. For example, postcode IV27 includes 107 distinct, named small 'communities'. Whilst, in 2007, there were 49 people receiving a total of 244 home care hours and 40 people receiving a total of 178.5 personal care hours, without a specific local survey it would be impossible to establish the number of home care hours supplied to individual communities.

Although the O4O project was obliged to approach service providers to locate the data required, this meant that the risk of non-supply was minimal and the request for data limited to the years in which O4O was operational. Some of the data sets supplied showed rises in demand (e.g. increased NHS 24 calls and emergency call-outs by the ambulance service) and others showed decreased uptake (e.g. numbers of hours of home care), but without suitable contextualisation these data are fairly meaningless. Longitudinal data over a number of years are required to show trends or changes and data need to be discussed with service providers and local people to help check for confounding effects. For example, home care hours may have decreased because the local authority cut home care hours or because it was difficult to recruit staff, rather than because demand fell.

In summary, even where available, routinely collected data from service providers have potential as a means of measuring the impact of community social enterprise interventions only if:

- data can be obtained at the appropriate level (e.g. by community or GP practice);
- longitudinal data sets are available that gathered data consistently over time;
- data are discussed with service provider and community representatives to contextualise them;
- it is not overly troublesome or costly to produce the data reports required.

What Worked in the O4O Evaluation?

Given the short duration of the O4O project, the most informative, acceptable and relatively inexpensive method for discovering impact was the iterative, qualitative interviewing. The interviews were informative because interviewees' perceptions of the types of impacts on their health, participation and community could be studied; interviews were open to adaptation of themes/questions and to unforeseen impacts arising. The interview data facilitated a degree of understanding of what was happening during the community social enterprise development process as people's actions and perceptions evolved in relation to changing circumstances. This conclusion is interesting and surprising. Policymakers tend to consider qualitative data less robust than quantitative data, largely as nuance and contingency are problematical and the meaning of discrete numbers is less easily disputed. But in this case, routine data were unavailable or unreliable and survey data inappropriate, costly and inconvenient to recipients. Thus, within the context of O4O, qualitative interviews helped both to describe and understand the process and outcomes of community social enterprises and to inform adaptation.

OTHER APPROACHES TO EVALUATION

Specific approaches to evaluating social enterprise have been developed (New Economics Foundation, 2000, 2009b; Cabinet Office, 2009; NHS

North West, 2009; Senscot, 2009; Pearce & Zadek, 2011), with one theme around converting social value into financial value. These methods provide a way of focusing socially oriented organisations on measuring financial outcomes. They identify and quantify outcomes and assign financial value. Methods may be used as one-off measurements or accrue to become social accounting tools. Some methods can be used to measure or forecast outcomes but with both the difficulty is identifying *all* of the pertinent likely impacts of a social enterprise. As an evidence base for different types of social organisations in different settings grows, then realistic, comparable assessments seem more likely.

SROI, a framework for measuring and accounting for value that incorporates social, environmental and economic costs and benefits (Cabinet Office, 2009) has, for some, become the gold standard for evaluating social enterprises, although, as Wood and Leighton (2010:28) concluded, 'SROI evaluations are relatively complex and resource intensive to carry out. Ascribing monetary values to soft intangible outcomes is a challenging process.' Nonetheless, SROI defines a framework and a process for social economy organisations to identify organisational outcomes, indicators and financial value so that they can show merit to investors in a consistent way. Applying SROI to evaluation involves six stages:

1. Establish the scope of the evaluation and identify key stakeholders.
2. Record the theory of impact and map envisaged impacts and outcomes.
3. Identify indicators and data that will measure the outcomes and 'monetise' them.
4. Collect evidence to establish impact.
5. Calculate benefits, subtract negatives and compare result to investment; then sensitivity test.
6. Share findings.

Various challenges within the SROI measurement process have been identified (Wood & Leighton, 2010). These include one-off measurement versus long-term impact (e.g. when do outcomes start to happen and how long do they last?). What is the relationship between inputs and outcomes (e.g. how important is leadership and mentoring and what is the effect of key individuals?). Whilst assessing monetary value is complex, there are formulae and examples within SROI guidance.

O4O's theoretical evaluative framework was comparable to SROI except that it did not attempt monetary values. However, outcomes *were* considered from the perspective of individuals, communities and service providers as stakeholder groups and the evaluation established a theory of outcomes production based on evidence and government policy. The

O4O example also highlighted further challenges for applying SROI techniques. First, developing a theory of how the community social enterprise will impact tends to be based on an optimistic assessment of what the researcher or developer *wants to happen*. In O4O, participating communities built an assortment of initiatives that were not originally envisaged, thereby raising the question, 'how does the evaluator cater for emergent/ evolving enterprise types?' A second challenge related to data deficits that meant it was difficult to measure some outcomes. Accounting for unforeseen impacts and subtracting the effects of detrimental impacts was a further challenge.

WHAT IS REALLY GOING ON WITH EVALUATION?

Evaluation is undeniably good practice. The process serves to distil the purpose of an intervention and the theory by which it is envisaged to achieve outcomes. An evaluation framework is a tool for both the enactor of a project and the evaluator, and ensures focus, transparency, robustness and clarity of purpose that mean a project can be communicated to others. Thinking about evaluation from the start of a project aligns with the principles of project management regarding the need for milestones, objectives and measurable outputs whilst evaluation findings are important for informing policy, persuading the public and developing knowledge. However, the apparently straightforward concept of evaluation conceals 'elephants in the room'. Policymakers ask for evidence but their reactions to projects, processes and the evidence base are not always rational (Greenhalgh et al, 2004; Walshe, 2007; Greenhalgh & Russell, 2006; Farmer & Currie, 2009). Policymakers will resort to stalling publication of evaluations that they have funded, perhaps through requesting repeated changes and additions or asking questions. Sometimes they will reject, explicitly or tacitly, findings on the basis of considering the methodology insufficiently robust; an accusation that is generally squared against qualitative evaluations. 'Stalling' and 'rejection' often occur because policymakers do not like, or *do not agree with*, the findings. In such situations it is difficult to establish what would represent an incontrovertible evaluation framework with a methodology that is unassailable by any of the stakeholders and findings which would thus have to be treated as robust. Perhaps only a randomised controlled trial would do but, as we have seen with O4O, many aspects of social policy evolve as policy is implemented and these processes would act to upset and confound a randomised controlled trial.

Reflecting on the experience of O4O, the question arises: what would success look like? For the research team it was about finding out whether communities could and would develop social enterprises and/or co-produce in line with government policy, and there was interest in processual elements such as how processes evolve and adaptations are made at different points and in different cases, and why. Within the project, Project Managers recorded progress, discussions and meetings, and looked at outputs and outcomes as they appeared and were construed, at that time, and discussed how these had occurred using the reflective, evaluative process discussed by Farmer and Steven in Chapter 4. In contrast, for funders and some stakeholders O4O should be evaluated in terms of outputs; that is, the production of tangible and sustainable new or enhanced local services produced through community social enterprise. This meant that where a service was not created, O4O was deemed to have failed.

Perhaps the most interesting and instructive perspective regarding the identification of 'success' was that of the 'service provider stakeholders' such as local health service and local authority managers. These went through a long phase of apathy before there was a discernible turning point which occurred due to a particular alignment of factors. First, the O4O project started to make progress with one community which had been in conflict with the local authority for many years over the potential closure of a residential care home. The local authority started to see that this was a situation that could be turned around, with a favourable outcome being community interest in running some sort of local care service through an O4O community social enterprise. Secondly, a new head of social services was appointed, who was favourable to service innovation – and a global financial crisis hit! The result was that both local authority and health care providers became interested in the potential and mechanisms for social enterprises running services in rural communities. Thereafter, O4O came to be regarded as a 'success' and 'an example' by these stakeholders, even though it failed to develop in one of the Highland communities. At this point, elements of the formal evaluation were clearly unimportant compared with the perception that there was a potential solution to a challenging problem affecting small rural communities across a large part of Scotland. The decision by some key stakeholders that the O4O project was a success meant that it gained repute and was then discussed as an example of innovation that could be stimulated in communities, rather than waiting for unpredictable grassroots emergence. Since this time (mid-2010) the environment for community social enterprise service provision has become more receptive in the UK where, as Hill discusses in Chapter 1, Prime Minister David Cameron has been promoting the concept of the Big Society. This amorphous concept, though unpopular during the election campaign, is now a focus of right-of-centre policy think-tanks that are looking increasingly at moving communities to doing things for themselves, retracting public service provision and encouraging mixed-economy alternatives; perceiving the public to be more malleable and therefore receptive to such ideas in 'an age of austerity'.

It remains to be seen how community social enterprise service provision will play out in practice because there is still a gulf between stakeholders accepting that these ideas might work and the practicalities of their happening on the ground in communities where barriers such as those revealed through O4O exist, including lack of human capacity for volunteering and the need for the right kind of leadership and mentoring.

ETHICS

In this chapter we have used the example of O4O and its evaluation in the Scottish region of Highland to highlight the methodological challenges of evaluating an intervention to develop community social enterprises. O4O was intended as a 'test' of government policy which implies that social enterprise can be ubiquitous and purports a range of beneficial outcomes. An issue that was always an undercurrent, but grew as involvement with communities became more and more complex, and which we now briefly discuss, is *ethics*.

In order to test the policy's tenets, the O4O project had to implement them. It is thus entirely possible to consider O4O as ethically problematical because: a) it could be viewed as promoting government policy; and b) it was using communities experimentally for social change which was energy-consuming and had the potential to fail. The dilemmas for Project Managers became increasingly large, and real, as they asked communities to assume more responsibility and used adaptations such as tailoring a social enterprise course so that it did not overtly feature business concepts as these were unacceptable to the community or, as one Project Manager put it, *'using stealth'*. The ethical dilemmas of this kind of implementation research are unresolved. Within O4O they were addressed through repeated discussions with communities about how to sustain social enterprises after the end of the project and by avoiding providing money from O4O to communities.

Perez et al (2009) note that little has been written about the ethics of inviting people to participate in community-based interventions and programmes, and the issue remains highly problematical. They highlight that an empowering stance and manipulation by government can be easily over-layered. Whilst ostensibly participation can be sold as bringing positive social change through making people the active subjects of change, Perez et al (2009:339) state that 'participatory strategies challenge existing conditions and bear the risk of increasing the vulnerability and marginalization of communities involved'. Action research projects may seek to introduce new methods of participation and imply obligation to participate that might be alternatively viewed as political and social manipulation (Ugalde, 1985). Collins and Green (1994) suggest that where inviting citizens to participate results in reduced service quality or carrying unbearable burdens it harms communities and clearly contravenes research ethics codes. Perez et al (2009) review various ethical codes for participatory action research, including seven ethical principles for research studies with human participants – social or scientific value, scientific validity, fair subject/participant selection, favourable risk–benefit ratio, independent review, informed consent, and respect for potential and enrolled participants (Emanuel et al, 2000) – and suggest that these are: open to interpretation (whose social or scientific value do we seek to pursue?); problematical (how do you gain consent from a community?); or could cause levels of awareness that might bias findings (alerting participants to potential problems through seeking informed consent, for example). They conclude that an ethical stance should see community members contributing as much as possible to research design, questions and methods.

CONCLUSIONS

SROI is the current method being promoted for evaluating social enterprise initiatives. Whilst this appears complex, in the O4O project it was relatively easy to identify the theory and stakeholders of interest but more difficult to engage stakeholders in measurement, identification of data and participation in primary data collection.

A basket of techniques for measuring the outcomes of social enterprise as a service provider was tested in O4O. Individual-level data-gathering was useful as it indicated health and social impacts on individuals. It was relatively easy and quick to conduct, made it straightforward to engage participants and was a practical way of obtaining useful information in the very short time that the O4O social enterprises had to make any impact. It was also valuable for eliciting nuances of change and the time points within the project that they were related to. Additionally, individuals' stories have resonance and can act to illustrate change to policymakers.

The community-level survey was the least successful due to selecting a unit of analysis where it would be difficult to identify change and to attribute it to a particular intervention. To convince service providers to divert money out of traditional services into potentially preventive measures such as might be provided by community social enterprises, it is important to show impacts on service demand and costs to providers. Ongoing quality monitoring data will also be key. However, most data on demand, costs and quality are inaccessible at individual community level and therefore difficult to align with the actions of a community social enterprise. As predicted by the evidence base on evaluating policy interventions, there are often factors at play other than 'robust evaluation evidence' that predict whether an initiative will be taken up, regarded as a success or rejected. In the case of O4O-delivered social enterprises there was initially only superficial interest from service providers, and only latterly, due to a combination of economic context and some small obvious successes that were brought to the attention of a new council official, did the potential for wider roll-out of the project become of interest.

Testing policy interventions through implementation research raises problematical ethical questions for academic researchers. Intriguingly, these would not exist were the academics to be evaluating policy implemented by the state or were public services evaluating their own interventions. Thus, this issue, in turn, questions how researchers will reconcile the new demands on them to be 'engaging researchers' with their traditional distanced and ethical principles.

REFERENCES

Berkman L.F., Glass T., Brissette I., & Seeman T.E. (2000), 'From Social Integration to Health: Durkheim in the new millennium', *Social Science & Medicine*, 51(6), pp. 843–857.

Birckmayer J.D. & Weiss C.H. (2000), 'Theory-Based Evaluation in Practice: What do we learn?', *Evaluation Review*, 24(4), pp. 407–431.

Cabinet Office (2009), *A Guide to Social Return on Investment*, London: New Economics Foundation.

Cabinet Office (2010), *Building the Big Society*. Retrieved from: http://www.cabinetoffice.gov.uk/media/407789/building-big-society.pdf (accessed 24 February 2012).

Chen H.-T. (2005), *Practical Program Evaluation*, Thousand Oaks, CA: Sage.

Cole G.E. (1999), 'Advancing the Development and Application of Theory-Based Evaluation in the Practice of Public Health', *American Journal of Evaluation*, 20(3), pp. 453–470.

Collins C. & Green A. (1994), 'Decentralization and Primary Health Care: Some negative implications in developing countries', *International Journal of Health Services*, 24, pp. 459–475.

Conservative Party (2010), *Big Society, not Big Government: Building a big society*, London: UK Conservative Party.

Department of Health (2007), *Welcoming Social Enterprise into Health and Social Care: A resource pack for social enterprise providers and commissioners*, Leeds: Department of Health Social Enterprise Unit.

Draper A.K., Hewitt G. & Rifkin S. (2010), 'Chasing the Dragon: Developing indicators for the assessment of community participation in health programmes', *Social Science & Medicine*, 71, pp. 1102–1109.

Economist (2010), 'Let's Hear Those Ideas', 14 August, pp. 55–57.

Emanuel E.J., Wendler D. & Grady C. (2000), 'What Makes Clinical Research Ethical?', *Journal of the American Medical Association*, 283(20), pp. 2701–2711.

Farmer J. & Currie M. (2009), 'Evaluating the Outcomes of Rural Health Policy', *Australian Journal of Rural Health*, 17, pp. 53–57.

Farmer J., Steinerowski A. & Jack S. (2008), 'Starting Social Enterprises in Remote and Rural Scotland: The best or the worst of circumstances?', *International Journal of Entrepreneurship and Small Business*, 6(3), pp. 450–464.

Fernandez-Ballesteros R. (2002), 'Social Support and Quality of Life Among Older People in Spain', *Journal of Social Issues*, 58(4), pp. 645–659.

Greenhalgh T. & Russell J. (2006), 'Reframing Evidence Synthesis as Rhetorical Action in the Policy-Making Drama', *Healthcare Policy*, 1(2), pp. 34–42.

Greenhalgh T., Robert G., MacFarlane F., Bate P. & Kyriakidou O. (2004), 'Diffusion of Innovations in Service Organizations: Systematic review and recommendations', *The Milbank Quarterly*, 82(4), pp. 581–629.

H.M. Treasury (2002), *The Role of the Voluntary and Community Sector in Service Delivery: A cross-cutting review*, London: H.M. Treasury.

H.M. Treasury (2004), *Cross-Cutting Review: Follow-up of the role of the Third Sector in service delivery*, London: H.M. Treasury.

H.M. Treasury (2005), *Exploring the Role of the Third Sector in Public Service Delivery and Reform*, London: H.M. Treasury.

H.M. Treasury & Cabinet Office (2006), *The Future Role of the Third Sector in Social and Economic Regeneration: Interim report*, London: H.M. Treasury.

Home Office (UK Government) (2003), *Building Civil Renewal: Government support for community capacity building and proposals for change*, London: Home Office.

Jump P. (2011), 'AHRC and the Big Society: "You use the language policymakers understand"', *Times Higher Education*, 28 March. Retrieved from: http://www.timeshighereducation.co.uk/story.asp?sectioncode=26&storycode=415641&c=1 (accessed 24 February 2012).

Khanlou N. & Peter E. (2005), 'Participatory Action Research: Considerations for ethical review', *Social Science & Medicine*, 60, pp. 2333–2340.

Kilpatrick S. & Abbott-Chapman J. (2005), *Community Efficacy and Social Capital: Modelling how communities deliver outcomes for members*, Hobart: University of Tasmania. Retrieved from: http://eprints.utas.edu.au/201/1/Kilpatrick-Abbott-Chapman-Stirling.pdf (accessed 24 February 2012).

Lum T.Y. & Lightfoot E. (2005), 'The Effects of Volunteering on the Physical and Mental Health of Older People', *Research on Aging*, 27(1), pp. 31–55.

Luoh M.-C. & Herzog A.R. (2002), 'Individual Consequences of Volunteer and Paid Work in Old Age: Health and mortality', *Journal of Health & Social Behaviour*, 43(4), pp. 490–509.

Lyon F. (2009), 'Measuring the Value of Social and Community Impact' in Hunter P. (Ed.), *Social Enterprise for Public Service: How does the third sector deliver?*, London: The Smith Institute, pp. 29–36.

Minkler M. & Wallerstein M. (2008), 'Introduction to Community Based Participatory Research: New issues and emphases' in Minkler M. & Wallerstein M. (Eds.), *Community Based Participatory Research for Health: From processes to outcomes*, San Francisco: Jossey Bass, pp. 371–392.

Morrow-Howell N., Hinterlong J., Rozario P.A. & Tang F. (2003), 'Effects of Volunteering on the Well-Being of Older Adults', *Journal of Gerontology: Social Sciences*, 54B(3), S173–S180.

New Economics Foundation (2000), *Prove It!*, London: New Economics Foundation.

New Economics Foundation (2009a), *Seven Principles for Measuring What Matters*, London: New Economics Foundation.

New Economics Foundation (2009b), *Tools For You: Approaches to proving and improving for charities, voluntary organisations and social enterprise*, London: New Economics Foundation.

NHS North West (2009), *NHS Cross-Regional Social Value Commissioning Project*, Exeter: NHS North West.

Nicholls J., Lawler E., Neitzert E. & Goodspeed T. (2009), *Guide to Social Return on Investment*, London: New Economics Foundation.

Nimegeer A., Farmer J., West C., Whiston S. & Heaney D. (2010), *Remote Service Futures: Health care service design with communities*, Inverness: Centre for Rural Health & NHS Highland.

Norman J. (2010), *The Big Society: The anatomy of the new politics*, Buckingham: University of Buckingham Press.

Office for National Statistics (2003), *Measuring Social Capital in the United Kingdom*, London: Office for National Statistics.

Pawson R. & Tilley N. (1997), *Realistic Evaluation*, London: Sage.

Pearce J. & Zadek S. (2011), *Social Accounting Framework*, London: New Economic Foundation.

Perez D., Lefevre P., Romero M.I., Sanchez L., de Vos P. & van der Stuyft P. (2009), 'Augmenting Frameworks for Appraising the Practices of Community-Based Health Interventions', *Health Policy & Planning*, 24, pp. 335–341.

Pollock A. (2008), 'Public Health Meets Law: Are there sufficient legal safeguards to ensure access to public health care for all?', *Medico-legal Journal*, 76(4), pp. 118–132.

Pommier J., Guevel M.-R. & Jourdan D. (2010), 'Evaluation of Health Promotion in Schools: A realistic evaluation approach using mixed methods', *BMC Public Health*, 10, pp. 43–55.

Rebellato J.L. (1997), *Etica de la Autonomia: Desde la practica de la psicologia con las comunidades*, Montevideo: Nordan.

Rifkin S.B. (1996), 'Rapid Rural Appraisal: Its use and value for health planners and managers', *Public Administration*, 74, pp. 509–526.

Scottish Social Enterprise Coalition (2007), *Bigger, Better, Bolder: Social enterprise solutions for Scotland*, Edinburgh: SSEC.

Senscot (2009), *Social Enterprise and the Healthy Working Lives Initiative*, Edinburgh: Senscot.

SQW Ltd. (2002), *Assessment of the Social Economy of the Highlands and Islands*, Report for Highlands & Islands Enterprise, Edinburgh: SQW Ltd.

Ugalde A. (1985), 'Ideological Dimensions of Community Participation in Latin American Health Programs', *Social Science & Medicine*, 21, pp. 41–53.

Walshe K. (2007), 'Understanding What Works – and Why – in Quality

Improvement: The need for theory-driven evaluation', *International Journal of Quality in Health Care*, 19(2), pp. 57–59.

Ware J.E., Kosinski M. & Keller S.D. (1996), 'A 12-Item Short-Form Health Survey', *Medical Care*, 34, pp. 220–223.

Weiss C. (1995), 'Nothing as Practical as Good Theory: Exploring theory-based evaluation for comprehensive community initiatives' in Connell J., Kubisch A., Schoor L. & Weiss C. (Eds.), *New Approaches to Evaluating Comprehensive Community Initiatives: Concepts, methods and contexts*, Washington DC: The Aspen Institute.

West C., Farmer J. & Whyte B. (2004), 'Implementing Computerised Workload Data Collection in Rural Primary Health Care', *Australian Journal of Rural Health*, 12, pp. 11–16.

Wilson F. (2009), 'Social Entrepreneurs and Public Service Delivery' in Hunter P. (Ed.), *Social Enterprise for Public Service: How does the third sector deliver?*, London: The Smith Institute, pp. 49–56.

Wood C. & Leighton D. (2010), *Measuring Social Value: The gap between policy and practice*, London: Demos.

Conclusion

Carol Hill, Jane Farmer and Sarah-Anne Muñoz

In countries with well-developed systems of public sector service provision, recent decades have seen an increased focus on community involvement in the mechanisms of state delivery. Interest in achieving an active role for citizens and communities in the co-production of services and amenities for the maintenance of the health and wellbeing of, and to build capacity for, sustainable communities continues to develop. In the UK, the 2010-elected Conservative-led coalition government is promoting a 'Big Society' agenda shaped by a neo-mutualist policy trajectory. This has elevated the role of social enterprises, charities and voluntary organisations as vehicles for service provision. It has placed the UK government in the vanguard of an international policy environment that is increasingly promoting the development of tangible policies around co-production and social enterprise.

In 2008, the UK-based New Economics Foundation proposed co-production, with its ethos of improving the moral and social health of the nation by applying the force of the collective to providing localised services and amenities, as a concept that would involve citizens working with the state for the common good. Once elected, the Conservative-led coalition government set about transforming its rather vague ideas about creating a Big Society, and embracing citizen involvement in co-production, into practical policies for change. This has seen co-production advance from exhortations as to the merits of community social enterprise to the creation of structural changes intended to compel ubiquitous social enterprise development. A social enterprise bank, a network of community organisers to support and steer neighbourhood organisations and a Big Society Network have been discussed or established.

During the period that the O4O: Older People for Older People (O4O) exemplar project of this book took place, the play of policy in the UK evolved from what might loosely be referred to as 'co-productive noises' into an established policy of co-production with community social enterprise at the forefront. This timeframe has enabled comparison of the practical experiences and lessons gleaned from O4O with the *modus operandi* of a contemporaneous government seeking to embed ideas and action to achieve pervasive community social enterprise; what Gewirth (1996) refers to as 'socialised' or 'collective' entrepreneurship.

Although the Big Society emanates from the right wing of UK politics and, as such, its alignment with terms such as 'socialised' and 'collective' is unusual, the UK's coalition government is clear that:

> The Big Society is a society with much higher levels of personal, professional, civic and corporate responsibility; a society where people come together to solve problems and improve life for themselves and their communities; a society where the leading force for progress is social responsibility, not state control. (Conservative Party, 2011)

It further suggests that under this agenda social enterprises, charities and voluntary groups should take a leading role in the design and delivery of public services and that, rather than being seen as provider of first choice, state activity should be geared to facilitating the provision of start-up support. In this way it proposes to 'give new powers and rights to neighbourhood groups: the "little platoons" of civil society' (Conservative Party, 2010). It will also draw upon a Big Society network of influential believers who will lead it by spanning boundaries between communities, business and politics (Coote, 2010).

The UK government's *Big Society, Not Big Government* document (Conservative Party, 2011) presents a picture of social enterprise as the means of addressing the ills of disadvantaged, urban communities. However, this stereotypical picture of challenged communities gives rise to as many questions as the issues social enterprise is purported to overcome. What, for example, of rural communities or communities with non-stereotypical, non-urban challenges? Why is social enterprise generally identified as useful for disadvantaged communities? If marginalisation of certain socio-economic groups has helped to generate a dysfunctional society, shouldn't social action present a way for all community members and communities to unite to begin to help themselves, and each other?

In contrast with the euphoric picture of 'healing society by involving it', critics of the Big Society suggest that its co-production agenda is a manipulative one in which the state sets the framework for what social action is allowable, invites citizens to be involved and then claims benefits from embracing civil society. Thus, if citizens do not become involved any failure to improve social conditions or provide services becomes their fault – by default. This view is espoused by Scott, who draws on Gramsci (2007) to suggest that government policy towards the collective production of public services cynically uses moral persuasion and ideological consent (Scott, 2010) to control and coerce – since it is hard to argue that involvement and reciprocal helping is other than good. Nonetheless, with co-production firmly embedded in policy across the UK political spectrum and further afield, there seem few alternative manifestos for innovative ways of meeting the needs of society into the future.

This book has drawn upon a large European Union-funded project which took place from 2007 to 2010. It was first envisaged in 2006, at a time when policymakers, service providers and researchers were high-lighting: the apocalyptic nature of demographic trends producing increas-ing proportions of older people in society; the ensuing disproportionately large numbers of older people in rural Europe; and the threat that tradi-tional methods of public service delivery would be unable to cope with the increasing older rural population. At the same time, social enterprise as a means of co-producing services, movements to shift the balance of health care from hospitals to the community and issues around how to cater for the needs of large numbers of people with a complex range of chronic con-ditions were being elevated in policy. As a result, multiple policy strands appeared to support the notion of enabling communities of older people to engage in social enterprise as a way of providing services that would enable other older people to live in their own homes and communities for longer.

Within the EU northern periphery countries that participated in O4O, teams of academic researchers, Project Managers, health and social care practitioners, and volunteers put the implication of this emergent policy strand to the test. Sceptical of universally beneficial outcomes from social enterprise and co-production, and intrigued as to the emergence of com-munity involvement policies across Europe, the O4O partners sought to investigate whether rural communities could and would establish social enterprises, and with what results. The interest in rural areas owed much to the rhetoric around the need for rural communities to self-generate resil-ience (Scottish Government, 2008) and evidence that rural settings present particular promoters (e.g. higher levels of volunteering, mutual help and social capital) and barriers (e.g. market failure and social mores around inter-community competition) to social enterprise development (Farmer et al, 2008). The interest in older people owed much to their presentation as an increasing burden on services and a growing ethos that older people can and should continue to contribute to society and be valued for doing so. O4O was therefore a 'lived experiment' that perhaps controversially united and sought to test the validity of several policy strands emergent in the mid-2000s, with real citizens and communities.

In Chapter 1, Hill's discussion of the evolution and inevitability of com-munity social enterprise shows how policy does not occur in a vacuum, and in Chapter 2 Skerratt outlines how mapping key concepts, ideas and policies across participant nations and regions makes it possible to predict areas of difference that will emerge when (social enterprise) policy is enacted. Indeed, O4O has shown that it is possible to overlay what transpires in different regions with a map of key differences around understandings of the concept of social enterprise, the culture of payment and policy, norms around what services are expected 'as of right' and from whom; and to match these in an explanatory story.

In Chapter 3, Muñoz and Steinerowski explain how various understandings of 'social enterprise' and 'social entrepreneur' impact on the drive for ubiquitous community social enterprise and highlight the misalignment between the individualism of entrepreneurship and the need to make communities collectively entrepreneurial. It becomes evident from their analysis that whilst communities have the potential to participate in developing and delivering services, many will require a framework that acknowledges their need for support to identify opportunities, leverage resources and build an enterprise. Indeed, there appears to be a key role for *community catalysts* or Project Managers as a 'force' that will tip communities from thinking about social enterprise to its enactment. However, by drilling down into the lived experience of a community catalyst, Farmer and Stephen (Chapter 4) uncover the stressful nature of this role and counter the perceived wisdom that community processes are essential precursors to successful outcomes when measured in terms of establishing social enterprise. Indeed, Radford and Shortall (Chapter 5) turn the rather cosy concept of community action as beneficial to all local citizens on its head, exposing the 'dark side' of community hegemony and the potential exclusionary impacts of strong community leaders; individuals that some evidence suggests are vital to community capacity-building. Radford and Shortall's work highlights the problems of an entrepreneurial approach to community social enterprise and may add weight to the case for a franchised or governed model of community social enterprise development, enabled by, and accountable to, the state.

Typically, the sustainability of an entrepreneurial business venture is measured in terms of its financial viability; that is, the potential to generate surplus for reinvestment. However, as Whitelaw shows in Chapter 6, sustainability, as it relates to community social enterprise, is an ill-defined, labyrinthine and misunderstood concept. It is a concept that requires a more nuanced (re)definition that acknowledges that: social needs may be relatively short term; a social enterprise can be organic and therefore evolve to meet changing needs; communities alter and local participation is often time-limited; and the legacy of circumstances is as pertinent to chances of longevity as financial viability. Were community social enterprise to measure its sustainability status in this wider context, rather than focusing on financial gain or survival, it would perhaps facilitate access to much needed external support.

Evaluating the impacts of community social enterprise is fraught with difficulties, as is the ability to evidence its capacity to meet its purported outcomes. As Farmer and Bradley argue in Chapter 7, robust evaluation relies on the availability of quality data at the level of the local community, yet service provider data are often only available at large-area level or from costly, cumbersome community surveys whilst timescales frequently mitigate against linking interventions with outcomes. This being the case, it is incumbent upon policymakers and public service providers to exercise caution and not be swayed by what they perceive to be a 'good news story' that can be used to promote policy imperatives. As O4O evidenced, stakeholders' qualitative descriptions of impacts often uncovered unforeseen negative effects from participating in community social enterprise. For example, far from helping mental wellbeing some volunteers became exhausted by their social enterprise activities and others were distressed by their intrusion into family life.

EMERGENT THEMES AND IDEAS

The experience of O4O has highlighted the light and dark sides of the policy thrust to engage citizens through government-led agendas for community social enterprise and co-production. Whilst, even after our large-scale study, we are unable to make a definitive comment on whether community social enterprise is beneficial for communities overall, we are able to highlight the difficulties of establishing social enterprises and to offer practical suggestions for the enactment of policy in ways that are least painful to, and most respectful of, citizens and communities.

Co-production and social enterprise feed on enthusiasms for community sustainability, ethical business and an interest in social capital as a means of building community capacity. However, they are also seen as mechanisms for offloading the expense of providing public services on to communities, particularly those in problematic situations such as rural settings, where commercial provision may not be viable. That social enterprise has the potential to combine lower-cost services and a facility for employing the 'hard to employ' is not in doubt. Indeed, as high-profile social entrepreneurs such as Muhammad Yunnus, the founder of Grameen Bank; Jamie Oliver, a celebrity chef offering training to hard-to-employ teenagers; and Bill Drayton, founder of Ashoka have shown, successful social enterprise is do-able, innovative and, indeed, inspiring. However, these same criteria give rise to the risk of such well-intentioned activities being adopted by political elites in order to sell social enterprise as a fashionable, liberating and socially responsible solution to the perceived fragmentation of society and mounting public sector costs – but without acknowledging the risks. And, as the example of O4O has shown, there are challenges to overcome if community social enterprise is to successfully provide, or co-produce, local public services.

Certainty of service delivery is essential to those who procure public services (e.g. councils or health services) and without assurance that a small community social enterprise will endure, handing over service provision will be problematical, particularly where failure will result in a gap in provision that procurers may not be able to (re)fill within budget. A safety net for provision is therefore essential and this may result in councils thinking it is safer to continue to provide services themselves.

Procurers also need assurance that community social enterprises will meet the criteria required of public sector and commercial organisations in relation to standards, reliability, accountability, health and safety, and quality. Thus, governance and accountability structures are vital, yet the experience of O4O has shown that governance, accountability and maintaining health and safety bureaucracy are problematic areas for developing community social enterprises and require significant support from (external) facilitators.

Social entrepreneurship literature highlights the concept of the lone entrepreneur but this does not align with the notion of co-production and imperatives for collective community action. It is clear that where governments seek community input to service provision, thought must be given to the process of mobilising communities. This is not catered for within policy where practical actions are at odds with the policy rhetoric and dependent on notions of the entrepreneur from a commercial business paradigm. In O4O, paid Project Managers acted as 'the entrepreneur'. They stimulated and facilitated entrepreneurial activity and their experiences inform our suggestion and view that where governments wish communities to be entrepreneurial they must first create enabling structures and that failing to do so will lead to uneven levels of capacity for, and enactment of, social enterprise.

O4O also reinforced conventional wisdom that a small number of 'usual suspects' (regular community leaders) lead and produce community activities and that concerted efforts to generate a wider pool of participants are unlikely to meet with success. Most active community members are already involved in other/multiple activities and, as a consequence, community enterprises are likely to run with small groups of (over)stretched people. This phenomenon was identified by Mycock and Tonge (2011) as highly problematic for building the Big Society. Furthermore, since community social enterprise for service provision comprises responsible, burdensome work, it may be difficult to source the requisite level of skills to devolve responsibility and plan for succession; for example, book-keeping, computing and financial management skills may reside with only a few members of a community who may not want, or be fit for, ongoing responsibility.

The role of community catalyst, facilitator or organiser has emerged as fundamental to harnessing a community's ideas, building confidence, pushing community members to organise and obtain funding, and in spanning the boundaries between the community and various external networks. The legitimacy of this role can derive either from external linkages (e.g. to a project, a university, a development agency or a public service) or through their identification as 'one of us' (a person from, or who knows, the local community) and is therefore sensitive to the local context and concerns. The ideal community catalyst should have the credibility of links with an external organisation yet 'talk the local language', and be able to empathise and mix freely with community members yet have the capacity to communicate with a variety of stakeholders, including policymakers, local people, regional development agencies and funders.

Given the breadth of the challenges it is hard to envisage the ubiquitous movement from provision by public services to provision by community social enterprise organisations. This seems particularly inauspicious in the failed market situations of rural areas unless social enterprises are established and operated under the aegis of some form of umbrella agency with a remit to ensure that services are sustainable and safe, and which is able to step in to provide an interim service should individual community social enterprise failure occur. A significant conclusion from O4O is that a supportive organisational structure designed to provide business, governance and accountability structures, and mechanisms for sustainability, is essential where states seek to develop widespread co-productive community social enterprise. Run as an arm's-length agency of local or state government, the core functions of such an umbrella organisation or franchisee should include:

- employing and dispatching community catalysts to make social enterprise happen in different communities;
- conducting context-appropriate, adaptive business planning and training for community social enterprises; and
- undertaking the bureaucracy for local community social enterprises.

A supportive umbrella organisation of this type would: create economies of scale by undertaking the same bureaucratic processes for multiple community social enterprises and collective marketing; actively seek and manage contracts; undertake recruitment and human resources functions; and link communities with sources of finance – which would also serve to support sustainability.

In her 1990 book *Governing the Commons* Nobel prize winner Eleanor Ostrom depicts communities as able to develop their own associations and reciprocal systems that allow them to share natural resources by implementing mechanisms of cyclical use. Ostrom's work suggests that when left to their own devices community members can and will establish associations to help themselves. Whilst this is true of the communities Ostrom studied, it is difficult to transplant the idea of collective arrangements established through the generations in traditional societies to the current situation across rural areas of highly developed countries. These places are characterised by dynamic and sometimes traumatic demographic and economic change, with citizens often living fragmented lives with disparate, out-of-community connections and strong expectations of service provision by the state. Thus, whilst writers such as Ostrom (1990) and Putnam (2000) have been hugely influential by providing innovative ideas, when their ethos is operationalised in diverse real-life circumstances the theory–practice dichotomy becomes all too apparent.

Our work suggests that those promoting community social enterprise would benefit from a sense of realism about the activities in which local citizens and volunteers will readily participate. Across a number of countries and regions O4O found that community participants were more likely to engage when operating within their own sphere of understanding. They were attracted to developing enterprises they could relate to and, with some notable exceptions, showed more interest in establishing social activities than co-producing formal or informal services. This suggests a role for an umbrella organisation driving the development of rural community social enterprise in supporting citizens to participate in a range of activities about which they are relatively uninformed or inexperienced (e.g. providing basic care or domestic services).

O4O raised the importance of context awareness to policy implementation and demonstrated ways in which context can have surprising and conclusive impacts. For example, despite belief that social enterprise would resonate in Finland, where context is shaped by both a mixed economy of care and a population of older people who are used to paying for (some) services, O4O had limited success. This may have been due, in part, to Finland's particular conceptualisation of social enterprise and the related need for a social enterprise to employ a specific proportion of hard-to-employ staff. In addition, the concept of volunteering is problematic for Scandinavia in general but Finland in particular lacks a culture of formal volunteering and voluntary organisations. The idea of the state harnessing volunteers was anomalous. In Greenland, the context for efforts to develop community social enterprise was conditioned by its culture of family rather than community cohesion and highly paternalistic public service provision. Here, the relatively recent trend for rural families to migrate to towns has left many elderly people isolated and the need to bring people together, to engage in shared activities, was recognised as an essential precursor of any move to develop social enterprise. Thus, context-specificity meant that Greenland failed to establish social enterprises bearing any resemblance to service provider organisations run on commercial enterprise principles.

In all of the O4O participant regions the readiness of parts of the macro context for social enterprise provision of services for older people is problematic, for whilst policy around co-production has been developing, the intended 'receiving sectors' remain unprepared. For example, despite abundant policy rhetoric around a shift from technical, acute service provision to preventative health and social care within homes and communities, the emphasis on technical, public service inputs for older people's services remains. In part, this is attributable to the monolithic structure and culture of health and care service provision in which hospitals, doctors and nurses are perceived to be the structural backbone. But it neglects evidence that a growing quantity of the care services consumed by older people with complex, chronic conditions could be better managed at home and within communities. Support and enthusiasm from health and social care structures have not moved in parallel with a policy trajectory that increasingly promotes co-production. A complementary move is required from public sectors that should set out those activities that citizens and communities might fruitfully undertake to provide community-based services.

WILL COMMUNITY SOCIAL ENTERPRISE HAPPEN?

The policy environment and the extent to which community engagement is in the *zeitgeist* suggest the inevitability of increased citizen, community, volunteer and not-for-profit involvement in service delivery. However, this could unfold in different ways. In remote and rural communities, where it is difficult and expensive to provide services due to diseconomies of scale, there is an opportunity for community social enterprise to provide a range of much needed basic services to help older and vulnerable people remain in their own homes and communities. Some communities, at some times, may be able to provide leaders and entrepreneurs who can design, lead and fund local social enterprises. However, O4O has highlighted the lengthy road that many communities must travel if they are to produce community social enterprises.

Based on the international experience of O4O, the need for state-supported 'supportive umbrella organisations' to nurture community social entrepreneurialism and assist communities to develop, maintain and evolve local enterprises is both self-evident and essential. Such mechanisms would recognise community social enterprise as a collective venture that will not arise from a pool of lone, heroic entrepreneurs, and that alleviating necessary bureaucracy will significantly help to effectively harness local interests, enthusiasms and energy. We suggest the need for policymakers to address these three key questions:

1. *What are they expecting of citizens* and, in that respect, are there limits to the type of services citizens might be expected to provide for each other?
2. *Can ubiquitous community social enterprise be enabled?* We have suggested the development of state-led supportive organisations as a precursor to community social enterprise. We recognise that whilst governments may want co-production and social enterprise they may not wish to erect state-supported structures to do this. Nonetheless, it is unrealistic to expect unsupported communities to spontaneously 'rise up and look after themselves and each other' in the ways that are needed.
3. *For whom, and for where, is community social enterprise intended?* There has been a tendency amongst policymakers to focus on deprived urban communities with stereotypical bleak, urban problems whilst ignoring the range of community contexts that exist. If community social enterprise is truly the panacea for social ills, an effective and efficient way of reducing state activity (and spending), and a way of developing localised, needs-led services, the policy focus must be broader and social enterprise embraced as a concept relevant for all communities.

Community social enterprise can happen in rural communities, but to make it ubiquitous, sustainable, effective and safe it requires a state-supported supportive umbrella organisation. States must be realistic, focused and structured in making rural community social enterprise happen and move away from pressurising communities to be more resilient without appropriate, context-aware, policies and support.

REFERENCES

Coote A. (2010), *Cutting It: The Big Society and the new austerity*, London: New Economics Foundation.

Conservative Party (2010), *The Conservative Manifesto 2010*. Retrieved from: http://ucrel.lancs.ac.uk/wmatrix/ukmanifestos2010/conservative.txt (accessed 24 February 2012).

Conservative Party (2011), *Big Society Not Big Government*. Retrieved from: www.conservatives.com/~/media/Files/Downloadable%20Files/Building-a-Big-Society.ashx? (accessed 20 April 2011).

Farmer J., Steinerowski A. & Jack S. (2008), 'Starting Social Enterprises in Remote and Rural Scotland: The best or the worst of circumstances?', *International Journal of Entrepreneurship and Small Business*, 6(3), pp. 450–464.

Gewirth A. (1996), *The Community of Rights*, Chicago: University of Chicago Press.

Gramsci A. (2007 [1971]), *Selections from the Prison Notebooks*, London: Lawrence & Wishart.

Mycock A. & Tonge J. (2011), 'A Big Idea for the Big Society? The advent of a National Citizen Service', *Political Quarterly*, 82(1), January–March, pp. 56–66.

New Economics Foundation (2008), *Co-production: A manifesto for growing the core economy*, London: New Economics Foundation.

Norman J. (2010), *The Big Society: The anatomy of the new politics*, Buckingham: University of Buckingham Press.

Ostrom E. (1990), *Governing the Commons: The evolution of institutions for collective action*, Cambridge: Cambridge University Press.

Putnam R. (2000), *Bowling Alone: The collapse and revival of American community*, New York: Simon & Schuster.

Scott M. (2010), 'Reflections on "The Big Society"', *Community Development Journal*, 46(1), pp. 132–137.

Scottish Government (2008), *Delivering for Remote and Rural Health Care*, final report of the Remote & Rural Workstream, Edinburgh: Scottish Government.

Index